An In-Depth Study

of the

Texas TEKS

(Reading TEKS 6-10)

*Anatomy of the TEKS *Mentor texts *Posters *Lesson plans *Sample questions *ELAR TEKS used cross-curricular *Real-Life scenarios of the TEKS including homelife, friendships, inside and outside of school applications *Parental Involvement *Book Correlations

By Randi Whitney

An In-Depth Study of the Texas TEKS

ISBN: 978-1-966301-15-8

Published by BIG Time Publishing Company

BIG Time Publishing Company
3502 Columbia Memorial Parkway, Kemah, TX 77565, 281-549-4466
randiwhitney.com

This book is a work of non-fiction. Any references to real events, people, or organizations are intended only to provide context and support the author's perspective and are used with permission when applicable.

All photos and drawings are original and belong to Randi Whitney.

First Edition: 2025
Printed in the United States of America

Randi Whitney's Library Card!
Enjoy all the books across multiple genres by Randi Whitney

Motivational Speaking!

Children's Books

Buffalo Nickel Ranch	Leaving Tracks
Who Let the Goat Out	The Blue Egg
I Love Buggy Rides	The Class with Heart
The Messes We Make	Leave Something Take Something
The Annual Cookie Tree	Tomato Boy
It's Valentines, of Course of Course	Every Letter Counts
The Community Can	Chocolate Chip Cookies
Be Three	Louis, Louis

Author Visits!

Young Children's Chapter Books

The Ranch Coin	The Cookie Tree Tradition
Buggy Rides	The Biggest Mess
The Great Goatsby	The Green Egg
The Community Colection	The Lost Medal

Early Reader Picture Books

The Other Side of the Nickel   The Goat's Gate

Educational Books

Reading for Retrieval	4 Dimensions of Comprehension
Writing for Purpose	Grammatical Matters
Teach BIG: Believe in Greatness – Bring Best	Lexicon Mysteries Solved
Practices Back	Fluency Flows
Teach BIG: Believe in Greatness – Study Guide	GAP Phonics: Preventing and Closing Gaps

Mystery/Thriller Novels

A Good Witness   The Knock   The Teacher Retreat   Twisted Poison

Christian Novels

The Last Day   The First Day

Motivational Books

Don't Spend Your CAN Years CAN'Ting

Preteen Christian Chapter Books

The Bookcase: Matthew	The Bookcase: John
The Bookcase: Mark	The Bookcase: Acts
The Bookcase: Luke	The Bookcase: Romans

SCAN ME!

randiwhitney.com
teachbig.com

Dear Fellow Educators,

I want to take a moment to pause and acknowledge you—the incredible heart and soul of our classrooms. Day after day, you pour your energy, creativity, and compassion into your students, often in the face of challenges that seem to multiply with every passing season. I see you. I understand the weight you carry, the endless tasks on your to-do list, and the deep desire to not just meet standards but to truly make a difference in the lives of your students.

In the midst of all this, we have the Texas Essential Knowledge and Skills (TEKS)—a guide, a foundation, and sometimes, let's be honest, a source of stress. But here's what I hope we can all remember: The TEKS are not just boxes to check or tests to pass—they are tools to equip our students for life.

Every strand, every student expectation, and every vertical alignment point toward something bigger than a grade on a report card. They point to skills that last a lifetime—the ability to think critically, to communicate effectively, to read with purpose, and to write with clarity. The TEKS are a bridge, connecting the lessons we teach in our classrooms to the world our students will one day navigate as adults.

I know that diving into the TEKS can feel overwhelming. The language can be dense, the expectations high, and the time short. That's why I've poured my heart into this book—not as a checklist, but as a companion, a guide, and maybe even a little bit of relief. My hope and my prayer are that these pages bring clarity where there's confusion, excitement where there's frustration, and joy where there's burnout.

Teaching the TEKS isn't just about compliance—it's about empowerment. When we teach these standards with intention, we're not just preparing students for the next test, the next grade, or even graduation. We're preparing them to analyze, question, create, and contribute to the world around them.

So, to each of you who shows up every day, despite the obstacles, with a commitment to your students and to these standards—I applaud you. I believe in you. And I hope this book serves as a small gift of encouragement and support in your journey.

Let's embrace the TEKS not as burdens, but as opportunities—to light a fire for learning, to cultivate curiosity, and to prepare our students not just for school, but for life beyond the classroom walls.

With gratitude, respect, and hope,
Randi Whitney

Teach BIG Mission Statement:
Empowering Teachers to Become Experts in
Content, Craft, and Compliments

At Teach BIG, we believe that great teaching is not accidental—it is intentional, passionate, and rooted in expertise. Our mission is to help every educator become an EXPERT in the three foundational pillars: Content, Craft, and Compliments. When teachers are equipped in all three areas, instruction becomes purposeful, relationships deepen, and student outcomes are transformed while using their required curriculum.

Let's break down what each pillar means:

◆ Content: Know What You Teach

Content is the core of instructional integrity. It's not just knowing the subject—it's understanding the standards, the vertical alignment, the academic vocabulary, the cognitive demand, and the connections between concepts. Teachers must be able to unpack standards, identify readiness priorities, and recognize how each skill builds across time and across disciplines.

When teachers are experts in content, they teach with clarity, confidence, and intentionality. They don't just follow a curriculum—they lead it with purpose.

◆ Craft: Know How to Teach It

Craft is the art of delivery. It's about designing lessons that are engaging, rigorous, and accessible for all learners. It includes questioning techniques, differentiation, pacing, classroom management, and instructional strategies that bring content to life. Craft is where expertise meets creativity.

When teachers master their craft, students don't just learn—they lean in. They are curious, involved, and connected to the content.

◆ Compliments: Know How to Connect

Compliments refer to the relationships, praise, feedback, and classroom culture that build trust and motivation. This pillar focuses on the social-emotional side of teaching—how to affirm effort, celebrate growth, and create a safe, inspiring learning environment.

Compliments elevate content by making learning personal. When students feel seen and valued, they are more likely to take academic risks, persevere through challenges, and rise to expectations.

How *An In-Depth Study of the Texas TEKS* Supports the "Content" Pillar

An In-Depth Study of the Texas TEKS is a powerful tool designed to strengthen the "Content" pillar of the Teach BIG mission. This book helps educators move beyond simply being familiar with the TEKS—it empowers them to become fluent in them.

Through clear explanations, unpacking models, vertical alignment insights, and real classroom examples, this resource helps teachers:

- Break down each TEKS into actionable instructional pieces
- Understand the intent, complexity, and instructional implications of each standard
- Identify readiness vs. supporting standards and how they appear on STAAR
- Build units and lessons with precise TEKS alignment
- Connect TEKS to questioning, assessment, and evidence-based feedback

In short, this book helps teachers turn the TEKS into tools—not tasks. It transforms standards from something teachers have to teach into something they understand, own, and use to drive learning forward.

When teachers master content, their instruction becomes intentional. When they develop their craft, their delivery becomes impactful. And when they lead with compliments, their classrooms become transformative.

That's what it means to Teach BIG.
And that's where expert teaching begins.

An In-Depth Study of the TEXAS TEKS

Forward for "Make It Make Sense: An In-Depth Study of the TEKS"

In education, we often focus on teaching specific skills and measuring students' ability to understand texts, but there's a bigger picture. The Texas Essential Knowledge and Skills (TEKS) standards are not just about teaching comprehension or ensuring students can pass an exam—they are a guide to help students navigate real-life situations. These standards are designed to cultivate cognitive patterns that extend far beyond the classroom, preparing students to think critically, solve problems, and connect ideas in their daily lives.

Each TEKS standard represents an important way the brain processes information. When students practice making inferences, evaluating evidence, or synthesizing new ideas, they are exercising the same cognitive skills they will need in their future careers, personal relationships, and decision-making moments. Whether it's analyzing a text in school or evaluating a real-life problem at home or in the workplace, the ability to think clearly, make connections, and draw conclusions is essential.

In "An In-Depth Study of the Texas TEKS," we explore how the TEKS standards are more than just educational benchmarks—they are frameworks for real-world thinking. This book will help you see how the same cognitive abilities measured in standardized tests are those we rely on when managing complex life situations, making thoughtful choices, and solving everyday problems. The TEKS are not merely about comprehension—they are about making sense of the world. By understanding and applying these standards, educators, students, and even parents can draw powerful connections between academic learning and the way we all navigate life.

The brain is capable of extraordinary connections when guided by these principles, and in the pages that follow, we will explore how each TEKS standard serves as a building block for mastering both academic content and life's greatest challenges.

For a list of all released data since 2022, please visit the Teach BIG website and click on the store link or visit Teachers Pay Teachers. We have disaggregated this data for all grades 3-10.

- Question Stem Vocabulary
- Question Stem Analysis
- Questions Grouped by TEKS Standard
- Frequency of Standards Charts
- Editing Standards Data
- Revising Standards Data
- Instructional Implications
- Comparative Analysis
- Alignment to Educational Goals
- TEKS to CCSS Crosswalk

Chapter Summary: An In-Depth Study of the Texas TEKS

Chapter 1: Inherent Challenges and Keywords

This chapter addresses the common challenges educators face when implementing the Texas TEKS in the classroom. It identifies barriers such as complexity, alignment with diverse student needs, and time constraints. To help educators navigate these challenges, the chapter provides a detailed glossary of keywords and phrases found in the TEKS, offering clarity and actionable definitions to guide lesson planning and delivery.

Chapter 2: Real-Life Applications of the TEKS

Real-world relevance is at the heart of this chapter. It explores how TEKS can be tied to everyday scenarios, making learning more meaningful and engaging for students. From applying comprehension skills to reading a recipe to analyzing advertisements for persuasive techniques, this chapter provides concrete examples and projects that connect the TEKS to students' lives, preparing them for real-world problem-solving.

Chapter 3: Opening Activities for the TEKS

This chapter is a treasure trove of creative and practical opening activities designed to spark student engagement while aligning with specific TEKS. Each activity introduces key concepts in an accessible way, setting the stage for deeper learning. Examples include icebreakers, quick discussions, brainstorming sessions, and interactive games tailored to various content areas and grade levels.

Chapter 4: Poems and Scripts to Explain the TEKS

Through poetry and scripted dialogues, this chapter offers imaginative ways to explain TEKS standards. Poems personify abstract concepts, making them more relatable, while scripts provide engaging, dialogue-driven explanations that capture students' attention. These creative tools help teachers introduce TEKS in a way that students can easily grasp and remember.

Chapter 5: Explanation of the TEKS by Content Area

This chapter offers a detailed breakdown of TEKS standards by subject, including English Language Arts, Math, Science, and Social Studies. Each section explains the purpose and expectations of the standards in the respective content area. Practical examples and instructional strategies are included to help teachers deliver the content effectively.

Chapter 6: Mentor Texts with Practice Passages (With and Without TEKS)

Focused on the use of mentor texts, this chapter provides a collection of exemplar passages aligned with specific TEKS. Each passage includes guided practice questions that address TEKS standards. To foster flexibility, some passages are presented without explicit TEKS labeling, encouraging teachers to create their own activities and assessments tailored to student needs.

Chapter 7: TEKS Categorized by the Four Dimensions

This chapter organizes the TEKS into four dimensions of learning: **Taught (content knowledge), Tap (textual evidence), Think (inference and analysis), and Toggle (comparative and relational skills)**. Each dimension is explained with examples and strategies, helping teachers design lessons that balance these critical elements and support comprehensive skill development.

Chapter 8: TEKS Posters

This chapter features ready-to-use posters for every TEKS standard. Each poster is designed to be visually engaging, with simplified explanations, key phrases, and student-friendly language. These posters serve as reference tools for both teachers and students, reinforcing learning objectives and keeping TEKS front and center in the classroom.

Chapter 9: Parental Involvement with the TEKS

Recognizing the vital role of parents in education, this chapter provides guidance on involving families in supporting TEKS-based learning. It includes tips for hosting parent workshops, creating home-based activities aligned with TEKS, and fostering communication between school and home. Sample letters, newsletters, and parent resources are included to enhance collaboration.

Chapter 10: Book Recommendations with TEKS-Correlated Questions

This chapter provides a curated list of children's books, novels, and nonfiction texts aligned with TEKS standards. Each recommendation includes discussion questions and activity ideas that correlate with specific TEKS, making it easy for teachers to integrate literature into their lessons while targeting essential skills.

Chapter 11: Nonfiction TEKS-Based Passage Practice with Stopgap Questions

Focused on nonfiction, this chapter offers practice passages aligned with TEKS. Each passage includes stopgap comprehension questions that encourage students to think critically as they read. These questions focus on key TEKS skills like summarizing, making inferences, and analyzing the author's purpose, helping students build confidence and mastery in understanding informational texts.

Chapter 12: An Escape Room Project based on the TEKS (6-10)

This chapter offers a comprehensive TEKS project centered around a book of your choice and an escape room theme. Additional projects are also described in this chapter. This chapter also offers station activities based on a provided passage.

Summary of An In-Depth Study of the Texas TEKS

An In-Depth Study of the Texas TEKS is a comprehensive guide designed to support educators in understanding, teaching, and applying the TEKS standards in meaningful ways. From addressing inherent challenges and providing practical resources like mentor texts and posters to fostering parental involvement and incorporating real-world applications, this book equips teachers with everything they need to create engaging, TEKS-aligned learning experiences. By offering creative approaches, such as poetry, scripts, and opening activities, alongside rigorous practice passages and assessment tools, the book empowers educators to inspire a lifelong love of learning while meeting state standards with confidence.

<u>Chapter 1</u>

*English Language Arts TEKS

*Inherent Challenges & Myths
Regarding Implementation

*Keywords for STAAR and the TEKS

The 13 Sections of TEKS for English Language Arts and Reading

TEKS #	Title	Description (Simplified)
1	Developing and Sustaining Foundational Language Skills: Oral Language	Focuses on listening, speaking, and discussing to improve oral language skills through active participation.
2	Developing and Sustaining Foundational Language Skills: Beginning Reading and Writing	Teaches foundational word structure skills like phonics, spelling, and print concepts to support reading and writing.
3	Developing and Sustaining Foundational Language Skills: Vocabulary	Encourages students to learn and use new words effectively in speaking and writing.
4	Developing and Sustaining Foundational Language Skills: Fluency	Builds reading fluency by focusing on speed, accuracy, and expression while understanding grade-level texts.
5	Developing and Sustaining Foundational Language Skills: Self-Sustained Reading	Promotes independent reading of grade-appropriate texts for a sustained period to build comprehension and stamina.
6	Comprehension Skills	Helps students use thinking and problem-solving strategies to understand and analyze complex texts deeply.
7	Response Skills	Teaches students to respond thoughtfully to texts they read, hear, or view, using evidence and critical thinking.
8	Multiple Genres: Literary Elements	Guides students to identify and analyze elements like characters, plot, setting, and theme in different literary works.
9	Multiple Genres: Genres	Focuses on recognizing and analyzing the specific characteristics, structures, and purposes of various genres.
10	Author's Purpose and Craft	Teaches students to examine how authors use language, techniques, and structure to achieve specific effects.
11	Composition: Writing Process	Guides students through the writing process (planning, drafting, revising, and editing) to create clear and legible texts.
12	Composition: Genres	Helps students write meaningful texts using the characteristics and structure of specific genres.
13	Inquiry and Research	Encourages students to ask questions, gather information, and conduct research for short-term or long-term projects.

Let's Look at one of the TEKS Through a Vertically Aligned Lens

8D (grades 3-5), 7D (grades 6-8), 6D (grades 9-12)

3rd - explain the influence of the setting on the plot.

4th - explain the influence of the setting, including historical and cultural settings, on the plot.

5th - analyze the influence of the setting, including historical & cultural settings, on the plot.

6th - analyze how the setting, including historical and cultural settings, influences character and plot development.

7th - analyze how the setting influences character and plot development. *

8th - explain how the setting influences the values and beliefs of characters.

9th - analyze how the setting influences the theme.

10th - analyze how historical and cultural settings influence characterization, plot, and theme across texts.

11th - analyze how the historical, social, and economic context of setting(s) influences the plot, characterization, and theme.

12th - evaluate how the historical, social, and economic context of setting(s) influences the plot, characterization, and theme.

Here's a helpful analogy using a common and relatable scenario: eating at a restaurant. This analogy will help clarify the difference between explaining, analyzing, and evaluating in a way that's easy to remember—and easy to teach to students.

Restaurant Analogy: Eating a Meal

Let's say you're at a restaurant trying a new dish. Here's how each thinking level applies:

◆ **Explain = Tell What Happened**
You describe the experience.
"I ordered spaghetti and meatballs. It came with garlic bread and a side salad."
You're simply stating the facts and describing the process. You're giving the "what."

→ In reading: "The character moved to a new town and made a new friend."

◆ **Analyze = Break It Down and Understand Why/How**
Now you look deeper at the parts and their relationships.
"The sauce was tangy and thick, and the meatballs were very tender. I think the chef added fresh herbs because there was a unique flavor. The bread balanced the acidity of the sauce."
You're looking at ingredients, flavors, textures—how the parts work together.

→ In reading: "The character made a new friend because they both felt like outsiders. Their friendship helped both characters feel more confident."

◆ **Evaluate = Judge or Assess Based on Criteria**
Now you form an opinion based on what you've experienced.
"This was one of the best spaghetti dishes I've had. The quality of ingredients and the homemade feel made it better than others I've tried. I would definitely recommend it."
You are deciding if it was effective, worthwhile, or high-quality—and explaining why.

→ In reading: "This was a strong ending to the story because it resolved the main conflict and showed how the characters had grown. It left me feeling intrigued."

Summary:

- Explain = Tell what happened
- Analyze = Break it down and understand how and why
- Evaluate = Make a judgment and justify it

Understanding the Anatomy of the TEKS

The **Texas Essential Knowledge and Skills (TEKS)** is a structured framework that outlines what students are expected to learn in each subject area and grade level. It provides clarity and consistency in the education system while allowing flexibility for instruction. Here's a breakdown of its anatomy:

---

1. Knowledge and Skills Statements

- **Definition**: These statements describe broad concepts and skills that students should develop over time.
- **Numbered 1 through 13**: Each number represents a specific domain or strand within the subject. For example, in English Language Arts, you might see strands like comprehension, writing, or response skills.
- **Purpose**: They serve as overarching goals for each subject and provide the foundation for the student expectations.

---

2. Student Expectations

- **Definition**: These are more specific learning outcomes that detail what students are expected to know and be able to do.
- **Labeled with Capital Letters**: Each knowledge and skills statement is broken into several specific expectations labeled (A), (B), (C), etc.
- **Purpose**: These expectations narrow the focus of the knowledge and skills statement into measurable learning objectives.

---

3. Breakouts within Student Expectations

- **Purpose**: Breakouts clarify how to implement and evaluate the student expectations by detailing components or options for teaching and assessing the skills.
- **Key Words**: The breakouts are categorized by four key terms: **and**, **including**, **or**, and **such as**. These words define the required or optional components within each expectation.

Breakout Words and Their Definitions

Word	Definition
And	Indicates that all listed elements must be included and taught separately.
Including	Indicates that the specified element(s) must be included, and they cannot be skipped.
Or	Indicates that at least one of the listed elements must be included, but it is not necessary to include all. Teachers can choose which to emphasize.
Such as	Indicates that the elements listed are examples and not required. Teachers have the flexibility to use other examples to meet the same expectation.

Chart for the TEKS Breakdown: (10) Author's Purpose and Craft

(10) Author's purpose and craft: listening, speaking, reading, writing, and thinking using multiple texts. The student uses critical inquiry to analyze the authors' choices and how they influence and communicate meaning within a variety of texts. The student analyzes and applies author's craft purposefully in order to develop his or her own products and performances. The student is expected to:

(A) explain the author's purpose and message within a text;

Part	Description	Details
Part 1: Knowledge and Skills Statement	Focuses on analyzing how authors use their choices to influence and communicate meaning. Students learn to evaluate and apply these techniques in their own work.	Students develop critical inquiry skills to understand an author's purpose and craft across various types of texts.
Part 2: Student Expectation	Explains what students are specifically required to do.	(A): Explain the author's purpose and message within a text.
Part 3: Breakout	Further clarifies the expectations by breaking them into smaller, specific tasks.	(i): Explain the author's purpose within a text. AND (ii): Explain the author's message within a text.

This chart clearly organizes the three parts of the TEKS, making it easy to understand the hierarchy from broad objectives (Knowledge and Skills Statement) to specific tasks (Breakout).

Number of Breakout TEKS for 4th Grade ELAR

<u>TEKS Category</u>	<u>Number of Breakouts</u>
1. Foundations of Language	12
2. Phonics and Spelling	57
3. Vocabulary	12
4. Fluency	3
5. Reading for Sustained Time	2
6. Reading Comprehension	24
7. Reading Response	8
8. Literary Elements	9
9. Genre-Specific Reading	17
10. Author's Purpose	14
11. Composition (Writing Process)	62
12. Composition (Genre-Specific)	8
13. Research and Inquiry	14

Notes:

1. **Threaded TEKS (Sections 1–5)**:
   o These TEKS are foundational skills threaded throughout the curriculum.
   o **Total Breakouts**: 86
2. **Specialized TEKS for Reading (Sections 6–10)**:
   o These TEKS focus on reading-specific skills and analysis.
   o **Total Breakouts**: 72
3. **Specialized TEKS for Writing (Section 11)**:
   o These TEKS emphasize the writing process and conventions.
   o **Total Breakouts**: 62
4. **Applied TEKS (Sections 12–13)**:
   o These TEKS focus on applying skills to composition genres and research.
   o **Total Breakouts**: 22
   o

Total number of Breakout TEKS is 242!
This is why we MUST use the threaded TEKS on an everyday basis.

This is also why certain TEKS appear tested more than others.
Sometimes Individual TEKS have many aspects.

TEKS Breakout Explanation

The following pages contain two lesson plans. These examples exemplify the significance for understanding the breakout TEKS. The first lesson you will see addresses the author's <u>purpose</u> and the 2nd lesson addresses the author's <u>message</u>.

This is relevant because they address different skills. However, they are both listed under TEKS 10A.

This is where the importance of understanding how breakout TEKS function. This particular TEKS contains the word "and". This means that what comes before the word "and" as well as what comes after the word "and" must both be addressed **separately**.

Too often, teachers are under the impression that author's purpose and the author's message are the same/similar since they are contained within the same TEKS and can be covered by the same set of lesson plans. This is not the case.

Teachers must address both pieces, or breakouts, of the TEKS that contain the word "and" or the word "including". This is an example of how lessons must be different to address the same TEKS number 10A.

If you are interested in having the complete TEKS set of lessons for every breakout TEKS, all 242 of them, we highly suggest the Teach BIG ELAR TEKS lesson plans. Each of the TEKS sections are addressed individually. This allows you to purchase one TEKS set or all of them based on the needs of the TEKS explanations that best suit your current knowledge base as a teacher.

<u>Keep in mind that these lesson plans are not curriculum specific but rather provide valuable understanding to educators for all 242 TEKS breakouts.</u>

The Teach BIG TEKS Lesson Plans can be found on amazon.com and on teachbig.com.

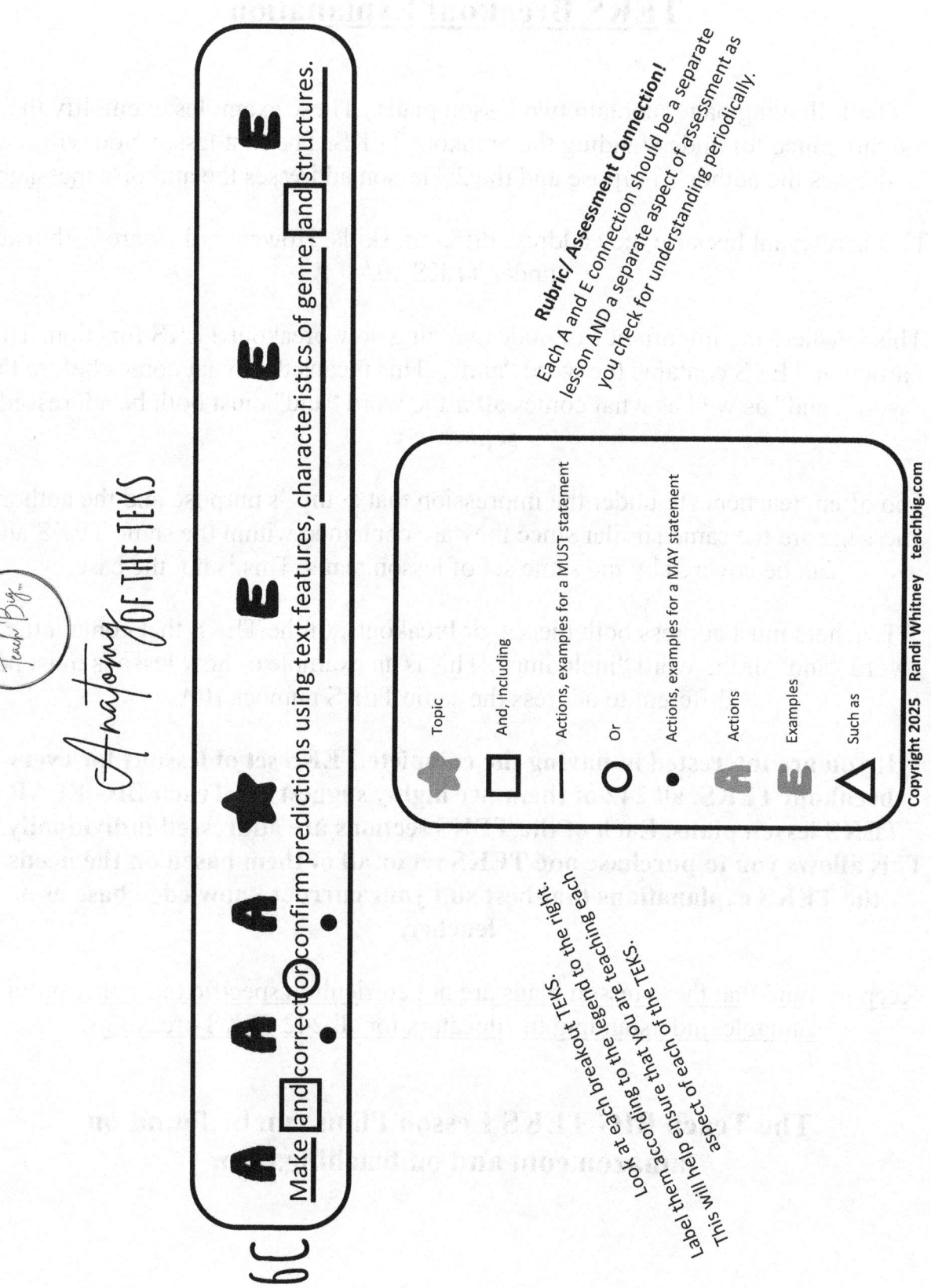

Anatomy OF THE TEKS

6C

Make and correct or confirm predictions using text features, characteristics of genre, and structures.

Rubric/ Assessment Connection!

Each A and E connection should be a separate lesson AND a separate aspect of assessment as you check for understanding periodically.

Topic ★

And, Including ☐

Actions, examples for a MUST statement |

Or ○

Actions, examples for a MAY statement •

Actions A

Examples E

Such as △

Look at each breakout and the legend to the right. Label them according to what you are teaching each. This will help ensure each of the TEKS.

Lesson Plan: Explaining the Author's <u>Purpose</u> Within a Text

---

Grade Level: 4th Grade
TEKS Focus: §110.16. (10)(A)(i) - Explain the author's purpose within a text
Objective:
Students will identify and explain the author's purpose in a text, going beyond basic categories (persuade, inform, entertain) to explore how the author's choices communicate meaning and achieve specific goals.

Materials Needed:

- Copies of short, diverse texts (e.g., a poem, a persuasive letter, an informational article, and a narrative)
- Anchor Chart: "Exploring Author's Purpose"
- Graphic Organizer: "Understanding the Author's Purpose" (sections for Text Type, Author's Purpose, Evidence from the Text, and How It Communicates Meaning)
- Whiteboard or chart paper and markers

Lesson Outline

1. Introduction (10 minutes)

Teacher Script:
*"Good morning, class! <u>Today, we're going to explore why authors write. Authors always have a purpose, or a reason, for creating a text. Sometimes it's to inform us about a topic, persuade us to believe something, or entertain us with a story</u> (there are many others: refer to **Reading for Retrieval** by Randi Whitney for a complete list with explanations). But an author's purpose can go even deeper. For example, they might want to inspire us, make us think about an issue, or teach us a lesson. Let's learn how to figure out an author's purpose by looking closely at the text."*

Explain the Concept:
"<u>The author's purpose is the reason they write. To figure out the purpose, we need to ask questions like:</u>"

1. What is the text about?
2. Why did the author write this text?
3. What does the author want the reader to think, feel, or do?

Write on the Board/Anchor Chart:
"Questions to Identify Author's Purpose:"

- *What is the author's main message?*
- *Who is the audience?*
- *What choices did the author make (e.g., words, tone, style)?*
- *How does the text make you think, feel, or act?*

---

2. Direct Instruction (10 minutes)

Teacher Script:
"Let's look at a text together and figure out the author's purpose. I'll read a short paragraph, and we'll analyze it step by step."

- **Example Text** (Persuasive Letter):
  "Dear Principal Johnson, recess is important for students' health and happiness. It gives us a chance to exercise, make friends, and take a break from learning. Please consider adding 10 more minutes to recess time so we can return to class refreshed and ready to learn!"

Model Thinking:

1. **What is the text about?**
   o *"This text is about recess and why it's important for kids."*
2. **Why did the author write this text?**
   o *"The author wrote this to convince the principal to add more time to recess."*
3. **What is the author's purpose?**
   o *"The author's purpose is to persuade the principal to make a change."*
4. **How does the author achieve this?**
   o *"The author uses reasons like exercise, friendship, and focus to make a strong argument."*

Write on the Board:

- *Text Type*: Persuasive Letter
- *Author's Purpose*: To persuade the principal to extend recess.
- *Evidence*: Mentions exercise, making friends, and returning refreshed.
- *How It Communicates Meaning*: Uses reasons and a polite tone to support the argument.

---

3. Guided Practice (15 minutes)

Activity: "Purpose Detectives"

1. Provide students with a variety of short texts to analyze in small groups. Examples:
   - A poem about nature.
   - An article about recycling.
   - A narrative about a child overcoming a challenge.
2. Students will:
   - Read the text together.
   - Use the "Understanding the Author's Purpose" graphic organizer to record:
     - The text type.
     - The author's purpose.
     - Evidence from the text that supports their idea.
     - How the author communicates meaning through their choices.
3. Groups will share their findings with the class.

Teacher Script:
"Now, in your groups, read your assigned text and think about why the author wrote it. Use the graphic organizer to write down the text type, the purpose, and evidence from the text. Be ready to explain how the author's choices help communicate their purpose."

---

4. Independent Practice (15 minutes)

Activity: "Explain the Author's Purpose"

1. Provide students with a new text to analyze independently.
   - **Examples**: A short informational passage, a fable, or a persuasive paragraph.
2. Students will:
   - Read the text and use the graphic organizer to record:
     - The text type.
     - The author's purpose.
     - Evidence from the text.
     - How the author communicates meaning.
   - Write a short paragraph explaining the author's purpose and how the text supports it.

Teacher Script:
"Now it's your turn! Read the new text and think about the author's purpose. Use the graphic organizer to record your ideas, and then write a paragraph explaining why you think the author wrote this text and how they achieved their purpose."

5. Closing & Reflection (10 minutes)

Class Discussion:

- Ask students to share examples of the author's purpose from their texts.
- Discuss as a group:
    o *"Why is it important to understand an author's purpose?"*
    o *"How does knowing the author's purpose help us become better readers?"*

Teacher Script:
"Let's reflect on what we learned today. Did you notice how authors make specific choices to achieve their purpose? Understanding why a text was written helps us connect with the message and think critically about what we read."

Wrap-Up Tip:
"The next time you read something, ask yourself: Why did the author write this? What do they want me to think, feel, or do? This will help you understand the text on a deeper level."

Assessment

- Review students' graphic organizers to ensure they correctly identified the text type, author's purpose, evidence, and how the purpose was communicated.
- Evaluate their paragraphs for clear and accurate explanations of the author's purpose.
- Observe group discussions and presentations for engagement and comprehension.

Extension Activity

Write for a Purpose:

- Students choose one of three purposes: to persuade, to inform, or to inspire (or any other they would like).
- They write a short paragraph on a topic of their choice (e.g., "Why we need class pets" or "How to take care of a plant") and share it with the class.
- Peers guess the author's purpose based on the text and explain their reasoning.

This activity helps students apply their understanding of author's purpose to their own writing and develop critical thinking skills.

Lesson Plan: Explaining the Author's <u>Message</u> Within a Text

Grade Level: 4th Grade
TEKS Focus: §110.16. (10)(A)(ii) - Explain the author's message within a text
Objective:
Students will identify and explain the author's message within a text by analyzing the text's content, tone, and details and how these elements communicate a deeper meaning or theme.

Materials Needed:

- A variety of short texts (e.g., a poem, a fable, a short story, and an informational article)
- Anchor Chart: "How to Identify the Author's Message"
- Graphic Organizer: "Understanding the Author's Message" (sections for Key Details, Message, and How It's Communicated)
- Whiteboard or chart paper and markers

Lesson Outline

1. Introduction (10 minutes)

Teacher Script:
"Good morning, class! Today, we're going to dig deeper into what authors want to say in their writing. Sometimes, an author's purpose—like to inform, entertain, inspire, convince, or persuade (there are many others: refer to **Reading for Retrieval** by Randi Whitney for a complete list with explanations)*—is clear, <u>but they also include a message, which is the big idea or lesson they want us to learn. The author's message helps us think more deeply about the text and connect it to our own lives</u>."*

Explain the Concept:
<u>*"The author's message is the big idea or takeaway they want us to understand. To figure out the message, we need to pay attention to key details, the tone, and the overall theme of the text. For example, in a story about teamwork, the message might be, 'Working together makes us stronger.' Let's practice finding the author's message together."*</u>

Write on the Board/Anchor Chart:
"How to Identify the Author's Message:"

1. **Look for Key Details**: What happens in the text? What is repeated or emphasized?
2. **Consider the Tone**: How does the author feel about the topic?
3. **Think About the Theme**: What is the big idea or life lesson?

---

2. Direct Instruction (10 minutes)

Teacher Script:
"Let's look at a short story together and figure out the author's message. I'll read it aloud, and we'll analyze it step by step."

- **Example Text (Fable)**:
  "Once there was a group of birds trapped in a net. Each bird tried to escape on its own, but the net wouldn't budge. Finally, one bird suggested they all fly together at the same time. When they worked as a team, they lifted the net and flew to safety."

Model Thinking:

1. **Look for Key Details**:
   o *"The birds were trapped and couldn't escape alone, but they worked together to lift the net."*
2. **Consider the Tone**:
   o *"The tone is hopeful and positive, showing that teamwork can solve problems."*
3. **Think About the Theme**:
   o *"The big idea is that teamwork is powerful. The author's message is, 'We can accomplish more when we work together.'"*

Write on the Board:

- *Key Details*: Birds trapped in a net, teamwork helped them escape.
- *Tone*: Hopeful, positive.
- *Author's Message*: We can accomplish more when we work together.

3. Guided Practice (15 minutes)

Activity: "Find the Message"

1. Provide students with a variety of short texts to analyze in small groups. Examples:
   o A poem about nature.
   o A short story about helping others.
   o An informational article about taking care of the environment.
2. Students will:
   o Read the text together.
   o Use the "Understanding the Author's Message" graphic organizer to record:
     ▪ Key details.
     ▪ The tone.
     ▪ The author's message.
   o Discuss how the author communicated the message through the text.
3. Groups will share their findings with the class.

Teacher Script:
"Now, in your groups, read your assigned text and think about the author's message. Use the graphic organizer to record key details, the tone, and the message you think the author wanted to share. Be ready to explain your ideas to the class!"

---

4. Independent Practice (15 minutes)

Activity: "Explain the Author's Message"

1. Provide students with a new text to analyze independently.
   o **Examples**: A short poem about perseverance or a narrative about making mistakes and learning from them.
2. Students will:
   o Read the text and use the graphic organizer to record:
     ▪ Key details.
     ▪ The tone.
     ▪ The author's message.
   o Write a short paragraph explaining the author's message and how the text supports it.

Teacher Script:
"Now it's your turn! Read the new text and think about the message the author is trying to share. Use the graphic organizer to record your ideas, and then write a paragraph explaining the message and how the text communicates it."

5. Closing & Reflection (10 minutes)

Class Discussion:

- Ask students to share the messages they identified in their texts.
- Discuss as a group:
  - *"Why do authors include messages in their writing?"*
  - *"How does understanding the author's message help us connect with the text?"*

Teacher Script:
"Let's reflect on what we learned today. Did you notice how authors use details, tone, and themes to communicate a message? Understanding the author's message helps us think more deeply about what we read and how it applies to our own lives."

Wrap-Up Tip:
"The next time you read a story, poem, or article, think about the big idea the author is trying to share. Ask yourself: What is the message, and how can I use it in my life?"

Assessment

- Review students' graphic organizers to ensure they correctly identified key details, the tone, and the author's message.
- Evaluate their paragraphs for clear and accurate explanations of the author's message and how it was communicated.
- Observe group discussions and presentations for engagement and comprehension.

Extension Activity

Create a Text with a Message:

- Students write a short story, poem, or letter that includes a clear message (e.g., "Never give up" or "Be kind to others").
- They share their work with the class, and peers identify the message and explain how the text communicates it.

This activity helps students apply their understanding of authors' messages to their own writing and fosters creativity and critical thinking.

ELAR TEKS for Reading Specifically

(6) Comprehension skills: listening, speaking, reading, writing, and thinking using multiple texts. The student uses metacognitive skills to both develop and deepen comprehension of increasingly complex texts. The student is expected to:

(A) establish purpose for reading assigned and self-selected texts;

(B) generate questions about text before, during, and after reading to deepen understanding and gain information;

(C) make and correct or confirm predictions using text features, characteristics of genre, and structures;

(D) create mental images to deepen understanding;

(E) make connections to personal experiences, ideas in other texts, and society;

(F) make inferences and use evidence to support understanding;

(G) evaluate details read to determine key ideas;

(H) synthesize information to create new understanding; and

(I) monitor comprehension and make adjustments such as re-reading, using background knowledge, asking questions, and annotating when understanding breaks down.

(7) Response skills: listening, speaking, reading, writing, and thinking using multiple texts. The student responds to an increasingly challenging variety of sources that are read, heard, or viewed. The student is expected to:

(A) describe personal connections to a variety of sources, including self-selected texts;

(B) write responses that demonstrate understanding of texts, including comparing and contrasting ideas across a variety of sources;

(C) use text evidence to support an appropriate response;

(D) retell, paraphrase, or summarize texts in ways that maintain meaning and logical order;(E) interact with sources in meaningful ways such as notetaking, annotating, freewriting, or illustrating;

(F) respond using newly acquired vocabulary as appropriate; and

(G) discuss specific ideas in the text that are important to the meaning.

(8) Multiple genres: listening, speaking, reading, writing, and thinking using multiple texts--literary elements. The student recognizes and analyzes literary elements within and across increasingly complex traditional, contemporary, classical, and diverse literary texts. The student is expected to:

(A) infer basic themes supported by text evidence;

(B) explain the interactions of the characters and the changes they undergo;

(C) analyze plot elements, including the rising action, climax, falling action, and resolution; and

(D) explain the influence of the setting, including historical and cultural settings, on the plot.

(9) Multiple genres: listening, speaking, reading, writing, and thinking using multiple texts-genres. The student recognizes and analyzes genre-specific characteristics, structures, and purposes within and across increasingly complex traditional, contemporary, classical, and diverse texts. The student is expected to:

(A) demonstrate knowledge of distinguishing characteristics of well-known children's literature such as folktales, fables, legends, myths, and tall tales;

(B) explain figurative language such as simile, metaphor, and personification that the poet uses to create images;

(C) explain structure in drama such as character tags, acts, scenes, and stage directions;

(D) recognize characteristics and structures of informational text, including:

(i) the central idea with supporting evidence;

(ii) features such as pronunciation guides and diagrams to support understanding; and

(iii) organizational patterns such as compare and contrast;

(E) recognize characteristics and structures of argumentative text by:

(i) identifying the claim;

(ii) explaining how the author has used facts for an argument; and

(iii) identifying the intended audience or reader; and

(F) recognize characteristics of multimodal and digital texts.

(10) Author's purpose and craft: listening, speaking, reading, writing, and thinking using multiple texts. The student uses critical inquiry to analyze the authors' choices and how they influence and communicate meaning within a variety of texts. The student analyzes and applies author's craft purposefully in order to develop his or her own products and performances. The student is expected to:

(A) explain the author's purpose and message within a text;

(B) explain how the use of text structure contributes to the author's purpose;

(C) analyze the author's use of print and graphic features to achieve specific purposes;

(D) describe how the author's use of imagery, literal and figurative language such as simile and metaphor, and sound devices such as alliteration and assonance achieves specific purposes;

(E) identify and understand the use of literary devices, including first- or third-person point of view;

Teaching the TEKS can be <u>challenging</u> for teachers due to various factors, including curriculum alignment, diverse student needs, and accountability pressures. What are some of the challenges?

1. Understanding and Interpreting TEKS

- **Challenge:** TEKS standards can be broad and open to interpretation, making it difficult for teachers to determine exactly what mastery looks like.
- **Impact:** Teachers may struggle with aligning lessons and assessments directly to the standards.
- **Solution:** Provide clear examples, professional development, and resources for unpacking the standards.

2. Differentiating Instruction

- **Challenge:** TEKS must be taught to a wide range of learners, including English Language Learners (ELLs), students with disabilities, and advanced learners.
- **Impact:** Tailoring lessons to meet all students' needs while covering the required standards can be time-consuming and overwhelming.
- **Solution:** Use scaffolding techniques, tiered activities, and differentiated resources.

3. Time Management

- **Challenge:** Teachers must cover all required TEKS within a limited time frame while ensuring depth of understanding.
- **Impact:** Balancing pacing and thorough instruction can lead to gaps in coverage or surface-level learning.
- **Solution:** Prioritize high-impact standards and integrate multiple TEKS into cohesive lessons.

4. Assessment Alignment

- **Challenge:** Creating assessments that truly measure student mastery of TEKS can be complex, especially for skills like critical thinking and analysis.
- **Impact:** Misaligned assessments may not accurately reflect students' progress.
- **Solution:** Use formative assessments and TEKS-aligned rubrics to monitor and adjust instruction.

5. Integration Across Subjects

- **Challenge:** Some TEKS require cross-curricular integration (e.g., reading skills in social studies or science), which can be difficult to coordinate.
- **Impact:** Teachers may feel siloed in their subject areas.
- **Solution:** Collaborate with colleagues across disciplines to design interdisciplinary units.

6. Accountability and High-Stakes Testing

- **Challenge:** The emphasis on STAAR testing and performance-based accountability puts pressure on teachers to focus on tested TEKS.
- **Impact:** This can result in "teaching to the test" and neglecting standards not covered by assessments.
- **Solution:** Balance test preparation with meaningful, holistic instruction.

7. Student Engagement

- **Challenge:** Keeping students engaged while teaching rigorous TEKS can be difficult, particularly with abstract or complex skills.
- **Impact:** Lack of engagement can hinder mastery and long-term retention.
- **Solution:** Use project-based learning, real-world connections, and interactive strategies to make TEKS relevant.

8. Resource Availability

- **Challenge:** Not all schools have access to high-quality TEKS-aligned materials or technology.
- **Impact:** Teachers may need to spend extra time creating or sourcing resources.
- **Solution:** Advocate for district support and share materials within teacher networks.

9. Professional Development

- **Challenge:** Teachers often lack sufficient training on effectively teaching specific TEKS or integrating new instructional strategies.
- **Impact:** This can lead to inconsistent implementation across classrooms.
- **Solution:** Provide targeted, ongoing professional development and mentoring opportunities.

10. Balancing TEKS with SEL and Real-World Skills

- **Challenge:** Incorporating social-emotional learning (SEL) and 21st-century skills while meeting TEKS can feel like an added burden.
- **Impact:** Important skills like collaboration, problem-solving, and empathy might take a backseat.
- **Solution:** Integrate SEL and real-world skills into TEKS instruction for a more holistic approach.

By addressing these challenges with effective strategies, collaboration, and support, teachers can ensure that they deliver TEKS instruction in a way that is meaningful, engaging, and impactful for all students.

Common <u>Myths</u> About the TEKS and the Truth Behind Them

1. **Myth: The TEKS Are Too Rigid and Limit Teacher Creativity**
   - **Truth:** The TEKS provide a framework, not a script. They outline what students need to learn but leave the *how* up to the teacher. Educators can use creative teaching strategies, projects, and real-world applications to bring the standards to life while staying aligned with the TEKS.
2. **Myth: The TEKS Are Only for State Assessments**
   - **Truth:** While state assessments are based on the TEKS, they serve a much larger purpose. The TEKS are designed to ensure students gain essential knowledge and skills for success in school, careers, and life—not just to perform well on tests.
3. **Myth: The TEKS Are Too Complex for Younger Students**
   - **Truth:** The TEKS are developmentally appropriate and vertically aligned to build knowledge progressively. While some standards may seem complex, they are designed to scaffold learning over time, starting with foundational skills in earlier grades.
4. **Myth: The TEKS Are the Same as a Curriculum**
   - **Truth:** The TEKS are **standards**, not a curriculum. They specify what students need to know and be able to do but do not dictate how lessons should be taught. Schools and districts develop curricula, lesson plans, and materials based on the TEKS.
5. **Myth: The TEKS Don't Allow for Differentiation**
   - **Truth:** The TEKS are broad enough to accommodate differentiation. Teachers can tailor lessons to meet diverse student needs, including those of English language learners, gifted students, and students with special needs, while staying aligned with the standards.
6. **Myth: The TEKS Are All About Academic Skills**
   - **Truth:** The TEKS encompass much more than academics. They include social-emotional learning, critical thinking, collaboration, and problem-solving skills, preparing students to be well-rounded individuals.
7. **Myth: The TEKS Are Updated Too Frequently**
   - **Truth:** The Texas Education Agency (TEA) reviews and revises the TEKS periodically, but updates occur after significant review and feedback cycles. This ensures the standards remain relevant and reflect the needs of modern education without unnecessary disruption.
8. **Myth: Teachers Must Teach Every TEKS Standard in Isolation**
   - **Truth:** The TEKS are meant to be integrated. Many standards naturally overlap, allowing teachers to address multiple TEKS in a single lesson or unit, fostering deeper learning and connections across disciplines.
9. **Myth: The TEKS Are the Same Across All Subjects**
   - **Truth:** Each subject has its own TEKS with unique goals, language, and emphasis. For example, the English Language Arts TEKS focus on comprehension, writing, and analysis, while the Science TEKS emphasize inquiry, experimentation, and critical thinking.

10. **Myth: Teachers Should Cover Every TEKS Equally**
      o **Truth:** Not all TEKS carry the same weight in the classroom. Teachers should prioritize the "readiness standards" (key concepts that are foundational for future learning) while addressing "supporting standards" as part of broader instruction.

How to Debunk These Myths

- **Stay informed:** Engage in professional development and study the TEKS deeply to understand their purpose and flexibility.
- **Collaborate:** Work with colleagues to share strategies, ideas, and insights about teaching the TEKS effectively.
- **Advocate for creativity:** Remember that the TEKS provide the "what" and leave room for the "how," allowing teachers to bring their personal strengths to the classroom.

By understanding the truth behind these myths, educators can use the TEKS as a valuable tool to guide student learning while fostering engagement and creativity.

Top 7 Things Educators Can Do to Better Understand the TEKS

1. **Compare the Grade Levels Before and After Their Own**
   - Understanding how skills progress and build over time is essential. Educators should study the TEKS for the grade level immediately before and after theirs to see how their instruction fits into the larger learning trajectory. This helps ensure seamless transitions and prepares students for future challenges.

2. **Analyze the Action Words**
   - Pay close attention to verbs such as "identify," "analyze," "compare," "evaluate," or "synthesize" in the TEKS. These action words indicate the expected level of rigor and guide educators on how deeply students should engage with the material.

3. **Pay Attention to What is Offset in Commas**
   - Often, phrases set off by commas provide additional context, conditions, or clarifications for the standard. These details are critical for understanding the full scope of what students are expected to learn or demonstrate.

4. **Break Down Each Standard into Manageable Parts**
   - Dissect the TEKS into smaller components to understand each expectation clearly. This makes it easier to create targeted lesson plans and ensures no part of the standard is overlooked.

5. **Study the Vertical Alignment**
   - Examine how TEKS standards progress across grade levels and content areas. This helps educators see the "big picture" of student learning and understand how their instruction contributes to long-term goals.

6. **Focus on the Content-Specific Language**
   - Identify the specific vocabulary, phrases, and terminology unique to each content area within the TEKS. Familiarity with this language ensures accurate instruction and assessment.

7. **Highlight Key Phrases That Signal Depth of Knowledge**
   - Words and phrases like "increasingly complex texts," "variety of sources," or "supported by text evidence" indicate higher-level thinking expectations. Recognize these signals to prepare lessons that meet the intended rigor.

Anatomy of a Common TEKS

Understanding the structure of a typical TEKS (Texas Essential Knowledge and Skills) standard requires breaking it down into its key components. Each part provides specific guidance on what students are expected to learn and how educators should approach instruction. Below is the "anatomy" of a TEKS:

---

1. Strand

- **What It Is:**
  The overarching category or domain that the standard falls under, such as "Comprehension Skills," "Response Skills," or "Author's Purpose and Craft."
- **Purpose:**
  Sets the broad focus of learning and instruction within the content area.

---

2. Knowledge Statement

- **What It Is:**
  A general statement that describes the goal of the strand. This is often written as an introductory sentence and serves as a summary of the skills and concepts to be developed.
- **Purpose:**
  Provides the "big picture" of what students should achieve by mastering the standard.
- **Example:**
  "The student uses metacognitive skills to develop and deepen comprehension of increasingly complex texts."

---

3. Student Expectation (SE)

- **What It Is:**
  The detailed, actionable components of the standard, often listed as subpoints (e.g., A, B, C, etc.). These specify what students should do, know, or produce.
- **Purpose:**
  Breaks the standard into measurable and teachable objectives.
- **Example:**
  "(A) Establish purpose for reading assigned and self-selected texts."

---

4. Action Words (Verbs)

- **What It Is:**
  The verbs in the student expectation that indicate what students are expected to do (e.g., "explain," "analyze," "compare," "evaluate").
- **Purpose:**
  Clarifies the depth and rigor of the expectation, aligning with Bloom's Taxonomy.
- **Example:**
  In "(A) explain the author's purpose and message," the verb "explain" signals a higher-order thinking skill that requires understanding and articulation.

5. Modifiers and Conditions

- **What It Is:**
  Phrases that specify how or in what context the action should be performed. These are often offset by commas and include details that narrow or expand the scope of the expectation.
- **Purpose:**
  Provides clarity and ensures consistency in instruction and assessment.
- **Example:**
  In "(C) make and correct or confirm predictions using text features, characteristics of genre, and structures," the conditions clarify the tools or strategies students should use.

6. Key Content Terms

- **What It Is:**
  Specific vocabulary or concepts students need to understand and apply, such as "figurative language," "text features," or "inferences."
- **Purpose:**
  Highlights essential knowledge that must be taught and mastered.
- **Example:**
  In "(E) make connections to personal experiences, ideas in other texts, and society," "connections" and "personal experiences" are the key concepts.

7. Complexity Level

- **What It Is:**
  The implied or explicit difficulty level of the expectation, often aligned with the progression of skills from lower to higher grades.

- **Purpose:**
  Helps educators understand the depth of knowledge required and how it builds over time.
- **Example:**
  A 4th-grade TEKS might require students to "explain," while a higher-grade TEKS may require them to "analyze."

---

8. Context or Examples (Optional)

- **What It Is:**
  Additional examples or scenarios sometimes included to illustrate how the standard might be applied.
- **Purpose:**
  Provides guidance for teachers by suggesting practical applications or interpretations.
- **Example:**
  "Including self-selected texts" clarifies that students have choice in their reading materials.

---

9. Grade-Level Progression (Vertical Alignment)

- **What It Is:**
  While not part of the individual TEKS, each standard is aligned with expectations from preceding and subsequent grades.
- **Purpose:**
  Ensures continuity and scaffolding of skills as students move through grade levels.
- **Example:**
  In earlier grades, students might "identify" main ideas, while later they are expected to "evaluate" and "synthesize" them.

Summary of TEKS Anatomy

A typical TEKS consists of **broad strands, clear knowledge statements, specific student expectations, action words, modifiers, key content terms, and optional examples.** Together, these components create a structured, measurable standard that guides instruction, ensures consistent expectations, and prepares students for academic success. Understanding this anatomy helps educators plan lessons, assess student progress, and align instruction with state standards.

List of the Most Important Words Found in the TEKS

Each term represents a critical concept or action essential for lesson planning, instructional delivery, and student mastery.

Section 6: Comprehension Skills

- Listening, Speaking, Reading, Writing, Thinking
- Metacognitive Skills
- Comprehension, Complex Texts
- Establish, Purpose
- Assigned, Self-Selected Texts
- Generate, Questions
- Before, During, After
- Deepen, Understanding
- Gain, Information
- Make, Correct, Confirm
- Predictions, Text Features, Genre, Structures
- Create, Mental Images
- Connections, Personal Experiences, Ideas, Society
- Inferences, Evidence, Support
- Evaluate, Details, Key Ideas
- Synthesize, Information, New Understanding
- Monitor, Adjustments, Comprehension
- Re-reading, Background Knowledge, Annotating

Section 7: Response Skills

- Listening, Speaking, Reading, Writing, Thinking
- Respond, Challenging Variety
- Describe, Personal Connections
- Sources, Self-Selected Texts
- Write, Responses, Understanding
- Comparing, Contrasting, Ideas
- Text Evidence, Support
- Retell, Paraphrase, Summarize
- Meaning, Logical Order
- Interact, Notetaking, Annotating, Freewriting, Illustrating
- Respond, Acquired Vocabulary
- Discuss, Specific Ideas, Meaning

Section 8: Multiple Genres - Literary Elements

- Listening, Speaking, Reading, Writing, Thinking
- Literary Elements, Traditional, Contemporary, Classical, Diverse Texts
- Infer, Basic Themes
- Text Evidence
- Explain, Interactions, Characters
- Changes, Undergo
- Analyze, Plot Elements
- Rising Action, Climax, Falling Action, Resolution
- Influence, Setting
- Historical, Cultural, Plot

Section 9: Multiple Genres - Genres

- Listening, Speaking, Reading, Writing, Thinking
- Genre-Specific, Characteristics, Structures, Purposes
- Demonstrate, Knowledge
- Distinguishing Characteristics
- Children's Literature, Folktales, Fables, Legends, Myths, Tall Tales
- Explain, Figurative Language
- Simile, Metaphor, Personification
- Poet, Images
- Structure, Drama
- Character Tags, Acts, Scenes, Stage Directions
- Recognize, Informational Text
- Central Idea, Supporting Evidence
- Pronunciation Guides, Diagrams
- Organizational Patterns, Compare, Contrast
- Recognize, Argumentative Text
- Claim, Facts, Audience, Reader
- Multimodal, Digital Texts

Section 10: Author's Purpose and Craft

- Listening, Speaking, Reading, Writing, Thinking
- Critical Inquiry, Analyze
- Authors' Choices, Influence
- Communicate, Meaning
- Explain, Author's Purpose, Message
- Text Structure, Contributes, Purpose
- Analyze, Print Features, Graphic Features
- Specific Purposes
- Describe, Imagery
- Literal Language, Figurative Language
- Simile, Metaphor
- Sound Devices, Alliteration, Assonance
- Identify, Understand
- Literary Devices
- First-Person, Third-Person

This compilation of key words provides a focused vocabulary for understanding and teaching the TEKS standards. Each term represents a critical concept or action essential for lesson planning, instructional delivery, and student mastery.

Understanding the <u>parts of speech</u> in the TEKS is a powerful tool for teachers because it provides clarity on the structure and intent of the standard.

1. Identifies Key Actions (Verbs)

- **Why it helps**: Verbs define the specific actions students are expected to perform, such as "make," "correct," "confirm," or "analyze."
- **Benefit**: Teachers can focus their lesson planning on building these skills. For example, if the TEKS includes verbs like "describe" or "explain," lessons should emphasize articulation and reasoning.

2. Highlights the Focus (Nouns)

- **Why it helps**: Nouns in the TEKS identify the concepts, topics, or content areas students need to learn.
- **Benefit**: Teachers can pinpoint the subject matter of the lesson. For instance, in "predictions using text features," the nouns "predictions" and "text features" reveal the content focus.

3. Clarifies Relationships (Conjunctions and Prepositions)

- **Why it helps**: Conjunctions ("and," "or") and prepositions ("using," "of") specify how different parts of the TEKS are connected.
- **Benefit**: Teachers can break down multi-part standards into manageable components. For example:
  - **"And"** means all elements must be taught separately.
  - **"Or"** offers flexibility, allowing one or the other to meet the TEKS.

4. Helps Deconstruct Breakouts

- **Why it helps**: Many TEKS contain breakout phrases introduced by words like "including," "such as," "or," and "and."
- **Benefit**: Teachers can determine which elements are required (e.g., "including") versus optional examples (e.g., "such as"). This avoids confusion over instructional priorities.

5. Supports Differentiated Instruction

- **Why it helps**: By knowing the parts of speech, teachers can tailor instruction for specific student needs. For instance:
    - Focus on verbs for students who struggle with the skills.
    - Emphasize nouns for students needing more content knowledge.

---

6. Guides Assessment Design

- **Why it helps**: The parts of speech in the TEKS reveal the expected outcomes.
- **Benefit**: Teachers can create assessments aligned with the TEKS by matching verbs (skills) to tasks (e.g., describe = written explanation) and nouns (content) to questions.

Example Application

Consider the TEKS 6C:
"Make and correct or confirm predictions using text features, characteristics of genre, and structures."

- **Verbs**: "Make," "correct," "confirm," "using" – Students must actively engage in these actions during lessons.
- **Nouns**: "Predictions," "text features," "characteristics of genre," "structures" – These are the specific areas to be addressed.
- **Conjunctions**: "And," "or" – Indicates some skills are cumulative ("and") while others are flexible ("or").
- **Prepositions**: "Using" – Specifies the tools or methods required to meet the TEKS.

By breaking this TEKS down, teachers know they need to:

1. Teach students how to **make predictions** and correct or confirm them.
2. Use specific tools like **text features**, **genre characteristics, and structures** to achieve this.

Conclusion: Knowing the parts of speech transforms the TEKS from a dense standard into a clear, actionable plan. It ensures that teachers:

- Understand exactly what the TEKS requires.
- Break the TEKS into teachable steps.
- Align instruction with the language and expectations of the TEKS.

This level of analysis not only makes the TEKS more accessible but also ensures instruction is focused, effective, and aligned with state standards.

The Grammar of TEKS (6C)

"Make and correct or confirm predictions using text features, characteristics of genre, and structures."

Word-by-Word Analysis

1. **Make** – Verb (base form; imperative mood, indicating an action to be done).
2. **and** – Conjunction (joins "make" and "correct or confirm").
3. **correct** – Verb (base form; imperative mood, indicating an action to be done).
4. **or** – Conjunction (offers a choice between "correct" and "confirm").
5. **confirm** – Verb (base form; imperative mood, indicating an action to be done).
6. **predictions** – Noun (plural; the object of the actions "make," "correct," and "confirm").
7. **using** – Verb (present participle; introduces the participial phrase "using text features, characteristics of genre, and structures," modifying the verb phrases "make and correct or confirm predictions").
8. **text** – Noun (singular; modifies "features").
9. **features** – Noun (plural; the first object of "using").
10. **characteristics** – Noun (plural; the second object of "using").
11. **of** – Preposition (shows the relationship between "characteristics" and "genre").
12. **genre** – Noun (singular; object of the preposition "of").
13. **and** – Conjunction (joins "characteristics" and "structures").
14. **structures** – Noun (plural; the third object of "using").

Explanation of Structure

- The sentence contains multiple **verbs** in the imperative mood: "make," "correct," "confirm," and "using."
- The **direct object** of these verbs is "predictions."
- The **participial phrase** "using text features, characteristics of genre, and structures" acts as an **adjective**, explaining *how* to make, correct, or confirm predictions.
- The **prepositional phrase** "of genre" modifies "characteristics," giving additional context.

This analysis helps clarify how each word functions within the sentence.

Tell Me More about Grammar and the TEKS

"Make and correct or confirm predictions using text features, characteristics of genre, and structures."

The word **"using"** is a **verb** in its **present participle** form, functioning as a **gerund** (a verb form that acts as a noun) or **part of a participial phrase**. In this context, it introduces the phrase **"using text features, characteristics of genre, and structures"**, which describes *how* predictions are made or confirmed.

In grammatical terms:

- **"using"** is functioning as the **head of a participial phrase** that modifies the action "make and correct or confirm predictions."

A **participial phrase** is a group of words that begins with a **participle** (a verb form used as an adjective) and includes any modifiers or complements. The phrase functions as an **adjective** in a sentence, describing or providing more information about a noun or pronoun.

Key Features of a Participial Phrase

1. **Starts with a participle**: Participles are verb forms that can act as adjectives. There are two types:
   - **Present participle**: Ends in **-ing** (e.g., running, using, swimming).
   - **Past participle**: Often ends in **-ed** or **-en** (e.g., baked, broken, frozen).
2. **Includes modifiers and complements**: A participial phrase may contain objects, adverbs, or prepositional phrases to complete its meaning.
3. **Acts as an adjective**: The entire participial phrase modifies a noun or pronoun.

Examples of Participial Phrases

1. **Present Participle Example**:
   - **Sentence**: The dog, **barking loudly at the mailman**, startled the neighbors.
   - **Participial Phrase**: "barking loudly at the mailman" modifies "The dog."
2. **Past Participle Example**:
   - **Sentence**: The cookies, **baked to perfection**, were cooling on the counter.
   - **Participial Phrase**: "baked to perfection" modifies "The cookies."
3. **With Modifiers and Complements**:
   - **Sentence**: The student, **running to catch the bus**, tripped on the sidewalk.
   - **Participial Phrase**: "running to catch the bus" modifies "The student."

How It Works in This Sentence

"Make and correct or confirm predictions using text features, characteristics of genre, and structures."

- **Participial Phrase**: "using text features, characteristics of genre, and structures."
- **Participle**: "using."
- **Function**: Modifies the verbs **"make and correct or confirm predictions"** by explaining *how* the predictions are to be approached.

TEKS (6) Analysis: Verbs (Skills) to Tasks and Nouns (Content) to Questions

TEKS (6)(A): Establish purpose for reading assigned and self-selected texts

- **Verbs (Skills):**
  - **Establish** → Task: Set a purpose for reading through reflection or planning.
- **Nouns (Content):**
  - **Purpose** → Question: What is the purpose of reading this text?
  - **Assigned and self-selected texts** → Question: How do assigned texts differ from self-selected texts when establishing purpose?

TEKS (6)(B): Generate questions about text before, during, and after reading to deepen understanding and gain information

- **Verbs (Skills):**
  - **Generate** → Task: Write or verbalize questions.
- **Nouns (Content):**
  - **Questions** → Question: What types of questions can you ask before, during, and after reading?
  - **Text** → Question: How does questioning a text help deepen understanding?
  - **Understanding and information** → Question: What specific information can be gained through questioning?

TEKS (6)(C): Make and correct or confirm predictions using text features, characteristics of genre, and structures

- **Verbs (Skills):**
  - **Make** → Task: State a prediction.
  - **Correct or confirm** → Task: Adjust or validate predictions based on evidence.
- **Nouns (Content):**
  - **Predictions** → Question: What predictions can you make about this text?
  - **Text features, characteristics of genre, structures** → Question: How do text features and genre help you predict what will happen?

TEKS (6)(D): Create mental images to deepen understanding

- **Verbs (Skills):**
  - o **Create** → Task: Visualize scenes or concepts described in the text.
- **Nouns (Content):**
  - o **Mental images** → Question: What mental image does this passage create for you?
  - o **Understanding** → Question: How do mental images help you better understand the text?

TEKS (6)(E): Make connections to personal experiences, ideas in other texts, and society

- **Verbs (Skills):**
  - o **Make** → Task: Articulate or document connections.
- **Nouns (Content):**
  - o **Connections** → Question: How does this text connect to your personal experiences?
  - o **Personal experiences, ideas in other texts, society** → Question: What parallels can you draw between the text and other ideas or societal themes?

TEKS (6)(F): Make inferences and use evidence to support understanding

- **Verbs (Skills):**
  - o **Make** → Task: Identify logical conclusions.
  - o **Use** → Task: Cite evidence from the text.
  - o **Support** → Task: Justify inferences with specific details.
- **Nouns (Content):**
  - o **Inferences** → Question: What inferences can you draw from the text?
  - o **Evidence** → Question: What evidence supports your inferences?
  - o **Understanding** → Question: How does this evidence deepen your understanding of the text?

TEKS (6)(G): Evaluate details read to determine key ideas

- **Verbs (Skills):**
  - o **Evaluate** → Task: Assess the importance of specific details.
  - o **Determine** → Task: Identify the key ideas.
- **Nouns (Content):**
  - o **Details** → Question: Which details in the text are most important?
  - o **Key ideas** → Question: What are the key ideas conveyed in this text?

TEKS (6)(H): Synthesize information to create new understanding

- **Verbs (Skills):**
  - **Synthesize** → Task: Combine information from multiple sources.
  - **Create** → Task: Formulate new insights.
- **Nouns (Content):**
  - **Information** → Question: What information can you combine from this text?
  - **New understanding** → Question: How does synthesizing information lead to a deeper understanding of the text?

TEKS (6)(I): Monitor comprehension and make adjustments such as re-reading, using background knowledge, asking questions, and annotating when understanding breaks down

- **Verbs (Skills):**
  - **Monitor** → Task: Track your comprehension as you read.
  - **Make adjustments** → Task: Use strategies like re-reading, annotating, or asking questions.
- **Nouns (Content):**
  - **Comprehension** → Question: How well do you understand the text?
  - **Adjustments** → Question: What strategies can you use to improve your understanding when it breaks down?

Summary

By breaking down the TEKS into verbs and nouns, teachers can better focus instruction on the specific **skills (verbs)** students need to develop and the **content (nouns)** students must understand. This approach ensures alignment with the TEKS and clarity in lesson design.

TEKS (7) Analysis: Verbs (Skills) to Tasks and Nouns (Content) to Questions

---

TEKS (7)(A): Describe personal connections to a variety of sources, including self-selected texts

- **Verbs (Skills):**
  - **Describe** → Task: Write or verbally explain how personal experiences relate to a source.
- **Nouns (Content):**
  - **Personal connections** → Question: How does this text relate to your personal experiences?
  - **Variety of sources** → Question: What types of texts or sources can you connect with personally?
  - **Self-selected texts** → Question: Why did you choose this text, and how does it connect to you?

TEKS (7)(B): Write responses that demonstrate understanding of texts, including comparing and contrasting ideas across a variety of sources

- **Verbs (Skills):**
  - **Write** → Task: Create written responses to show comprehension.
  - **Demonstrate** → Task: Prove understanding through clear communication.
  - **Compare and contrast** → Task: Identify similarities and differences between ideas in texts.
- **Nouns (Content):**
  - **Responses** → Question: How can you use writing to demonstrate your understanding of this text?
  - **Understanding of texts** → Question: What does this text mean, and how can you show your understanding?
  - **Variety of sources** → Question: How do the ideas in these texts compare or contrast?

TEKS (7)(C): Use text evidence to support an appropriate response

- **Verbs (Skills):**
  - **Use** → Task: Select and incorporate textual evidence into a response.
  - **Support** → Task: Justify a response using evidence from the text.
- **Nouns (Content):**
  - **Text evidence** → Question: What evidence from the text supports your response?

    o **Appropriate response** → Question: How does this evidence strengthen your response to the question or prompt?

TEKS (7)(D): Retell, paraphrase, or summarize texts in ways that maintain meaning and logical order

- **Verbs (Skills):**
  - **Retell** → Task: Verbally recount the events or ideas in the text.
  - **Paraphrase** → Task: Restate the text's ideas in your own words.
  - **Summarize** → Task: Write or explain a brief overview of the main points.
  - **Maintain** → Task: Ensure the meaning and logical order of the original text are preserved.
- **Nouns (Content):**
  - **Texts** → Question: What are the main ideas or events in this text?
  - **Meaning and logical order** → Question: How does your retelling or summary maintain the text's meaning and order?

TEKS (7)(E): Interact with sources in meaningful ways such as notetaking, annotating, freewriting, or illustrating

- **Verbs (Skills):**
  - **Interact** → Task: Engage actively with the text through various strategies.
  - **Notetaking, annotating, freewriting, illustrating** → Tasks: Take notes, mark key points, write thoughts, or create visual representations.
- **Nouns (Content):**
  - **Sources** → Question: How can you interact with this source in a way that helps you understand it better?
  - **Meaningful ways** → Question: Which method (notetaking, annotating, freewriting, or illustrating) works best for you, and why?

TEKS (7)(F): Respond using newly acquired vocabulary as appropriate

- **Verbs (Skills):**
  - **Respond** → Task: Write or speak using new vocabulary.
  - **Using** → Task: Apply newly learned words in context.
- **Nouns (Content):**
  - **Newly acquired vocabulary** → Question: What new words have you learned, and how can you use them in your response?
  - **Appropriate** → Question: How does your use of vocabulary enhance your response?

TEKS (7)(G): Discuss specific ideas in the text that are important to the meaning

- **Verbs (Skills)**:
  - ○ **Discuss** → Task: Verbally explore ideas with peers or teachers.
  - ○ **Identify** (implied) → Task: Pinpoint key ideas in the text.
- **Nouns (Content)**:
  - ○ **Specific ideas** → Question: What are the key ideas in this text that contribute to its meaning?
  - ○ **Meaning** → Question: How do these specific ideas support the overall meaning of the text?

TEKS (8) Analysis: Verbs (Skills) to Tasks and Nouns (Content) to Questions

TEKS (8)(A): Infer basic themes supported by text evidence

- **Verbs (Skills):**
  - **Infer** → Task: Draw logical conclusions about the theme from the text.
  - **Support** → Task: Use evidence from the text to justify the inferred theme.
- **Nouns (Content):**
  - **Basic themes** → Question: What is the theme of this text?
  - **Text evidence** → Question: What evidence from the text supports your understanding of the theme?

TEKS (8)(B): Explain the interactions of the characters and the changes they undergo

- **Verbs (Skills):**
  - **Explain** → Task: Write or verbally describe character interactions and their significance.
  - **Describe** (implied) → Task: Outline how characters interact and evolve in the story.
- **Nouns (Content):**
  - **Interactions of the characters** → Question: How do the characters interact with each other, and what do these interactions reveal?
  - **Changes they undergo** → Question: What changes do the characters experience, and what causes these changes?

TEKS (8)(C): Analyze plot elements, including the rising action, climax, falling action, and resolution

- **Verbs (Skills):**
  - **Analyze** → Task: Break down the plot into its key elements and evaluate their roles.
- **Nouns (Content):**
  - **Plot elements** → Question: What are the main elements of the plot?
  - **Rising action** → Question: What events build tension in the story?
  - **Climax** → Question: What is the turning point of the story?
  - **Falling action** → Question: How do events unfold after the climax?
  - **Resolution** → Question: How is the story's conflict resolved?

TEKS (8)(D): Explain the influence of the setting, including historical and cultural settings, on the plot

- **Verbs (Skills)**:
  - **Explain** → Task: Describe how the setting impacts the story's events and characters.
- **Nouns (Content)**:
  - **Influence of the setting** → Question: How does the setting affect the characters and plot development?
  - **Historical settings** → Question: How do historical elements in the setting shape the events of the story?
  - **Cultural settings** → Question: How do cultural aspects of the setting impact the story's themes and characters?
  - **Plot** → Question: How is the plot influenced by the setting's time and place?

TEKS (9) Analysis: Verbs (Skills) to Tasks and Nouns (Content) to Questions

TEKS (9)(A): Demonstrate knowledge of distinguishing characteristics of well-known children's literature such as folktales, fables, legends, myths, and tall tales

- **Verbs (Skills):**
  - **Demonstrate** → Task: Provide examples, explanations, or comparisons of the characteristics.
- **Nouns (Content):**
  - **Distinguishing characteristics** → Question: What makes folktales, fables, legends, myths, and tall tales unique?
  - **Well-known children's literature** → Question: How do these forms of children's literature reflect cultural or moral values?

TEKS (9)(B): Explain figurative language such as simile, metaphor, and personification that the poet uses to create images

- **Verbs (Skills):**
  - **Explain** → Task: Describe how figurative language conveys meaning or imagery.
- **Nouns (Content):**
  - **Figurative language** → Question: What is a simile, metaphor, or personification, and how do they create images?
  - **Images** → Question: How does the poet use figurative language to create vivid mental pictures?

TEKS (9)(C): Explain structure in drama such as character tags, acts, scenes, and stage directions

- **Verbs (Skills):**
  - **Explain** → Task: Describe how the structural elements of drama contribute to understanding the play.
- **Nouns (Content):**
  - **Structure in drama** → Question: What role do acts, scenes, and stage directions play in a drama?
  - **Character tags** → Question: How do character tags help the reader or viewer follow the dialogue?

TEKS (9)(D): Recognize characteristics and structures of informational text, including:

(i) the central idea with supporting evidence

- **Verbs (Skills):**
  - **Recognize** → Task: Identify the main idea and evidence within an informational text.
- **Nouns (Content):**
  - **Central idea** → Question: What is the central idea of this text?
  - **Supporting evidence** → Question: What details or examples support the central idea?

(ii) features such as pronunciation guides and diagrams to support understanding

- **Verbs (Skills):**
  - **Recognize** → Task: Identify features and explain how they contribute to understanding.
- **Nouns (Content):**
  - **Features** → Question: How do pronunciation guides and diagrams help you understand the text?

(iii) organizational patterns such as compare and contrast

- **Verbs (Skills):**
  - **Recognize** → Task: Identify and describe organizational patterns.
- **Nouns (Content):**
  - **Organizational patterns** → Question: How does the author use compare and contrast to present information?

TEKS (9)(E): Recognize characteristics and structures of argumentative text by:

(i) identifying the claim

- **Verbs (Skills):**
  - **Recognize** → Task: Identify and label the author's main argument.
  - **Identify** → Task: Locate the claim within the text.
- **Nouns (Content):**
  - **Claim** → Question: What is the author's main argument or position?

(ii) explaining how the author has used facts for an argument

- **Verbs (Skills):**
  - **Explain** → Task: Describe how factual evidence supports the argument.
- **Nouns (Content):**
  - **Facts** → Question: What evidence does the author use to support their argument?

(iii) identifying the intended audience or reader

- **Verbs (Skills):**
  - **Identify** → Task: Determine the target audience of the text.
- **Nouns (Content):**
  - **Intended audience or reader** → Question: Who is the author writing this argument for, and how can you tell?

TEKS (9)(F): Recognize characteristics of multimodal and digital texts

- **Verbs (Skills):**
  - **Recognize** → Task: Identify and describe unique features of multimodal or digital texts.
- **Nouns (Content):**
  - **Characteristics of multimodal and digital texts** → Question: What makes a multimodal or digital text different from a traditional text?

TEKS (10) Analysis: Verbs (Skills) to Tasks and Nouns (Content) to Questions

---

TEKS (10)(A): Explain the author's purpose and message within a text

- **Verbs (Skills)**:
    - ○ **Explain** → Task: Provide a clear written or verbal explanation of the author's purpose and message.
- **Nouns (Content)**:
    - ○ **Author's purpose** → Question: Why did the author write this text?
    - ○ **Author's message** → Question: What idea or lesson does the author want readers to take away?

TEKS (10)(B): Explain how the use of text structure contributes to the author's purpose

- **Verbs (Skills)**:
    - ○ **Explain** → Task: Analyze and describe how the text structure supports the author's intent.
    - ○ **Contributes** (implied) → Task: Connect specific structures to the author's purpose.
- **Nouns (Content)**:
    - ○ **Text structure** → Question: What text structure is used in this passage (e.g., cause-effect, problem-solution), and how does it work?
    - ○ **Author's purpose** → Question: How does the structure help the author achieve their purpose?

TEKS (10)(C): Analyze the author's use of print and graphic features to achieve specific purposes

- **Verbs (Skills)**:
    - ○ **Analyze** → Task: Break down and evaluate how the author uses print and graphic elements to enhance their purpose.
- **Nouns (Content)**:
    - ○ **Print features** → Question: What print features (e.g., bold text, headings) are used, and how do they emphasize key ideas?
    - ○ **Graphic features** → Question: How do the graphic elements (e.g., charts, illustrations) contribute to the text's meaning?
    - ○ **Specific purposes** → Question: What purpose is the author trying to achieve with these features?

TEKS (10)(D): Describe how the author's use of imagery, literal and figurative language such as simile and metaphor, and sound devices such as alliteration and assonance achieves specific purposes

- **Verbs (Skills)**:
  - **Describe** → Task: Articulate how specific language and sound devices enhance the author's intent.
- **Nouns (Content)**:
  - **Imagery** → Question: What mental images does the author create, and how do they support the text's purpose?
  - **Literal language** → Question: How does straightforward language clarify the author's message?
  - **Figurative language** → Question: How do similes or metaphors deepen the reader's understanding of the text?
  - **Sound devices** → Question: What effect do alliteration and assonance have on the tone or rhythm of the text?
  - **Specific purposes** → Question: How do these devices help the author achieve their goals?

TEKS (10)(E): Identify and understand the use of literary devices, including first- or third-person point of view

- **Verbs (Skills)**:
  - **Identify** → Task: Recognize literary devices in the text.
  - **Understand** → Task: Explain how these devices contribute to meaning or perspective.
- **Nouns (Content)**:
  - **Literary devices** → Question: What literary devices are used in this text, and where are they located?
  - **First-person point of view** → Question: How does the first-person point of view affect how the reader understands the story?
  - **Third-person point of view** → Question: What does the third-person perspective reveal about the events or characters?

Summary

Breaking down these TEKS into **verbs (skills)** and **nouns (content)** provides a roadmap for instruction, ensuring that tasks and questions target the required skills while addressing the key content areas. By focusing on both **what students need to do** and **what they need to know**, teachers can create clear, purposeful lessons aligned with these TEKS.

List of Verbs Found Within Each TEKS

Section 6: Comprehension Skills

- **(A):** establish
- **(B):** generate, deepen, gain
- **(C):** make, correct, confirm, use
- **(D):** create, deepen
- **(E):** make, connect
- **(F):** make, use, support
- **(G):** evaluate, determine
- **(H):** synthesize, create
- **(I):** monitor, make, re-read, use, ask, annotate

Section 7: Response Skills

- **(A):** describe
- **(B):** write, demonstrate, compare, contrast
- **(C):** use, support
- **(D):** retell, paraphrase, summarize, maintain
- **(E):** interact, notetake, annotate, freewrite, illustrate
- **(F):** respond, use
- **(G):** discuss

Section 8: Multiple Genres - Literary Elements

- **(A):** infer, support
- **(B):** explain, interact, undergo
- **(C):** analyze, include
- **(D):** explain, influence

Section 9: Multiple Genres - Genres

- **(A):** demonstrate, distinguish
- **(B):** explain, use, create
- **(C):** explain
- **(D):** recognize, support
  - o **(i):** identify
  - o **(ii):** support
  - o **(iii):** compare, contrast
- **(E):** recognize
  - o **(i):** identify
  - o **(ii):** explain, use
  - o **(iii):** identify
- **(F):** recognize

Section 10: Author's Purpose and Craft

- **(A):** explain
- **(B):** explain, contribute
- **(C):** analyze, achieve
- **(D):** describe, achieve
- **(E):** identify, understand

Summary of Key Verbs Across All Sections

The verbs emphasize **actionable skills** such as:

- **Higher-order thinking:** infer, analyze, evaluate, synthesize
- **Application:** use, create, support, recognize
- **Communication:** explain, describe, discuss, write
- **Interaction:** connect, interact, compare, contrast

This list highlights the active nature of the TEKS and can be used for lesson planning, assessments, and instructional focus.

TEKS/STAAR Keywords

Here is a breakdown of each word, its definition, and an example question for each word within the context of a STAAR Test question. Each question is linked to a specific TEKS:

---

1. Identify

- **Definition:** To find or recognize something in the text.
- **Example Question:**
  "In the passage, **identify** the main problem the character faces."
  (TEKS 3.9B): "Identify the central idea and supporting details in a text."

---

2. Explain

- **Definition:** To make something clear by describing it in more detail or by revealing relevant facts.
- **Example Question:**
  "Read the passage and **explain** how the main character's actions help solve the problem."
  (TEKS 4.6D): "Explain the sequence of events in a text."

---

3. Analyze

- **Definition:** To examine something carefully and in detail in order to understand it better.
- **Example Question:**
  "**Analyze** how the author uses descriptive language to create a mood of suspense in the story."
  (TEKS 5.9D): "Analyze how the author's use of language contributes to meaning."

---

4. Evaluate

- **Definition:** To judge or assess the value, quality, or importance of something.
- **Example Question:**
  "**Evaluate** the effectiveness of the character's decision to confront the villain at the end of the story."
  (TEKS 4.10B): "Evaluate how well the plot structure supports the theme."

5. Develop

- **Definition:** To build or improve something gradually, over time.
- **Example Question:**
  "In what way does the author **develop** the theme of friendship throughout the story?"
  (TEKS 5.9A): "Analyze how the author develops the theme through plot and character actions."

6. Organize

- **Definition:** To arrange or structure things in a specific order or pattern.
- **Example Question:**
  "How does the author **organize** the events in the passage to create a sense of mystery?"
  (TEKS 4.10A): "Describe the structure of a text, including its sequence of events."

7. Synthesize

- **Definition:** To combine different elements from multiple sources to form a complete idea.
- **Example Question:**
  "After reading the two articles, **synthesize** the information to explain how weather affects animal behavior."
  (TEKS 5.10E): "Synthesize information across multiple texts to understand ideas."

8. Discuss

- **Definition:** To talk about a topic or write about it in detail, considering different aspects.
- **Example Question:**
  "**Discuss** how the setting influences the main events in the story."
  (TEKS 4.6A): "Discuss how setting influences plot development."

9. Describe

- **Definition:** To give a detailed account of something.
- **Example Question:**
  "**Describe** the character's actions that lead to the solution of the conflict."
  (TEKS 3.8B): "Describe the character's actions and their role in resolving the plot."

10. Reflect

- **Definition:** To think deeply or carefully about something.
- **Example Question:**
  "After reading the story, **reflect** on how the character's journey relates to your own experiences."
  (TEKS 5.6F): "Reflect on how personal experiences relate to a character's journey."

11. Defend

- **Definition:** To support an argument or position with evidence.
- **Example Question:**
  "**Defend** your opinion on whether the main character made the right choice at the end of the story using evidence from the text."
  (TEKS 5.10D): "Use text evidence to defend a response or position."

Summary of Differences:

- **Identify** asks the student to **find** information.
- **Explain** requires the student to **clarify** information.
- **Analyze** requires a **detailed examination** of parts of the text.
- **Evaluate** asks the student to **judge** or **assess**.
- **Develop** focuses on how an idea or theme is **built** throughout the text.
- **Organize** focuses on how the structure is **arranged**.
- **Synthesize** asks the student to **combine** information from multiple sources.
- **Discuss** means to **consider** or **write about** a topic in detail.
- **Describe** requires the student to **give a detailed account**.
- **Reflect** asks for a **deep personal thought** or connection.
- **Defend** requires the student to **support** an opinion with evidence.

Each question type helps students engage with the text in different ways, encouraging comprehension, critical thinking, and reflection.

Chapter 2

Real-Life Applications of the TEKS

Introduction: The TEKS are designed to help students develop critical thinking and comprehension skills that apply not just to the classroom but to their everyday lives. By relating these standards to real-life situations, students can understand their broader significance and how they help navigate everyday experiences, family interactions, and social settings.

Below are examples of how these TEKS standards can be applied in practical, real-world scenarios.

Real-Life Applications for TEKS (6) Comprehension Skills

(A) Establish purpose for reading assigned and self-selected texts

- **Home:** A student reads a recipe with the purpose of baking cookies with family.
- **Friendships:** They read instructions for a board game to understand the rules and explain them to friends.
- **Outside School:** They read a wildlife guide with the purpose of identifying animals during a nature hike.
- **In School:** They set a purpose to find key facts while reading a science article for a project.

(B) Generate questions about text before, during, and after reading

- **Home:** They ask, "What will happen next?" while reading a bedtime story and discuss the ending with their parents.
- **Friendships:** During a shared storytime, they ask their friends questions about characters' motivations.
- **Outside School:** They watch a movie at the park and ask questions about its themes to deepen understanding.
- **In School:** They generate questions during a read-aloud to help understand challenging concepts.

(C) Make and correct or confirm predictions using text features, genre, and structures

- **Home:** They predict the outcome of a story based on its illustrations and genre and confirm or adjust their guess as they read.
- **Friendships:** They guess the ending of a comic book their friend is reading based on dialogue and visuals.
- **Outside School:** They use captions in a museum exhibit to predict what the next display will showcase.
- **In School:** They predict the results of a science experiment after reading the procedural text.

(D) Create mental images to deepen understanding

- **Home:** They visualize the setting of a fantasy novel and describe it to their family during dinner.
- **Friendships:** They imagine and act out a scene from a favorite book with their friends during play.
- **Outside School:** While attending a play, they visualize the characters' actions based on the dialogue.
- **In School:** They draw what they imagine while listening to a poem during English class.

(E) Make connections to personal experiences, ideas in other texts, and society

- **Home:** They connect a story about helping others to their own experiences doing chores.
- **Friendships:** They relate teamwork in a novel to working with friends during a soccer game.
- **Outside School:** They connect themes in a movie to lessons about kindness taught at their local church or community group.
- **In School:** They link a historical fiction book to lessons about the same time period in history class.

(F) Make inferences and use evidence to support understanding

- **Home:** They infer a character's feelings based on dialogue in a story their parent reads aloud.
- **Friendships:** They infer why a friend might be upset based on their tone and actions.
- **Outside School:** They infer why an animal behaves a certain way after observing it in a zoo exhibit.
- **In School:** They use text evidence from a book to explain their inferences about the main character's motivations.

(G) Evaluate details read to determine key ideas

- **Home:** They summarize the main points of a family newsletter.
- **Friendships:** They evaluate details in a rulebook to decide which parts are the most important for gameplay.
- **Outside School:** They identify the main takeaway from a presentation at a museum.
- **In School:** They highlight key points in a reading passage during a group activity.

(H) Synthesize information to create new understanding

- **Home:** They combine what they learned from a cooking show and a recipe book to create their own meal.
- **Friendships:** They integrate what they learned from different superhero comics to design their own superhero.
- **Outside School:** They use knowledge from multiple sources to create a nature journal during a hike.
- **In School:** They synthesize information from multiple articles to write a report on environmental conservation.

(I) Monitor comprehension and make adjustments

- **Home:** They re-read a confusing part of a story their parent read aloud.
- **Friendships:** They ask their friends clarifying questions while playing a game with complex instructions.
- **Outside School:** They pause and ask questions about the rules of a community event if they don't understand.
- **In School:** They annotate a passage and refer to their notes to clarify meaning during class discussions.

Real-life applications of TEKS (7) Response Skills

(A) Describe personal connections to a variety of sources, including self-selected texts

- **Home:** A 4th grader connects a story about family traditions to their own holiday celebrations, like cooking a special dish with their parents.
- **Friendships:** While reading a book about teamwork, they relate the characters' struggles to their soccer team's challenges during a recent game.
- **Outside School:** They watch a nature documentary and share how it reminds them of a camping trip they went on with family.
- **In School:** During class discussion, they explain how a character's determination to succeed mirrors their experience studying for a tough test.

(B) Write responses that demonstrate understanding of texts, including comparing and contrasting ideas across a variety of sources

- **Home:** The student writes about how two bedtime stories, like *The Tortoise and the Hare* and *The Lion and the Mouse*, share themes of perseverance but differ in their characters' strategies.
- **Friendships:** They compare two superhero comics with friends, noting how one focuses on bravery while the other emphasizes teamwork.
- **Outside School:** At a community library, they write a book review comparing a new release with a classic they've read before.
- **In School:** The student writes a response comparing the depiction of natural disasters in a nonfiction article and a fictional story.

(C) Use text evidence to support an appropriate response

- **Home:** The student explains why they liked a specific character in a book by citing examples of their actions and dialogue.
- **Friendships:** While discussing a shared favorite movie, they use evidence from the script to argue why a particular scene is impactful.
- **Outside School:** During a museum visit, they use information from an exhibit description to explain their favorite artifact to their family.
- **In School:** In a reading response, they use direct quotes from a text to support their inference about a character's motivation.

(D) Retell, paraphrase, or summarize texts in ways that maintain meaning and logical order

- **Home:** After reading a chapter with their family, they summarize the key events to explain what happens next.
- **Friendships:** They retell the plot of a favorite TV show episode to their friends during lunch, ensuring the sequence of events is clear.
- **Outside School:** They paraphrase a wildlife guide's explanation of an animal's behavior to describe it during a nature walk.
- **In School:** The student summarizes the main ideas of a nonfiction text during a group activity in class.

(E) Interact with sources in meaningful ways such as notetaking, annotating, freewriting, or illustrating

- **Home:** They take notes while reading a cookbook with their parents to highlight the steps for a favorite recipe.
- **Friendships:** They annotate a shared comic book, underlining funny or important parts to discuss with their friends.
- **Outside School:** While attending a science fair, they sketch illustrations of an experiment setup to better understand it.
- **In School:** During a reading workshop, they highlight key points in an article and jot down questions in the margins.

(F) Respond using newly acquired vocabulary as appropriate

- **Home:** They use words like "ingenious" or "perseverance" from a book in conversations with their parents about a sibling's creative project.
- **Friendships:** While talking to friends, they describe a character in a shared story as "resilient," a word they recently learned in class.
- **Outside School:** They use new vocabulary like "ecosystem" or "predator" during a discussion about animals at the zoo.
- **In School:** During a book talk, they incorporate vocabulary words from the text to describe the setting and plot.

(G) Discuss specific ideas in the text that are important to the meaning

- **Home:** They discuss how a character's bravery helped them succeed in a family movie and what lesson they learned.
- **Friendships:** During a book club with friends, they explain why the theme of loyalty is central to the story they're reading.
- **Outside School:** After watching a community theater play, they share how the setting contributed to the overall story.
- **In School:** They participate in a class discussion about how the author uses the resolution to reinforce the story's message.

Real-life applications of TEKS (8) Multiple Genres: Literary Elements

(A) Infer basic themes supported by text evidence

- **Home:**
    - A student reads a family story about working together to solve problems and infers that the theme is teamwork. They apply this by helping their siblings clean up after dinner.
- **Friendships:**
    - While reading a story about friendship, the student infers the theme of forgiveness after seeing how the characters apologize to each other. They use this lesson to make up with a friend after an argument.
- **Outside School:**
    - At a community play, the student notices the theme of bravery as the main character faces challenges and connects it to their own experience of trying something new.
- **In School:**
    - During class discussions, they infer the theme of perseverance in a historical fiction book by citing moments when the characters refuse to give up.

(B) Explain the interactions of the characters and the changes they undergo

- **Home:**
    - While reading a bedtime story with their family, the student explains how a shy character becomes confident after helping others. They relate this to their own experience of gaining confidence by volunteering at home.
- **Friendships:**
    - The student observes how characters in a story resolve their differences and use a similar approach to work through disagreements with friends.
- **Outside School:**
    - At a library event, they describe how characters in a story about animals work together to survive, showing the importance of cooperation.
- **In School:**
    - During a group reading activity, they explain how the protagonist changes from selfish to kind and how other characters influence this transformation.

(C) Analyze plot elements, including the rising action, climax, falling action, and resolution

- **Home:**
  - While watching a family movie, the student identifies the rising action (the buildup of challenges), the climax (the turning point), and the resolution (how everything gets resolved).
- **Friendships:**
  - When recounting a funny story to friends, the student organizes the events into rising action, climax, and resolution to make the story more engaging.
- **Outside School:**
  - During a storytelling event, they analyze how the storyteller builds suspense to reach the climax and bring closure in the resolution.
- **In School:**
  - They break down the plot of a short story during a reading lesson, labeling key moments as rising action, climax, falling action, and resolution.

(D) Explain the influence of the setting, including historical and cultural settings, on the plot

- **Home:**
  - While reading a story set in the past, the student explains how the historical setting (e.g., the Great Depression) influences the characters' struggles to find work and food.
- **Friendships:**
  - They discuss how a fantasy story's magical setting changes the way characters solve problems compared to real life.
- **Outside School:**
  - During a visit to a historical site, the student explains how the events they learn about were shaped by the location and cultural norms of the time.
- **In School:**
  - In a classroom discussion, they analyze how the cultural setting in a folktale affects the characters' traditions and actions.

Real-life applications of TEKS (9) Multiple Genres

(A) Demonstrate knowledge of distinguishing characteristics of well-known children's literature such as folktales, fables, legends, myths, and tall tales

- **Home:** The student identifies *The Tortoise and the Hare* as a fable and shares its moral of perseverance with younger siblings during bedtime stories.
- **Friendships:** During play, they create their own tall tale about a superhero friend with exaggerated abilities, inspired by *Paul Bunyan.*
- **Outside School:** At a storytelling festival, they recognize a local legend and discuss its importance to their community's culture.
- **In School:** The student categorizes books in a class library, distinguishing myths, fables, and folktales based on their characteristics.

(B) Explain figurative language such as simile, metaphor, and personification that the poet uses to create images

- **Home:** The student notices a metaphor in a family conversation, like "time is flying by," and explains its meaning.
- **Friendships:** While joking with friends, they use similes, such as "You're as fast as a cheetah!" to make their stories more entertaining.
- **Outside School:** They read a poem in a park brochure describing trees as "dancing in the wind" and share how it creates a vivid image of the setting.
- **In School:** The student identifies personification in a class poem, such as "The moon whispers secrets to the stars," and explains its effect on the mood.

(C) Explain structure in drama such as character tags, acts, scenes, and stage directions

- **Home:** While putting on a family play, the student uses stage directions like "stand center stage" to guide their performance.
- **Friendships:** They write a short skit with friends, dividing it into scenes and adding character tags for clarity.
- **Outside School:** During a theater visit, they recognize how the transitions between acts and scenes shape the story.
- **In School:** The student analyzes a class play script, identifying character tags and stage directions to prepare for a performance.

(D) Recognize characteristics and structures of informational text

(i) The central idea with supporting evidence

- **Home:** While reading a family health magazine, the student identifies the main idea of an article about eating vegetables and cites supporting evidence, such as specific nutritional benefits.
- **Friendships:** During a group project, they determine the main idea of an article about teamwork and use it to brainstorm strategies for their task.
- **Outside School:** They summarize the central idea of a museum exhibit on dinosaurs and share it with their family.
- **In School:** The student highlights the main idea and supporting evidence in a science textbook about the water cycle.

(ii) Features such as pronunciation guides and diagrams

- **Home:** They use a pronunciation guide in a recipe book to correctly pronounce "quinoa" while helping prepare dinner.
- **Friendships:** While reading a manual for a board game, they reference diagrams to understand the setup and explain it to friends.
- **Outside School:** At a zoo, they study a diagram of an animal's habitat to understand its needs.
- **In School:** The student interprets a diagram in a history textbook to explain the layout of a historic fort.

(iii) Organizational patterns such as compare and contrast

- **Home:** The student compares two family pets' behaviors and writes about their differences in a journal.
- **Friendships:** While discussing two movies with friends, they contrast the characters and plotlines.
- **Outside School:** They compare the rules of two sports they're learning at a community center.
- **In School:** The student identifies the compare-and-contrast structure in a nonfiction text about different ecosystems.

(E) Recognize characteristics and structures of argumentative text

(i) Identifying the claim

- **Home:** The student identifies the claim in a commercial, such as "This toothpaste is the best for kids!"
- **Friendships:** During a debate about which video game is better, they recognize their friend's claim and provide their own counterpoint.

- **Outside School:** They read a flyer promoting recycling and identify the claim that recycling reduces waste.
- **In School:** The student analyzes an article about school uniforms, identifying the claim and supporting evidence.

(ii) Explaining how the author has used facts for an argument

- **Home:** While reading a family newsletter, they notice how facts about screen time are used to support limiting TV hours.
- **Friendships:** During a discussion about choosing a team captain, they point out facts friends use to argue why a specific person is the best choice.
- **Outside School:** At a library event, they explain how a speaker used statistics to support their argument for protecting local wildlife.
- **In School:** The student identifies factual evidence in an opinion article about reducing homework to support the author's point of view.

(iii) Identifying the intended audience or reader

- **Home:** They notice that a magazine article about parenting tips is written for parents and explain why the advice is tailored to that audience.
- **Friendships:** They recognize that a birthday invitation is intended for their group of friends and note the use of casual language and fun images.
- **Outside School:** The student explains how a park brochure about safety tips is aimed at families visiting the area.
- **In School:** They identify the audience for a persuasive essay written to the principal about adding recess time.

(F) Recognize characteristics of multimodal and digital texts

- **Home:** They interact with a cooking app by watching videos and reading instructions to help make dinner with their family.
- **Friendships:** They create a digital slideshow with images and captions to share photos and memories from a fun outing.
- **Outside School:** The student explores a museum's interactive exhibit that combines video, text, and diagrams to explain historical events.
- **In School:** They use an educational website with videos, quizzes, and infographics to complete a research assignment.

Real-life applications of TEKS (10) Author's Purpose and Craft

(A) Explain the author's purpose and message within a text

- **Home:**
  - The student reads a family recipe book and identifies the purpose as instructional—to teach how to prepare meals. They use this knowledge to cook with their parents.
- **Friendships:**
  - They explain that a comic book's purpose is to entertain and share funny moments with friends during a sleepover.
- **Outside School:**
  - While attending a community event, they recognize that a speaker's message about recycling aims to persuade the audience to take action.
- **In School:**
  - The student identifies the author's purpose in a persuasive article about school uniforms and explains its message to their classmates during a group discussion.

(B) Explain how the use of text structure contributes to the author's purpose

- **Home:**
  - They notice how a chore chart uses a list structure to clearly organize tasks for family members, making it easier to follow instructions.
- **Friendships:**
  - While reading a storybook with friends, they explain how the chronological structure helps build suspense leading to the climax.
- **Outside School:**
  - The student points out how a pamphlet at a local museum uses a cause-and-effect structure to show how pollution affects animals.
- **In School:**
  - During a reading lesson, they explain how the problem-and-solution structure in an article about endangered species highlights the importance of conservation efforts.

(C) Analyze the author's use of print and graphic features to achieve specific purposes

- **Home:**
  - The student uses bolded text and headings in a family manual to quickly locate troubleshooting tips for an appliance.
- **Friendships:**
  - They analyze how speech bubbles in a comic book help convey dialogue and emotions to make the story more engaging.
- **Outside School:**
  - While visiting a zoo, they notice how graphic features like diagrams and maps make it easier to understand an exhibit's information.
- **In School:**
  - They analyze a nonfiction article in a textbook, explaining how captions and charts support the main ideas in the text.

(D) Describe how the author's use of imagery, literal and figurative language such as simile and metaphor, and sound devices such as alliteration and assonance achieves specific purposes

- **Home:**
  - The student reads a bedtime story and points out a simile, such as "the night was as quiet as a mouse," to explain how it sets the tone.
- **Friendships:**
  - They notice how a poem in a birthday card uses alliteration, like "happy hugs and heartfelt hopes," to make it more cheerful and memorable.
- **Outside School:**
  - During a community play, they recognize how a metaphor like "the world is a stage" helps convey a deeper meaning.
- **In School:**
  - In a poetry unit, they describe how imagery in a poem, such as "golden rays of sunshine," paints a vivid mental picture for the reader.

(E) Identify and understand the use of literary devices, including first- or third-person point of view

- **Home:**
  - The student explains that a journal entry written in the first person helps them understand the author's personal experiences and emotions.
- **Friendships:**
  - They notice how a story written in third person lets them know more about all the characters, which helps them better explain the plot to friends.
- **Outside School:**
  - At a storytelling event, they identify the use of first-person point of view in a folktale and share how it makes the story feel more personal.
- **In School:**
  - During a reading lesson, they compare two stories—one written in first person and one in third person—and discuss how the perspective changes the reader's understanding.

Conclusion: Teaching the TEKS standards not only enhances students' comprehension of texts but also builds critical life skills that they can apply in everyday situations. Whether making decisions, understanding instructions, or analyzing experiences, these standards help students navigate the complexities of family, friends, and their community. As they grow, these skills equip them to engage more meaningfully in the world around them.

Chapter 3

Opening Activities for the TEKS

Here are three quick and easy <u>opening activities</u> for each of the specified TEKS standards:

TEKS (6) Comprehension Skills:

(A) Establish purpose for reading assigned and self-selected texts

1. **Book Cover Purpose Chart:**
   Display book covers or titles. Have students write why they might read each book (e.g., "to learn something new," "for fun").
2. **What's the Goal?**
   Provide a short passage and ask, "Why would someone read this text?" Discuss answers like entertainment, information, or persuasion.
3. **Read and Share:**
   Let students choose a book from the class library and share their purpose for reading (e.g., "I want to learn about sharks.").

(B) Generate questions about text before, during, and after reading

1. **Question Cards:**
   Give students a sentence starter like, "I wonder…" or "Why did…" and have them write a question about a text's title or cover.
2. **Stop and Ask:**
   Pause halfway through reading a passage and ask students to generate questions about what might happen next.
3. **Question Relay:**
   In small groups, students pass around a text and each write a question about it, building on each other's ideas.

(C) Make and correct or confirm predictions using text features, characteristics of genre, and structures

1. **Predict the Plot:**
   Show students the title and first sentence of a story and ask them to predict what will happen next.
2. **Cover Clues:**
   Display a book cover and ask students to predict the genre, plot, and theme based on the image and title.
3. **Prediction Check:**
   Stop reading halfway through a short passage and have students confirm or adjust their predictions.

(D) Create mental images to deepen understanding

1. **Draw the Scene:**
   Read a descriptive paragraph and ask students to draw what they imagine.
2. **Close Your Eyes:**
   Read aloud a vivid description and ask students to close their eyes and picture the scene. Then discuss.
3. **Illustrate a Sentence:**
   Give each student a sentence from a story to illustrate, focusing on sensory details.

(E) Make connections to personal experiences, ideas in other texts, and society

1. **Text-to-Self Chart:**
   After reading a short story, ask students to write one sentence about how it connects to their own life.
2. **Connections Carousel:**
   Post prompts like "Text-to-Text" and "Text-to-World" around the room. Students rotate and write connections for each.
3. **Story Share:**
   Read a short passage and ask, "Does this remind you of anything in your life?" Discuss as a class.

(F) Make inferences and use evidence to support understanding

1. **Inference Clues:**
   Provide a short scenario and ask students to infer what's happening (e.g., "The ground was wet, and kids were holding umbrellas").
2. **Who Am I? Game:**
   Write a character's actions and dialogue on the board. Students infer traits and back them up with evidence.
3. **Quote Detective:**
   Give a short quote from a text and ask, "What can we infer about this character or situation?"

(G) Evaluate details read to determine key ideas

1. **Highlighter Hunt:**
   Provide a paragraph and have students highlight key ideas versus supporting details.
2. **Main Idea Match:**
   Write sentences on cards (main idea and details). Students sort them into the correct categories.
3. **Key Idea Quiz:**
   Read a short text aloud and ask, "What's the most important thing the author wants us to know?"

(H) Synthesize information to create new understanding

1. **Mix and Match Facts:**
   Give two texts on the same topic. Students combine facts to write a new sentence or understanding.
2. **Double Bubble Map:**
   Compare two texts using a Venn diagram, then write a summary of what they learned.
3. **Text Blend:**
   After reading two short passages, students write a paragraph summarizing the most important ideas from both.

(I) Monitor comprehension and make adjustments

1. **Fix-It Chart:**
   Give a text with tricky parts. Students list what confused them and strategies they used to fix it (e.g., re-reading).
2. **Stop and Summarize:**
   Pause after every paragraph and have students summarize or ask, "Did that make sense?"
3. **Annotate the Text:**
   Hand out short texts for students to annotate, marking parts they understand and parts they need to revisit.

TEKS (7) Response Skills:

(A) Describe personal connections to a variety of sources, including self-selected texts

1. **Connection Web:**
   Write a text title in the center of the board. Students draw lines and write how the text connects to their own experiences (e.g., "This story reminds me of a trip I took to the zoo").
2. **Turn and Talk:**
   After reading a short story, have students turn to a partner and share one way the story connects to their life, such as a similar event or feeling.
3. **Post-It Connections:**
   Provide sticky notes and ask students to write one personal connection to a class read-aloud. Post them on a "Connections Wall."

(B) Write responses that demonstrate understanding of texts, including comparing and contrasting ideas across a variety of sources

1. **Quick Compare:**
   Show two short stories or videos and ask students to write one similarity and one difference. Example: "Both characters are brave, but one faces a bully, and the other faces a storm."
2. **T-Chart Response:**
   Create a T-chart labeled "Text 1" and "Text 2." Students fill in one idea from each text to compare and contrast them.
3. **Venn Diagram:**
   Provide a blank Venn diagram for students to compare two characters, settings, or events in two texts.

(C) Use text evidence to support an appropriate response

1. **Quote Finder:**
   After reading a passage, ask students to find a quote that answers a specific question (e.g., "What shows the character is brave?").
2. **Text Evidence Chart:**
   Create a chart with two columns: "My Answer" and "Text Evidence." Students fill in both after reading a short paragraph.
3. **Evidence Match:**
   Provide sentences with claims (e.g., "The character is kind") and have students match them to quotes from the text.

(D) Retell, paraphrase, or summarize texts in ways that maintain meaning and logical order

1. **Five-Finger Retell:**
   Teach students to retell using five fingers: Who, Where, What, Problem, and Solution. They share their retell with a partner.
2. **Summarize in 10 Words:**
   Challenge students to summarize a text in exactly 10 words, ensuring it captures the main ideas.
3. **Paraphrase Pairs:**
   Read a sentence or paragraph aloud and ask students to paraphrase it for a partner.

(E) Interact with sources in meaningful ways such as notetaking, annotating, freewriting, or illustrating

1. **Quick Notes:**
   Provide a short passage and have students jot down 2-3 key ideas or questions about it.
2. **Annotate the Text:**
   Hand out a short text and ask students to highlight a favorite sentence, circle unknown words, or write a quick note in the margin.
3. **Draw What You Read:**
   After reading a descriptive paragraph, have students quickly sketch what they imagined.

(F) Respond using newly acquired vocabulary as appropriate

1. **Word Match Response:**
   Give students a list of new vocabulary words and challenge them to use one in a sentence about the text.
2. **Quick Write with Vocabulary:**
   Ask students to write a short paragraph about the text, using at least two new vocabulary words correctly.
3. **Vocabulary Sentence Swap:**
   Students write a sentence using a new word from the text, then swap with a partner to guess its meaning based on context.

(G) Discuss specific ideas in the text that are important to the meaning

1. **Big Idea Discussion:**
   After reading, ask students to share what they think the most important idea in the text was and why.
2. **Idea Ranking:**
   Write three ideas from the text on the board. Students rank them in order of importance and explain their reasoning.
3. **Discussion Circles:**
   In small groups, students discuss specific questions about the text, such as "Why do you think the character made that choice?"

TEKS (8) Multiple Genres - Literary Elements:

(A) Infer basic themes supported by text evidence

1. **Theme Guess Game:**
   Write short quotes from well-known stories (e.g., *The Tortoise and the Hare*). Ask students to infer the theme and explain their reasoning.
   Example: "Slow and steady wins the race" → Perseverance.
2. **Theme Match-Up:**
   Create cards with themes (e.g., teamwork, honesty) and short story summaries. Students match the theme to the story and explain why.
3. **Think-Pair-Share:**
   Read a paragraph aloud and ask students to infer a possible theme. They discuss with a partner before sharing with the class.

(B) Explain the interactions of the characters and the changes they undergo

1. **Character Change Map:**
   Show an excerpt where a character's attitude or behavior changes. Ask students to draw or list how the character was at the beginning versus the end.
2. **Dialogue Dive:**
   Provide lines of dialogue from two characters in a story. Students infer how their relationship changes based on the interactions.
   Example: "I didn't like you at first, but now you're my best friend."
3. **Role-Play Changes:**
   Assign roles to students to act out a character's journey (e.g., shy to brave). Afterward, discuss the changes and what caused them.

(C) Analyze plot elements, including the rising action, climax, falling action, and resolution

1. **Plot Puzzle:**
   Provide scrambled events from a story. Students work in groups to arrange them in order: rising action, climax, falling action, resolution.
2. **Climax Highlight:**
   Read a short story excerpt and ask, "What is the most exciting or important moment in this text?" Discuss why that's the climax.
3. **Plot Line Diagram:**
   After reading a brief passage, students draw a basic plot line and label each part (rising action, climax, etc.).

(D) Explain the influence of the setting, including historical and cultural settings, on the plot

1. **Setting Swap:**
   Ask students, "What would happen if this story's setting was different?" Provide examples like changing *Little House on the Prairie* to a modern-day city.
2. **Setting Detective:**
   Read a short excerpt and ask students to identify clues about the time and place. Discuss how the setting affects the characters' actions.
3. **Timeline Connection:**
   Present a historical or cultural setting (e.g., medieval times) and ask students how it shapes a story's plot, such as how limited technology impacts the characters' problem-solving.

TEKS (9) Multiple Genres - Genres:

(A) Demonstrate knowledge of distinguishing characteristics of well-known children's literature such as folktales, fables, legends, myths, and tall tales

1. **Genre Match:**
   Provide a list of story summaries (e.g., *The Tortoise and the Hare, Paul Bunyan*). Students match each summary to its genre (fable, myth, etc.).
2. **Story Sorting:**
   Provide titles or descriptions of stories on slips of paper. Students sort them into categories: folktale, fable, myth, legend, or tall tale.
3. **Guess the Genre:**
   Read the beginning of a story aloud (e.g., "Once upon a time, a giant lived in the mountains…"). Students guess the genre and explain why.

(B) Explain figurative language such as simile, metaphor, and personification that the poet uses to create images

1. **Figurative Language Scavenger Hunt:**
   Display lines of poetry or short texts around the room. Students find examples of similes, metaphors, and personification and label them.
2. **Figurative Fix:**
   Write literal phrases (e.g., "The sun is bright") on the board. Students rewrite them with figurative language (e.g., "The sun is a golden ball in the sky").
3. **Quick Draw:**
   Provide a simile or metaphor (e.g., "Her smile was as bright as the sun") and ask students to quickly draw what it describes.

(C) Explain structure in drama such as character tags, acts, scenes, and stage directions

1. **Script Scramble:**
   Provide a short script with the parts mixed up (character tags, stage directions, dialogue). Students organize it correctly.
2. **Drama Decoder:**
   Show an excerpt from a play and ask students to identify character tags, acts, scenes, and stage directions.
3. **Act It Out:**
   Provide a short scene with stage directions. Students take turns reading their parts and following the directions.

(D) Recognize characteristics and structures of informational text

(i) The central idea with supporting evidence

1. **Main Idea Match:**
   Provide a paragraph and three possible main ideas. Students choose the correct one and underline the evidence.
2. **Title It!:**
   Read a short paragraph aloud and ask students to create a title that reflects the main idea.
3. **Evidence Chart:**
   Provide a central idea (e.g., "Rainforests are important") and a paragraph. Students highlight evidence supporting the idea.

(ii) Features such as pronunciation guides and diagrams

1. **Pronunciation Practice:**
   Provide words with pronunciation guides (e.g., "pterodactyl /ˌter-ə-ˈdak-təl/") and have students practice saying them aloud.
2. **Diagram Labeling:**
   Display a diagram (e.g., a plant's parts) with blank labels. Students fill in the missing terms based on a short description.
3. **Find the Feature:**
   Show a page from a textbook. Students identify and explain how features like captions or diagrams help understanding.

(iii) Organizational patterns such as compare and contrast

1. **Same and Different:**
   Provide two short passages and ask students to write one similarity and one difference.
2. **Sorting Sentences:**
   Give students mixed sentences from a compare-and-contrast passage. They sort them into "Compare" and "Contrast" columns.
3. **Venn Diagram Practice:**
   Provide two topics (e.g., cats and dogs) and have students use a Venn diagram to compare and contrast key details.

(E) Recognize characteristics and structures of argumentative text

(i) Identifying the claim

1. **Claim Clues:**
   Display a short advertisement or persuasive statement. Students identify the claim (e.g., "This product is the best!").
2. **Agree or Disagree:**
   Provide a simple claim (e.g., "School uniforms improve learning") and have students decide if they agree or disagree.
3. **Claim and Reason:**
   Write several claims and reasons. Students match each claim with its supporting reason.

(ii) Explaining how the author has used facts for an argument

1. **Fact Check:**
   Provide a paragraph with both facts and opinions. Students highlight the facts and explain how they support the argument.
2. **Strongest Argument:**
   Give a short argumentative text with multiple points. Students choose the strongest point and explain why.
3. **Fact Hunt:**
   Show a short article. Students find and write down two facts the author uses to support their argument.

(iii) Identifying the intended audience or reader

1. **Who's It For?:**
   Provide a flyer, ad, or article and ask students to identify the target audience (e.g., kids, parents, teachers).
2. **Audience Analysis:**
   Show two texts on the same topic (e.g., recycling) aimed at different audiences. Students compare how the language and style change.
3. **Rewrite for an Audience:**
   Provide a sentence (e.g., "This toy is the best!"). Students rewrite it for different audiences, such as kids and parents.

(F) Recognize characteristics of multimodal and digital texts

1. **What's the Mode?:**
   Show a video clip, infographic, or webpage. Students identify the different modes (e.g., visuals, audio, text) and their purpose.
2. **Multimodal Match-Up:**
   Provide examples of multimodal texts (e.g., a video with subtitles, an infographic). Students explain how each mode supports understanding.
3. **Design a Digital Ad:**
   Students create a quick sketch for a digital ad, including visuals, text, and a slogan to grab attention.

TEKS (10) Author's Purpose and Craft:

(A) Explain the author's purpose and message within a text

1. **Purpose Sort:**
   Provide short text excerpts (e.g., an ad, a poem, a news article). Students sort them into categories: persuade, inform, or entertain.
2. **Why Did They Write It?**
   Display a paragraph (e.g., a story about recycling). Students write one sentence explaining the author's purpose and the message.
3. **Purpose Discussion:**
   Show a commercial video clip and ask, "What is the purpose? What is the message the author wants us to take away?"

(B) Explain how the use of text structure contributes to the author's purpose

1. **Text Structure Match-Up:**
   Provide examples of different text structures (e.g., problem-solution, cause-effect). Students match each structure with a purpose (e.g., to explain a problem).
2. **What's the Structure?:**
   Show a short passage and ask students to identify its structure and how it supports the author's purpose.
   Example: A recipe's list format contributes to the purpose of giving step-by-step instructions.
3. **Structure Detective:**
   Use a nonfiction paragraph and ask, "Why did the author use this structure? How does it help us understand the text better?

(C) Analyze the author's use of print and graphic features to achieve specific purposes

1. **Feature Hunt:**
   Display a page from a nonfiction book. Students identify and explain how features like headings, captions, or bold text help the reader.
2. **Compare and Contrast Graphics:**
   Show two visuals (e.g., a bar graph and a diagram). Ask students which is more effective for understanding the author's message and why.
3. **Highlight the Purpose:**
   Use an advertisement or infographic. Students highlight text and graphics, explaining how they work together to achieve the purpose.

(D) Describe how the author's use of imagery, literal and figurative language such as simile and metaphor, and sound devices such as alliteration and assonance achieves specific purposes

1. **Figurative Language Match:**
   Provide examples of similes, metaphors, and alliteration. Students match each example to its effect (e.g., "creates a vivid image").
2. **Imagery Illustrations:**
   Read a sentence with strong imagery (e.g., "The golden sun dipped below the horizon"). Students draw what they picture and explain how the language creates the image.
3. **Sound Effect Search:**
   Share a poem with alliteration or assonance. Students underline the examples and explain how they enhance the poem's tone or rhythm.

(E) Identify and understand the use of literary devices, including first- or third-person point of view

1. **Point of View Sort:**
   Provide sentences written in first and third person. Students sort them and explain how the point of view affects the reader's understanding.
   Example: "I felt scared" (first person) vs. "She felt scared" (third person).
2. **Rewrite the Perspective:**
   Take a paragraph written in first person and have students rewrite it in third person (or vice versa). Discuss how this changes the narrative.
3. **Who's Telling the Story?:**
   Read a passage and ask, "Who is telling the story? How does their perspective influence the details shared?"

<u>Chapter 4</u>

Poems and Teacher Training Scripts to Explain the TEKS

Short Poems to help students recall what the ELAR TEKS Content

(6) Comprehension Skills

- **(A) Establish Purpose for Reading:**

  Before you read, ask yourself why,
  To learn, to enjoy, or just to try?
  A purpose set helps guide your way,
  So you can understand what's on display.

- **(B) Generate Questions:**

  Ask questions before, during, and when you're done,
  They help you learn, and make reading fun!
  What do you wonder? What do you see?
  Questions lead to discovery!

- **(C) Make Predictions:**

  Look at the pictures, titles, and more,
  Guess what will happen, what's in store.
  Check your guess as you read along,
  Was your prediction right or wrong?

- **(D) Create Mental Images:**

  Picture the story inside your head,
  See the colors, hear what's said.
  When you imagine what's going on,
  Your understanding will grow strong.

- **(E) Make Connections:**

  Connect the book to what you know,
  To places you've been, or a TV show.
  Link the text to your own life too,
  And understanding will shine through!

- **(F) Make Inferences:**

  Read between the lines, and take a look,
  At what's not said, but is in the book.
  Use clues to guess what's really true,
  That's an inference, and you can do it too!

- **(G) Evaluate Details:**

  What's the most important part?
  Think it through, give it heart.
  Decide what matters most to you,
  That's how you'll know what's key and true.

- **(H) Synthesize Information:**

  Take what you've read from here and there,
  Mix it together with thought and care.
  Combine the pieces into something new,
  And you'll create a bigger view!

- **(I) Monitor Comprehension:**

  If something's tricky, don't be shy,
  Go back and reread, give it a try.
  Ask questions, or look for clues,
  Until the meaning comes to you!

(7) Response Skills

- **(A) Describe Personal Connections:**

  How does this story remind you of you?
  Think of a time when something felt true.
  Make connections to your own life,
  To understand the text with less strife.

- **(B) Write Responses:**

  Write what you think and what you see,
  Compare the stories thoughtfully.
  Put your ideas on the page with care,
  To show you've learned, to show you care!

- **(C) Use Text Evidence:**

  Find the part that proves you're right,
  Use the text as your guiding light.
  When you give answers, use the clues,
  Text evidence is what you'll choose.

- **(D) Retell, Paraphrase, or Summarize:**

  Retell the story short and sweet,
  Tell the beginning, middle, and what's complete.
  Keep it clear, keep it neat,
  A summary helps the lesson repeat.

- **(E) Interact with Sources:**

  Take notes, doodle, or write down thoughts,
  Interact with reading, connect the dots.
  Drawing pictures or jotting words,
  Helps you understand what you've heard.

- **(F) Use Newly Acquired Vocabulary:**

  New words help us learn each day,
  Use them in what you think or say.
  Vocabulary helps us grow,
  Using new words lets others know.

- **(G) Discuss Important Ideas:**

  Talk about what matters most,
  The main ideas, the big idea post.
  Share your thoughts and what you've found,
  In a discussion, learning's all around!

---

(8) Multiple Genres - Literary Elements

- **(A) Infer Themes Supported by Text Evidence:**

  What's the lesson, what's the theme?
  Use the story to find the gleam.
  Look at the actions, look at the end,
  To see what message the book will send.

- **(B) Explain Interactions of Characters:**

  Who changed, and why did they grow?
  How did they treat each other, what did they show?
  Explain how they acted, what did they do,
  And how did they change from start to new?

- **(C) Analyze Plot Elements:**

  What's the climax, where's the peak?
  What happened after? Was it weak or sleek?
  Break down the story, bit by bit,
  So you can understand all of it!

- **(D) Explain the Influence of Setting:**

  Where does the story take place today?
  Does it change how the characters play?
  Explain how setting shapes the plot,
  The place and time can change a lot!

(9) Multiple Genres - Genres

- **(A) Characteristics of Well-Known Children's Literature:**

  Folktales, fables, legends, and myths,
  Stories we love to grow up with.
  Learn the differences, they're not the same,
  Each has a lesson, or a hero's name!

- **(B) Explain Figurative Language:**

  Similes say "like" or "as,"
  Metaphors compare, no "like," no "has."
  Personification makes objects real,
  Figurative language helps us feel!

- **(C) Explain Structure in Drama**
  Characters talk with tags on the side,
  Stage directions show how feelings hide.
  Scenes and acts move the story along,
  Like parts of a play or verses in song!
  Drama has structure—just like a book,
  With parts that tell us where to look!

- **(D) Recognize Characteristics of Informational Text**
  Facts and ideas are what you'll find,
  In texts that grow your curious mind!
  The central idea stands bold and true,
  With evidence stacked to support it too.
  Text features help—like maps and charts,
  To understand all the nonfiction parts!

- **(E) Recognize Characteristics of Argumentative Text**
  A claim is made—the author's view,
  Then facts are used to prove it true.
  They tell their side with strong support,
  To share an idea or build a report.
  And don't forget—each text is planned,
  For readers they hope will understand!

(10) Author's Purpose and Craft

- **(A) Explain the Author's Purpose:**

  Why did the author write this book?
  Was it to teach, to share, or just to hook?
  Understand the message, clear as day,
  So you can see what they wanted to say.

- **(B) Explain How Text Structure Contributes to Purpose:**

  How did the way the book was built,
  Help the author make their quilt?
  The way it's written helps you see,
  The author's purpose, clear as can be!

- **(C) Analyze the Author's Use of Print and Graphic Features**

  Did they bold it, box it, make it pop?
  Use pictures, labels, charts that stop?
  Print and graphics lead the way,
  To help you learn what words can't say.

- **(D) Describe the Author's Use of Imagery and Figurative Language**

  Can you see it? Hear it? Taste it too?
  That's imagery working just for you!
  With similes, sounds, and metaphors bright,
  The author paints pictures with pure delight.

- **(E) Identify and Understand Literary Devices (Point of View)**

  Is it "I" who tells the tale you hear?
  Or someone else who's far or near?
  First person sees from inside the show,
  Third person sees from high or low!

Teacher Script: Introducing TEKS (6) Comprehension Skills

Please know that the following scripts are only intended as a guide so that you can receive the best scope of the message that needs to be relayed to students. Please feel free to word the explanations in the best way for your students.

Teacher:

*"Today, we're going to talk about some really important skills that will help you become great readers and thinkers. These skills will guide you when you read, listen, speak, write, or think about stories, articles, or any text. We'll call these our **Comprehension Skills** because they help us understand and make sense of what we read or hear."*

(A) Establish Purpose for Reading Assigned and Self-Selected Texts

Teacher:

*"Let's start with **establishing purpose**. This means thinking about why you're reading something before you start. Are you reading for fun? To learn something new? To find an answer to a question? Knowing your purpose helps you focus.*

For example, if you're reading a recipe, your purpose is to learn how to cook something delicious. But if you're reading a comic book, your purpose might just be to laugh and enjoy the story!"

Possible Student Question:

"Why does it matter if I know my purpose? Can't I just read?"

Teacher Response:

"Good question! Knowing your purpose helps you pay attention to what's most important. For example, if you're reading to find out about pandas, you'll look for facts about pandas instead of focusing on unrelated details."

(B) Generate Questions About Text Before, During, and After Reading

Teacher:

"Next, let's talk about asking questions. A great reader is always curious! Before you read, you might ask, 'What will this book be about?' While reading, you might ask, 'What will happen next?' After reading, you could ask, 'What did I learn?' Asking questions helps you stay engaged and understand the text better."

Possible Student Question:
"What if I don't know what questions to ask?"

Teacher Response:
"Start simple! Look at the title, pictures, or headings, and ask yourself what you want to know. As you read, keep wondering about the characters, events, or facts."

(C) Make and Correct or Confirm Predictions

Teacher:
"Making predictions is like being a detective. You use clues from the text, like pictures, headings, or what you already know about the genre, to guess what might happen next. Then, as you keep reading, you see if your prediction was correct or if you need to change it."

Example:
"If you see a story titled The Lost Puppy, you might predict that the story will be about someone finding a puppy. As you read, you can check if your prediction is correct."

Possible Student Question:
"What if my prediction is wrong?"

Teacher Response:
"That's okay! Predictions aren't about being right or wrong; they're about thinking ahead and staying curious."

(D) Create Mental Images to Deepen Understanding

Teacher:
"Creating mental images means making a movie in your mind while you read. If the book says, 'The sun set over the ocean, painting the sky with orange and pink,' you can picture a colorful sunset in your head. This helps the story come alive!"

Possible Student Question:
"What if I can't picture anything?"

Teacher Response:
"Try reading the sentence again and focus on the words that describe colors, shapes, or actions. You can also imagine something similar you've seen before."

(E) Make Connections to Personal Experiences, Ideas in Other Texts, and Society

Teacher:
"Making connections means thinking about how what you're reading relates to your life, other books, or the world. For example, if you read about a character who's nervous about their first day of school, you might remember how you felt on your first day of school."

Possible Student Question:
"Why is making connections important?"

Teacher Response:
"It helps you understand the characters and events better because you can relate them to something you already know."

(F) Make Inferences and Use Evidence to Support Understanding

Teacher:
"Making inferences is like solving a mystery. You use clues from the text and what you already know to figure out something the author didn't say directly. For example, if a character is shivering and wearing a heavy coat, you can infer that it's cold outside."

Possible Student Question:
"What if I infer something wrong?"

Teacher Response:
"That's okay! You can reread the text and look for more clues to adjust your inference."

(G) Evaluate Details Read to Determine Key Ideas

Teacher:
"Evaluating details means deciding what's most important in a text. For example, if you're reading about sharks, the key idea might be that sharks are important for the ocean's ecosystem, and details like their size or diet support that idea."

Possible Student Question:
"How do I know which details are important?"

Teacher Response:
"Ask yourself: 'Does this detail help me understand the main idea? Or is it just extra information?'"

(H) Synthesize Information to Create New Understanding

Teacher:
"Synthesizing means taking all the information you read and combining it to create a new understanding. For example, if you read one article about how plants grow and another about how animals depend on plants, you might realize that plants are crucial for life on Earth."

Possible Student Question:
"Is synthesizing the same as summarizing?"

Teacher Response:
"Not exactly. Summarizing is about restating what the text says, but synthesizing means combining ideas from different texts or your own thoughts to create something new."

(I) Monitor Comprehension and Make Adjustments

Teacher:
"Monitoring comprehension means paying attention to whether you understand what you're reading. If something doesn't make sense, you can reread, look up a word, or ask a question to help you figure it out."

Possible Student Question:
"What if I still don't understand after rereading?"

Teacher Response:
"That's a great time to ask for help! You can also use pictures, headings, or even look for a simpler explanation in a different book."

Teacher Wrap-Up:
"These comprehension skills help you become an active reader. You're not just reading words—you're thinking, asking questions, and connecting ideas. Now let's practice one of these skills together!"

Teacher Script: Introducing TEKS (7) Response Skills

Please know that the following scripts are only intended as a guide so that you can receive the best scope of the message that needs to be relayed to students. Please feel free to word the explanations in the best way for your students.

Teacher:
*"Today, we're going to talk about some important skills that great readers, listeners, and thinkers use to respond to what they read, hear, or see. These are called **Response Skills** because they help us connect with texts and share our ideas about them. Let's go through each one together with examples you can relate to."*

(A) Describe personal connections to a variety of sources, including self-selected texts

Teacher:
"When you read or watch something, does it ever remind you of something in your life? This is called making a personal connection. For example, if you read a story about a character who feels nervous on the first day of school, you might think about how you felt on your first day of school. Making personal connections helps you understand the text better."

Possible Student Question:
"What if I can't think of a personal connection?"

Teacher Response:
"That's okay! Instead, you can think about other books you've read or things you've seen on TV that are similar. Those are connections too."

(B) Write responses that demonstrate understanding of texts, including comparing and contrasting ideas across a variety of sources

Teacher:
"Sometimes, we read two texts that are alike in some ways but different in others. For example, one story might be about a boy training for a race, and another might be about a girl preparing for a spelling bee. You can compare them by writing about how both characters worked hard, but their goals were different. This shows that you understand both stories."

Possible Student Question:
"Do I have to write a long response every time?"

Teacher Response:
"Not at all! Even one or two sentences comparing the stories is a great start. For example, 'Both characters were determined, but one trained for a race, and the other studied for a spelling bee.'"

(C) Use text evidence to support an appropriate response

Teacher:
"When you share your thoughts about a text, it's important to back them up with evidence from the text. For example, if you say, 'The character is brave,' you can use evidence like, 'The text says she entered the dark forest even though she was scared.' This shows you're paying attention to the details."

Possible Student Question:
"What if I can't find any evidence in the text?"

Teacher Response:
"Look closely at what the characters say and do or at the descriptions in the text. If you're still not sure, you can ask me or a friend for help!"

(D) Retell, paraphrase, or summarize texts in ways that maintain meaning and logical order

Teacher:
"Retelling, paraphrasing, and summarizing are ways to share the most important parts of a text. Retelling is when you explain the story in your own words but include all the key events. Summarizing is when you share only the main ideas, like saying, 'This story is about a boy who finds a lost dog and returns it to its owner.'"

Possible Student Question:
"What's the difference between retelling and summarizing?"

Teacher Response:
"Great question! Retelling includes more details and happens in the same order as the story. Summarizing is shorter and only focuses on the big ideas."

(E) Interact with sources in meaningful ways such as notetaking, annotating, freewriting, or illustrating

Teacher:
"When you read or listen to something, you can interact with it by jotting down notes, underlining key parts, or drawing pictures of what you imagined. For example, if you're reading a story about a dragon, you could draw the dragon or write a note about how it's described in the text. These activities help you remember and understand better."

Possible Student Question:
"What if I don't like drawing or writing?"

Teacher Response:
"That's okay! You can choose the method that works best for you. For example, you might like highlighting important parts or just jotting down a quick thought."

(F) Respond using newly acquired vocabulary as appropriate

Teacher:
"Every time you read or listen to something, you have the chance to learn new words. For example, if you learn the word 'courageous' in a story, you can use it to describe another character who shows bravery. Using new words shows that you're growing as a reader and thinker."

Possible Student Question:
"What if I'm not sure how to use a new word?"

Teacher Response:
"That's normal! Start by looking at how it's used in the text, and try using it in your own sentence. If you're still unsure, ask a friend or me for help."

(G) Discuss specific ideas in the text that are important to the meaning

Teacher:
"When you discuss a text, it's important to focus on the big ideas that matter most. For example, in a story about friendship, you might talk about how the characters helped each other or what the author wanted you to learn about being a good friend."

Possible Student Question:
"What if I think something is important, but others don't agree?"

Teacher Response:
"That's okay! Different people notice different things in a text. Just explain why you think it's important, and listen to what others think too. That's how we learn from each other."

Teacher Wrap-Up:
"These response skills are like tools that help us think about what we read, hear, or see. They make reading more interesting and help us connect with texts in meaningful ways. Now let's practice one of these skills together!"

Teacher Script: Introducing TEKS (8) Multiple Genres—Literary Elements

Please know that the following scripts are only intended as a guide so that you can receive the best scope of the message that needs to be relayed to students. Please feel free to word the explanations in the best way for your students.

Teacher:
*"Today, we're going to learn about the building blocks of stories. These are called **literary elements**. When we understand these elements, we can figure out the message of the story, how the characters grow, how the plot works, and how the setting influences everything. Let's dive in!"*

(A) Infer Basic Themes Supported by Text Evidence

Teacher:
*"Have you ever read a story and thought, 'This is teaching me a lesson'? That's called finding the **theme**. The theme is the big idea or message the author wants you to understand.*

For example, in The Tortoise and the Hare, the theme is perseverance—how slow and steady wins the race. To figure out the theme, you look at what happens in the story and use evidence to support your idea."

Possible Student Question:
"What if there's more than one theme in a story?"

Teacher Response:
"Great question! Many stories have more than one theme. For example, a story can be about bravery and friendship. It's okay to find more than one, as long as you can explain your thinking with evidence from the story."

(B) Explain the Interactions of the Characters and the Changes They Undergo

Teacher:
"Stories are all about characters and how they interact with each other. Sometimes, characters argue, help each other, or grow as people.

For example, let's say we're reading about a character who starts out shy but becomes confident after making a new friend. You could explain how that friendship helped the character change."

Possible Student Question:
"What if a character doesn't change?"

Teacher Response:
"Good observation! Some characters, called static characters, stay the same. For example, a wise mentor in a story might remain calm and steady to guide others."

(C) Analyze Plot Elements, Including the Rising Action, Climax, Falling Action, and Resolution

Teacher:
*"The **plot** is like the roadmap of the story—it's what happens from beginning to end. Every story has certain parts:*

1. ***Rising Action**—the build-up where the characters face challenges.*
2. ***Climax**—the most exciting part or the turning point.*
3. ***Falling Action**—what happens after the climax.*
4. ***Resolution**—how the story ends.*

Let's think about The Three Little Pigs. The climax is when the wolf tries to blow down the brick house, and the resolution is when the pigs are safe."

Possible Student Question:
"How can I tell what the climax is?"

Teacher Response:
"The climax is usually the part where you're on the edge of your seat, wondering what's going to happen. It's the big moment when everything changes for the characters."

(D) Explain the Influence of the Setting, Including Historical and Cultural Settings, on the Plot

Teacher:
*"The **setting** is where and when the story takes place. The setting can be a time in history, like the Civil War, or a place, like a magical forest. The setting influences the plot because it affects what the characters do and the challenges they face.*

For example, if a story takes place in the Arctic, the characters might struggle with freezing temperatures and need to find food and shelter. If the story happened in a desert instead, their challenges would be very different!"

Possible Student Question:
"What if the setting doesn't seem important?"

Teacher Response:
"Even if it's not obvious, the setting often influences how characters behave or what problems they face. Think about how a story in the past might have no technology, which makes solving problems harder."

Teacher Wrap-Up:

*"These literary elements—**theme, characters, plot, and setting**—are the key to understanding stories. They help us figure out why things happen and what the story is trying to teach us. Let's practice together by reading a short story and identifying these elements!"*

Teacher Script: Introducing TEKS (9) Multiple Genres

Please know that the following scripts are only intended as a guide so that you can receive the best scope of the message that needs to be relayed to students. Please feel free to word the explanations in the best way for your students.

Teacher:
*"Today, we're going to learn about different types of texts, or **genres**, and how to understand what makes each one special. Stories, poems, informational articles, and even online content all have unique characteristics, and we can learn how to recognize and analyze them. This will help us become better readers, writers, and thinkers!"*

(A) Demonstrate Knowledge of Distinguishing Characteristics of Well-Known Children's Literature

Teacher:
"Have you ever read a story like The Tortoise and the Hare or Paul Bunyan? These stories belong to different genres like fables, folktales, myths, legends, and tall tales. Each genre has its own characteristics.

For example, a fable like The Tortoise and the Hare teaches a moral, or lesson, like 'slow and steady wins the race.' A tall tale, like Paul Bunyan, uses exaggeration, such as Paul being so big he created the Grand Canyon by dragging his axe."

Possible Student Question:
"How can I tell what genre a story is?"

Teacher Response:
"Look for clues! If it teaches a lesson with talking animals, it's probably a fable. If it has exaggerated characters or events, it's likely a tall tale. The details in the story will help you figure it out."

(B) Explain Figurative Language Such as Simile, Metaphor, and Personification

Teacher:
"Authors use figurative language to make their writing more interesting and create vivid images.

- *A **simile** compares two things using 'like' or 'as,' like 'Her smile was as bright as the sun.'*
- *A **metaphor** compares things without using 'like' or 'as,' like 'The classroom was a zoo.'*
- ***Personification** gives human traits to objects or animals, like 'The wind whispered through the trees.'*

These help us imagine what the author is describing."

Possible Student Question:
"How can I figure out if something is a simile or a metaphor?"

Teacher Response:
"Great question! Look for the words 'like' or 'as.' If they're there, it's a simile. If not, and it's comparing two things directly, it's a metaphor."

(C) Explain Structure in Drama

Teacher:
"Drama, or plays, is written in a unique way. It has:

- *Character tags: These show who is speaking.*
- *Acts and scenes: These divide the play into sections, like chapters in a book.*
- *Stage directions: These tell actors what to do, like 'walk to the center of the stage.'*

For example, if we read a play about a school talent show, it might have two acts: Act 1 could be about preparing for the show, and Act 2 could be the actual performance."

Possible Student Question:
"What's the difference between a play and a story?"

Teacher Response:
"A play is meant to be performed, so it uses dialogue and stage directions, while a story is written to be read."

(D) Recognize Characteristics and Structures of Informational Text

Teacher:
"Informational texts give us facts and information. Here's how they're structured:

1. *Central Idea with Supporting Evidence: The main idea is like the big picture, and the evidence gives details to support it.*
2. *Features Like Pronunciation Guides and Diagrams: These help us understand better, like a pronunciation guide for tricky words or a diagram showing how something works.*
3. *Organizational Patterns Like Compare and Contrast: Some texts compare things, like apples and oranges, to show similarities and differences."*

Possible Student Question:
"How do I know the central idea of a text?"

Teacher Response:
"Look for repeated ideas or what the whole text is mainly about. Ask yourself, 'What does the author want me to learn?'"

(E) Recognize Characteristics and Structures of Argumentative Text

Teacher:
"An argumentative text is meant to persuade you to agree with the author's point of view. Here's how to recognize it:

1. ***The Claim:*** *This is the author's main argument or opinion, like 'Everyone should recycle.'*
2. ***Facts for the Argument:*** *The author uses facts to support the claim, like 'Recycling saves energy.'*
3. ***Intended Audience:*** *The author writes differently depending on who they're trying to convince, like kids or parents."*

Possible Student Question:
"How do I know if a fact supports the claim?"

Teacher Response:
"Good question! A fact supports the claim if it explains why the claim is true or gives evidence to back it up."

(F) Recognize Characteristics of Multimodal and Digital Texts

Teacher:
"Multimodal and digital texts combine words, images, and sounds to share information. For example, a website about space might have text explaining the planets, videos showing rocket launches, and pictures of astronauts. Each part helps you understand the topic better."

Possible Student Question:
"How is multimodal text different from regular text?"

Teacher Response:
"Regular text is just words, like a storybook. Multimodal text adds visuals, sounds, or videos to make learning more interactive and fun."

Teacher Wrap-Up: *"These genres and text structures are all around us—in books, websites, plays, and more. Recognizing them helps us understand what we're reading and how authors communicate their ideas. Now let's explore these together with some examples!"*

Teacher Script: Introducing TEKS (10) Author's Purpose and Craft

Please know that the following scripts are only intended as a guide so that you can receive the best scope of the message that needs to be relayed to students. Please feel free to word the explanations in the best way for your students.

Teacher:
*"Today, we're going to talk about how authors make choices in their writing to communicate ideas. These choices, like what they write about and how they write it, are called **author's craft**. By understanding an author's purpose and their craft, we can become better readers, writers, and thinkers."*

(A) Explain the Author's Purpose and Message Within a Text

Teacher:
*"Let's start with the **author's purpose**. Authors write with a reason in mind. They might want to:*

- *__Persuade__ you to believe or do something,*
- *__Inform__ you about something, or*
- *__Entertain__ you with a story.*

For example, if you read a commercial that says, 'Eat Healthy Snacks to Feel Great!' the author's purpose is to persuade you to eat healthy foods. The message is that eating healthy makes you feel better."

Possible Student Question:
"What if the text doesn't seem to fit one of those purposes?"

Teacher Response:
"Good question! Some texts might have more than one purpose. A story about a superhero might entertain you but also persuade you to be brave or kind."

(B) Explain How the Use of Text Structure Contributes to the Author's Purpose

Teacher:
*"Now let's talk about **text structure**, or how a text is organized. Authors choose different structures to help them achieve their purpose.*

For example:

- *A **cause-and-effect** structure shows how one event leads to another.*
- *A **problem-and-solution** structure presents a problem and explains how to solve it.*
- *A **sequence** structure lists steps in order, like a recipe.*

If the author's purpose is to teach you how to make slime, they might use a sequence structure with numbered steps."

Possible Student Question:
"How do I figure out what structure the author used?"

Teacher Response:
"Look at the way the text is organized. Are there steps? Is the author comparing two things? Those clues will help you figure it out.

(C) Analyze the Author's Use of Print and Graphic Features to Achieve Specific Purposes

Teacher:
*"Authors also use **print and graphic features** to help you understand their message.*

- *__Print features__ include bold words, headings, and bullet points to make information stand out.*
- *__Graphic features__ include pictures, charts, and diagrams to visually explain ideas.*

For example, in a book about sharks, the author might bold the word 'predator' and include a diagram of a shark's teeth to show how they hunt."

Possible Student Question:
"Why do authors use pictures or bold words?"

Teacher Response:
"They use these features to grab your attention and make the information easier to understand. It's like adding highlights to the most important parts."

(D) Describe How the Author's Use of Imagery, Figurative Language, and Sound Devices Achieves Specific Purposes

Teacher:
"Authors use language to paint pictures in your mind and make their writing more interesting.

- *__Imagery__ uses words to describe how something looks, feels, smells, tastes, or sounds.*
- *__Figurative language__ includes:*
  - *__Similes__, like 'Her smile was as bright as the sun,' to compare two things.*
  - *__Metaphors__, like 'Time is a thief,' to make a point creatively.*
  - *__Personification__, like 'The wind whispered,' to give human qualities to non-human things.*
- *__Sound devices__ include:*
  - *__Alliteration__, like 'Peter Piper picked a peck,' where words start with the same sound.*

     o   *Assonance, like 'The rain in Spain stays mainly in the plain,' where vowel sounds repeat."*

Possible Student Question:

"Why do authors use figurative language instead of just saying things plainly?"

Teacher Response:

"Great question! Figurative language makes writing more engaging and helps the reader imagine what the author is describing. It's like adding flavor to your favorite food!"

(E) Identify and Understand the Use of Literary Devices, Including First- or Third-Person Point of View

Teacher:

*"The **point of view** is the perspective the author uses to tell the story:*

- ***First-person** point of view uses 'I' or 'we,' so the narrator is part of the story. Example: 'I walked into the spooky house.'*
- ***Third-person** point of view uses 'he,' 'she,' or 'they,' so the narrator is outside the story. Example: 'She walked into the spooky house.'*

The author chooses the point of view to help you connect with the story in a certain way. A first-person story might feel more personal, while a third-person story might give you a bigger picture of what's happening."

Possible Student Question:

"How does the point of view change how I understand the story?"

Teacher Response:

"Good question! In first-person, you only know what the narrator knows or feels. In third-person, you might see what all the characters are thinking, so you get more information."

Teacher Wrap-Up:

"Authors make choices about their purpose, structure, language, and point of view to communicate their ideas in the best way. Understanding these choices helps us enjoy stories, learn new things, and even improve our own writing. Let's practice analyzing these elements together!"

Chapter 5

Explanation of the TEKS by Content Area

Here's a <u>student-friendly explanation</u> for each TEKS standard:

(6) Comprehension Skills:

- **(A) Establish purpose for reading assigned and self-selected texts:**
  - *Explanation:* This means figuring out why you are reading something before you start. Are you reading for fun, to learn something, or to follow instructions?
  - *Example:* If you're reading a comic book, you might be reading for fun. If you're reading a science article, you're reading to learn new information.
- **(B) Generate questions about text before, during, and after reading to deepen understanding and gain information:**
  - *Explanation:* You should ask questions while you read. What do you wonder about before starting? Are you curious about anything as you read? What new questions do you have after you finish?
  - *Example:* If you're reading about space, you might ask, "How do astronauts train?" while reading, and "What does space feel like?" afterward.
- **(C) Make and correct or confirm predictions using text features, characteristics of genre, and structures:**
  - *Explanation:* Make guesses about what will happen next in the story, and see if you were right.
  - *Example:* If you see a picture of a superhero flying, you might predict that the hero will save someone in trouble.
- **(D) Create mental images to deepen understanding:**
  - *Explanation:* While reading, imagine pictures in your mind of what's happening in the story.
  - *Example:* If the book describes a forest, picture the trees, the animals, and how it might feel to be there.
- **(E) Make connections to personal experiences, ideas in other texts, and society:**
  - *Explanation:* Think about how what you're reading connects to your life, another book, or something happening in the world.
  - *Example:* If you read a book about a kid moving to a new school, think about how you felt when you started a new grade.
- **(F) Make inferences and use evidence to support understanding:**
  - *Explanation:* Use clues from the story to figure out things the author doesn't tell you directly.
  - *Example:* If a character is shivering and wearing a coat, you can infer that it's cold outside.
- **(G) Evaluate details read to determine key ideas:**
  - *Explanation:* Decide what the most important ideas are in what you're reading.
  - *Example:* In a book about animals, the key idea might be that all animals need food, water, and shelter to survive.
- **(H) Synthesize information to create new understanding:**
  - *Explanation:* Take everything you've learned from the text and put it together to form a big idea.
  - *Example:* After reading a book about plants and a book about insects, you might realize how they help each other grow and survive.

- **(I) Monitor comprehension and make adjustments such as re-reading, using background knowledge, asking questions, and annotating when understanding breaks down:**
  - *Explanation:* If you don't understand something, stop and try to figure it out by re-reading, thinking about what you already know, or asking questions.
  - *Example:* If a paragraph is confusing, go back and read it again more slowly or ask someone to explain it.

(7) Response Skills:

- **(A) Describe personal connections to a variety of sources, including self-selected texts:**
  - *Explanation:* Tell how what you're reading reminds you of your own life or something you've read before.
  - *Example:* If you read about a family going on a vacation, you might think of a trip you took with your family.
- **(B) Write responses that demonstrate understanding of texts, including comparing and contrasting ideas across a variety of sources:**
  - *Explanation:* Write about what you learned from the story and how it is similar to or different from other things you've read.
  - *Example:* Compare how two stories have different endings or how two characters solved their problems in different ways.
- **(C) Use text evidence to support an appropriate response:**
  - *Explanation:* When you answer a question about the text, include quotes or details from the text to back up your answer.
  - *Example:* If you say that the main character is brave, find a part in the story where the character shows bravery.
- **(D) Retell, paraphrase, or summarize texts in ways that maintain meaning and logical order:**
  - *Explanation:* Tell the story again in your own words while keeping the important parts in the right order.
  - *Example:* After reading a fairy tale, retell it by explaining what happened at the beginning, middle, and end.
- **(E) Interact with sources in meaningful ways such as notetaking, annotating, freewriting, or illustrating:**
  - *Explanation:* Show that you understand the text by taking notes, writing your thoughts, or drawing pictures about what you read.
  - *Example:* After reading, draw your favorite part or take notes on new facts you learned.
- **(F) Respond using newly acquired vocabulary as appropriate:**
  - *Explanation:* Use new words you learned from the text when talking or writing about it.
  - *Example:* If you learn the word "habitat" while reading about animals, use it in your discussion about where animals live.
- **(G) Discuss specific ideas in the text that are important to the meaning:**
  - *Explanation:* Talk about the big ideas in the story and why they matter.
  - *Example:* After reading a story about teamwork, discuss how the characters worked together to solve their problem.

(8) Multiple Genres - Literary Elements:

- **(A) Infer basic themes supported by text evidence:**
  - *Explanation:* Figure out the lesson or message of the story by looking at what happens and what the characters learn.
  - *Example:* In a story where friends help each other, the theme might be "friendship is important."
- **(B) Explain the interactions of the characters and the changes they undergo:**
  - *Explanation:* Describe how the characters treat each other and how they grow or change throughout the story.
  - *Example:* If a character starts off shy but becomes brave, explain what made that change happen.
- **(C) Analyze plot elements, including the rising action, climax, falling action, and resolution:**
  - *Explanation:* Break down the story into parts – the events that lead up to the most exciting part, the climax (big moment), and how the story ends.
  - *Example:* After reading a mystery, explain how the events built up to the big reveal of "who did it."
- **(D) Explain the influence of the setting, including historical and cultural settings, on the plot:**
  - *Explanation:* Talk about how the time and place where the story happens affect what happens in the story.
  - *Example:* If a story takes place in the past, explain how that makes things different from today.

(9) Multiple Genres - Genres:

- **(A) Demonstrate knowledge of distinguishing characteristics of well-known children's literature such as folktales, fables, legends, myths, and tall tales:**
  - *Explanation:* Recognize what makes different types of stories, like folktales or fables, special.
  - *Example:* A fable has a moral or lesson, while a tall tale has exaggerated characters that do impossible things.
- **(B) Explain figurative language such as simile, metaphor, and personification that the poet uses to create images:**
  - *Explanation:* Understand how authors use special language, like comparing things, to paint a picture in your mind.
  - *Example:* If the author says, "The clouds were cotton candy in the sky," they're using a metaphor to compare clouds to candy.
- **(C) Explain structure in drama such as character tags, acts, scenes, and stage directions:**
  - Explanation: Understand how plays are written and organized, like who is talking, where they are, and what they're doing.

   o Example: If a script says "JAY (excited): I can't wait!" — "JAY" is the character tag, "(excited)" is the stage direction, and this all happens in a certain scene or act of the play.

- **(D) Recognize characteristics and structures of informational text, including:**
  (i) the central idea with supporting evidence;
  (ii) features such as pronunciation guides and diagrams to support understanding; and
  (iii) organizational patterns such as compare and contrast:
  - o Explanation: Learn how nonfiction texts give information clearly using facts, features, and structure to help you understand.
  - o Example: An article about volcanoes may use bold words and a diagram to explain eruptions, with the central idea supported by facts and examples.

- **(E) Recognize characteristics and structures of argumentative text by:**
  (i) identifying the claim;
  (ii) explaining how the author has used facts for an argument; and
  (iii) identifying the intended audience or reader:
  - o Explanation: Understand how an author tries to convince you of something using a main point (claim), facts, and reasons.
  - o Example: If a writer says, "We should have longer recess because it helps us focus," that's a claim. They may give facts about brain breaks to support it, and they might be writing to a principal or teacher.

- **(F) Recognize characteristics of multimodal and digital texts:**
  - o Explanation: Identify how texts that use more than just words—like pictures, videos, and audio—help you learn and understand information.
  - o Example: A website about animals might include a video of a lion roaring, a photo of its habitat, and captions to explain the picture. That's a multimodal (many-mode) text!

(10) Author's Purpose and Craft:

- **(A) Explain the author's purpose and message within a text:**
    - *Explanation:* Understand why the author wrote the story and what they want you to learn or think about.
    - *Example:* The author might write a story to teach you to never give up, even when things get tough.
- **(B) Explain how the use of text structure contributes to the author's purpose:**
    - *Explanation:* Notice how the way the story is organized helps you understand the author's message.
    - *Example:* If the author tells the story in steps, it might be to show you how something changes over time.
- **(C) Analyze the author's use of print and graphic features to achieve specific purposes:**
    - Explanation: Notice how authors use bold words, titles, pictures, captions, and charts to help you understand what's important.
    - Example: If the author bolds the word "photosynthesis" and includes a diagram showing how plants make food, they're helping you focus on that key concept.
- **(D) Describe how the author's use of imagery, literal and figurative language such as simile and metaphor, and sound devices such as alliteration and assonance achieves specific purposes:**
    - Explanation: Understand how authors use sensory words and fun language—like comparing things or repeating sounds—to help you imagine, feel, or remember what you're reading.
    - Example: If the author writes, "Buzzing bees bounced by the blossoms," they're using alliteration and imagery to help you hear and picture the scene.
- **(E) Identify and understand the use of literary devices, including first- or third-person point of view:**
    - Explanation: Figure out who is telling the story and how it affects what you know and feel about the characters and events.
    - Example: If the narrator says, "I opened the door and gasped," it's first person. If they say, "She opened the door and gasped," it's third person.

TEKS reworded for students with examples for each skill showing how it can be helpful in their real lives:

(6) Comprehension Skills: Listening, Speaking, Reading, Writing, and Thinking

These skills help us understand things we read, listen to, and talk about in a deeper way.

- **(A) Set a Goal for Reading**
  What it means: Think about *why* you're reading something. Is it for fun? To learn? Knowing your reason helps you pay more attention.
  Example: If you read a story to learn about friendship, it's easier to spot how characters treat each other and how it teaches about being a good friend.
- **(B) Ask Questions Before, During, and After Reading**
  What it means: Asking questions helps you get curious and learn more from what you read.
  Example: Before starting a story about space, you might ask, "What's it like on the moon?" Asking questions can make reading feel like a fun adventure!
- **(C) Make and Check Predictions**
  What it means: Guess what might happen next based on what you've already read.
  Example: If a story mentions a dark, stormy sky, you might predict that something mysterious will happen. Checking if you're right keeps the story exciting!
- **(D) Make Mental Pictures**
  What it means: Imagine the story in your head like a movie to help you understand it better.
  Example: If you're reading about a big, green forest, picture it as you read to feel like you're really there.
- **(E) Make Connections**
  What it means: Think about how what you're reading connects to your life, other stories, or things happening in the world.
  Example: If a character is nervous about a big test, you might remember a time you felt the same way, which helps you relate to the character.
- **(F) Make Smart Guesses**
  What it means: Use clues from the story to figure things out that aren't directly said.
  Example: If a character is shivering, you can guess it's cold, even if the story doesn't say so.
- **(G) Find Key Ideas**
  What it means: Look for the most important details to understand what the story is mainly about.
  Example: In a story about a family road trip, the key idea might be about spending time together, rather than just the places they visit.
- **(H) Put Ideas Together to Understand**
  What it means: Combine different ideas you read to form a new, big idea.

Example: If a book tells about animals' fur, food, and shelter, putting it all together helps you understand how animals survive.

- **(I) Check for Understanding and Reread if Confused**
  What it means: Stop to make sure you're understanding. If not, read it again or ask questions.
  Example: If you're confused about a character's actions, go back and reread that part to make sense of it.

---

(7) Response Skills: Listening, Speaking, Reading, Writing, and Thinking

These skills help us respond to what we read or hear in ways that show we understand.

- **(A) Share Personal Connections**
  What it means: Tell how the story reminds you of something in your life.
  Example: If a character moves to a new school, you could talk about a time you met new friends.
- **(B) Write What You Learned**
  What it means: Show you understand by writing about what you read or how it's similar to other stories.
  Example: After reading two stories about animals, you could write about how both animals face challenges but in different ways.
- **(C) Use Proof from the Text**
  What it means: Use details from the story to back up what you're saying.
  Example: If you say a character is brave, you could show a part where they stood up for a friend.
- **(D) Retell or Summarize the Story**
  What it means: Tell the main parts of the story in your own words.
  Example: After reading a fairy tale, you might retell it by describing what the hero did, how they changed, and how the story ended.
- **(E) Interact with Text**
  What it means: Take notes, make drawings, or write down ideas about what you read to remember it better.
  Example: While reading, draw a picture of the main character to better imagine them.
- **(F) Use New Words**
  What it means: Try out new words you learn from reading in your own sentences.
  Example: If you learn the word "courage," you could say, "It took courage to try skateboarding for the first time."
- **(G) Talk About Important Ideas**
  What it means: Share what ideas in the story were most important to you and why.
  Example: After reading about teamwork, talk about how each character's actions made the team stronger.

(8) Multiple Genres: Understanding Story Elements

These skills help us understand different parts of stories and how they work together.

- **(A) Find the Theme or Lesson**
  What it means: Figure out the main lesson or message the story is trying to tell.
  Example: In "The Tortoise and the Hare," the theme might be that "slow and steady wins the race."
- **(B) Describe How Characters Act and Change**
  What it means: Notice how characters behave and what they learn or how they change.
  Example: If a character starts shy and later becomes confident, talk about how and why that change happened.
- **(C) Talk About Story Parts Like Climax**
  What it means: Identify parts of the story, like the beginning, big events, and ending.
  Example: Point out the climax, like when the hero faces their biggest challenge.
- **(D) Explain the Setting's Impact**
  What it means: Notice how the time or place affects the story.
  Example: If a story is set in a desert, the setting might mean the characters deal with heat and lack of water.

---

(9) Multiple Genres: Understanding Different Types of Texts

These skills help us learn what makes different types of writing special.

- **(A) Recognize Types of Stories**
  What it means: Learn the special features of stories like fables or myths.
  Example: A fable often has animals as characters and teaches a lesson.
- **(B) Understand Special Words like Similes**
  What it means: Learn how authors use words to create pictures, like "brave as a lion."
  Example: If a character's smile is "bright as the sun," it means they're very happy.
- **(C) Know How Plays are Structured**
  What it means: Notice special parts in plays, like characters' names before they speak.
  Example: In a play, you might see "Jill: I'm excited!" which shows Jill is the one talking.
- **(D) Recognize Informational Text Features**
  What it means: Notice things like diagrams or bold words that help explain information.
  Example: In a book about space, a diagram might show the planets in order.
- **(E) Identify Argument Parts**
  What it means: Spot parts of an argument, like the main point and supporting facts.
  Example: In a debate about recycling, you might find reasons why recycling helps the planet.
- **(F) Identify Digital Text Features**
  What it means: Notice unique features in online texts, like clickable links or videos.
  Example: In an online article, a link might take you to a picture or video about the topic.

(10) Author's Purpose and Craft

These skills help us think about why and how an author writes a certain way.

- **(A) Explain the Author's Purpose**
  What it means: Think about why the author wrote the story.
  Example: An author might write a funny story just to make readers laugh.
- **(B) Explain How Structure Helps Purpose**
  What it means: Notice how the way the text is organized helps us understand it better.
  Example: In a how-to book, steps are numbered to make instructions easier to follow.
- **(C) Notice Pictures or Bold Text**
  What it means: Look at pictures, charts, or bold words that help explain important parts.
  Example: A bolded word like "HERO" shows it's a main idea in the story.
- **(D) Describe Imagery or Sound in Language**
  What it means: Notice words that make you see, hear, or feel something, like "buzzing bees."
  Example: "Soft as a whisper" makes you imagine something gentle and quiet.
- **(E) Understand Point of View**
  What it means: Know who is telling the story, like "I" (first-person) or "they" (third-person).
  Example: "I walked to the store" feels more personal than "She walked to the store."
- **(F) Notice the Author's Voice**
  What it means: Pay attention to how the author's choice of words gives the story a unique feel.
  Example: A friendly voice might use words like "Hey there!" while a serious voice might say, "This is important."
- **(G) Identify Stories Within Stories (Anecdotes)**
  What it means: Look for small stories the author uses to make a point or give an example.
  Example: In a lesson about kindness, the author might tell a story about someone helping a neighbor.

These simplified TEKS with examples give kids a practical understanding of each skill, showing them how these skills can apply in real life and make reading more enjoyable and insightful.

Here's a reworded version of the TEKS standards in student-friendly language, with <u>playground</u> examples for each:

(6) Comprehension Skills: Listening, Speaking, Reading, Writing, and Thinking

These skills help us understand more about things we read, listen to, and talk about with others.

- **(A) Set a Purpose for Reading**
  What it means: Think about why you're reading or learning something.
  Playground Example: If you're reading the rules of a game, your purpose is to learn how to play correctly. Knowing this helps you pay more attention to the rules.
- **(B) Ask Questions**
  What it means: Asking questions before, during, and after reading helps you learn more.
  Playground Example: Before a new game starts, you might ask, "What are the rules?" or "How do you win?" This helps you understand the game better.
- **(C) Make Predictions**
  What it means: Guess what might happen next based on what you already know.
  Playground Example: If you see your friend getting close to the basketball hoop, you might predict they'll shoot the ball.
- **(D) Create Mental Images**
  What it means: Imagine what you're reading as a picture in your mind.
  Playground Example: If a friend describes a game with a treasure hunt, picture the playground as a map to make the game feel real and exciting.
- **(E) Make Connections**
  What it means: Think about how what you're learning or reading connects to things you know, other stories, or the world around you.
  Playground Example: If a friend gets hurt, you might remember a time you were hurt and needed a friend, helping you know how to comfort them.
- **(F) Use Clues to Figure Out Meaning**
  What it means: Use details to understand things not directly said.
  Playground Example: If you see someone with their arms crossed and frowning, you might guess they're upset about something, even if they don't say it.
- **(G) Find Key Ideas**
  What it means: Look for the main points to understand the most important parts.
  Playground Example: If the teacher explains safety rules, the key ideas might be "stay safe" and "watch out for others."
- **(H) Put Ideas Together to Understand**
  What it means: Combine what you know to understand things in a new way.
  Playground Example: If you see someone who's new at a game and struggling, you can use what you know about playing and being new to offer help.
- **(I) Check for Understanding**
  What it means: Make sure you understand, and ask questions if you're confused.

Playground Example: If a friend explains a new game but you don't understand, you could ask them to show you how it works.

---

(7) Response Skills: Listening, Speaking, Reading, Writing, and Thinking

These skills help us show that we understand what we've read or heard.

- **(A) Make Personal Connections**
  What it means: Relate what you read or learn to your own experiences.
  Playground Example: If you hear a story about a kid who felt left out, you might think of a time you felt left out, too, which helps you understand the story better.
- **(B) Write or Share What You Learned**
  What it means: Show you understand by talking or writing about it.
  Playground Example: After learning a new game, you could explain it to a friend to show you understand how it works.
- **(C) Use Proof from the Text**
  What it means: Use specific details to back up what you're saying.
  Playground Example: If you say the game's rule is "no pushing," you can point to where it's written in the rule book.
- **(D) Retell or Summarize the Story**
  What it means: Share the main parts in your own words.
  Playground Example: After playing a game, you could summarize it by explaining how each person takes a turn and how the game ends.
- **(E) Take Notes or Draw to Remember**
  What it means: Take notes or draw pictures to remember what you've learned.
  Playground Example: You might make a drawing of the field positions in a soccer game to remember them better.
- **(F) Use New Words**
  What it means: Use new vocabulary you've learned.
  Playground Example: If you learn the word "teammate," you could say, "My teammate passed the ball to me!"
- **(G) Discuss Important Ideas**
  What it means: Talk about the main ideas you learned.
  Playground Example: After hearing a story about sharing, you could discuss why sharing is important when playing games with others.

---

(8) Multiple Genres: Understanding Story Elements

These skills help us understand the different parts of stories and how they work.

- **(A) Find the Theme or Lesson**
  What it means: Figure out the main lesson or message.

Playground Example: If a story on the playground is about teamwork, you can discuss how working together makes the game more fun.

- **(B) Describe How Characters Act and Change**
  What it means: Notice how characters behave and what they learn.
  Playground Example: If someone starts a game by being shy and becomes more confident, you can talk about how playing helped them open up.
- **(C) Identify Story Parts Like Climax**
  What it means: Recognize parts like the main events and the story's ending.
  Playground Example: In a game, you might think of the most exciting part, like the final goal, as the "climax."
- **(D) Explain the Setting's Impact**
  What it means: Think about how the place or time affects the story.
  Playground Example: Playing hide-and-seek in a playground with lots of trees might make it easier to hide than if you were playing on a soccer field.

---

(9) Multiple Genres: Understanding Different Types of Texts

These skills help us understand what makes different types of writing special.

- **(A) Recognize Types of Stories**
  What it means: Learn what makes different kinds of stories unique.
  Playground Example: A tall tale might be about a super-strong kid who can throw a ball across the whole field, which sounds funny and exaggerated.
- **(B) Understand Figurative Language**
  What it means: Notice when language helps you imagine things, like "as quick as lightning."
  Playground Example: If someone says, "She ran like a cheetah," you imagine someone running really fast.
- **(C) Know How Plays Are Structured**
  What it means: Recognize special parts of a play, like characters speaking to each other.
  Playground Example: In a skit on the playground, you might say lines for your character and know when someone else's turn is to speak.
- **(D) Identify Informational Text Features**
  What it means: Recognize things like bold words or diagrams that explain more.
  Playground Example: If you see a diagram showing the positions in a kickball game, it helps you know where everyone stands.
- **(E) Identify Parts of an Argument**
  What it means: Spot main points in an argument, like a claim and supporting facts.
  Playground Example: If two kids are discussing the best playground game, one might say "tag is best because it's fun and everyone can play."
- **(F) Recognize Digital Texts**
  What it means: Notice unique features in online or digital texts, like videos or buttons.
  Playground Example: If you see a video showing how to play dodgeball, the video makes learning the rules easier.

(10) Author's Purpose and Craft

These skills help us think about why and how an author writes.

- **(A) Explain the Author's Purpose**
  What it means: Understand why the author wrote something.
  Playground Example: If a story about sharing is read aloud, the purpose might be to show why sharing is important on the playground.
- **(B) Explain How Text Structure Helps Purpose**
  What it means: Notice how the way a text is organized helps you understand it better.
  Playground Example: If rules for a game are listed step-by-step, it's easier to learn how to play.
- **(C) Notice Graphics or Bold Text**
  What it means: Look at pictures or bold words that make ideas stand out.
  Playground Example: If the rule "No running near swings" is in bold, it shows it's really important for safety.
- **(D) Describe Imagery or Sound in Language**
  What it means: Notice words that create a picture in your mind or sound interesting.
  Playground Example: If a game is described as "exciting as a rollercoaster," it helps you feel the thrill of playing.
- **(E) Understand Point of View**
  What it means: Know who is telling the story, like "I" or "they."
  Playground Example: If a kid says, "I felt excited," it's their point of view, making the story feel more personal.
- **(F) Notice Author's Voice**
  What it means: Pay attention to the author's style or mood in writing.
  Playground Example: If a story about winning a game sounds playful, it shows the writer wants it to feel fun.
- **(G) Recognize Small Stories or Examples (Anecdotes)**
  What it means: Spot little stories used to explain a point or give examples.
  Playground Example: If a story about friendship includes a part about one friend helping another after a fall, it shows why friendship matters.

These simplified TEKS make each skill understandable, showing how these skills can apply in real-life playground situations and help kids learn and play better together.

Here's a student-friendly breakdown of the TEKS standards with lunchroom examples to help them understand how these skills can apply in <u>real-life scenarios.</u>

---

(6) Comprehension Skills: Listening, Speaking, Reading, Writing, and Thinking

These skills help us understand and think about things we read, hear, and talk about with others.

- **(A) Set a Purpose for Reading**
  What it means: Think about why you're reading or listening to something.
  Lunchroom Example: If you're reading the cafeteria menu, your purpose is to decide what you want to eat. Knowing this helps you pay more attention to the choices.
- **(B) Ask Questions**
  What it means: Asking questions before, during, and after reading helps you learn more.
  Lunchroom Example: When you see a new food, you might ask, "What's in this?" or "Does it taste spicy?" Asking questions helps you decide if you want to try it.
- **(C) Make Predictions**
  What it means: Guess what might happen next based on what you already know.
  Lunchroom Example: If you see your friend carrying a messy taco, you might predict they'll need lots of napkins!
- **(D) Create Mental Images**
  What it means: Imagine what you're reading or hearing as a picture in your mind.
  Lunchroom Example: If a friend describes how delicious the pizza tastes, imagine the gooey cheese and crispy crust to help you decide if you want to try it.
- **(E) Make Connections**
  What it means: Think about how what you're learning connects to things you know or your experiences.
  Lunchroom Example: If a friend brings food from a different culture, you might connect it to something similar you've tried before or seen on TV.
- **(F) Use Clues to Figure Out Meaning**
  What it means: Use details to understand things not directly said.
  Lunchroom Example: If someone's staring at their food and looking disappointed, you might guess they don't like it, even if they don't say so.
- **(G) Find Key Ideas**
  What it means: Look for the main points to understand what's most important.
  Lunchroom Example: When reading about cafeteria rules, the key idea might be "clean up after yourself" and "be respectful."
- **(H) Put Ideas Together to Understand**
  What it means: Combine different ideas to understand new things.
  Lunchroom Example: If you notice the line is long and kids seem unhappy with the food, you might understand that the cafeteria is very busy and the wait is causing frustration.
- **(I) Check for Understanding**
  What it means: Make sure you understand, and ask questions if you're confused.

Lunchroom Example: If you don't understand a cafeteria rule, like "no sharing food," you could ask a teacher to explain why it's important.

---

(7) Response Skills: Listening, Speaking, Reading, Writing, and Thinking

These skills help us show that we understand what we've read or heard.

- **(A) Make Personal Connections**
  What it means: Relate what you read or learn to your own experiences.
  Lunchroom Example: If you read a rule about no running in the cafeteria, you might connect it to a time when someone almost slipped because of running.
- **(B) Write or Share What You Learned**
  What it means: Show you understand by talking or writing about it.
  Lunchroom Example: After learning about a healthy food choice, you could tell a friend why eating fruit is good for you.
- **(C) Use Proof from the Text**
  What it means: Use specific details to back up what you're saying.
  Lunchroom Example: If you say sharing food isn't allowed, you can show the rule on the cafeteria poster.
- **(D) Retell or Summarize**
  What it means: Share the main parts in your own words.
  Lunchroom Example: After listening to the cafeteria rules, you could retell them to a new student so they understand how to behave at lunch.
- **(E) Take Notes or Draw to Remember**
  What it means: Write down or draw ideas to remember what you learned.
  Lunchroom Example: You might draw a picture of the food groups after learning about healthy lunches to remember what to pick.
- **(F) Use New Words**
  What it means: Use new vocabulary you've learned.
  Lunchroom Example: If you learn the word "nutritious," you could say, "Eating an apple is nutritious and helps keep me healthy!"
- **(G) Discuss Important Ideas**
  What it means: Talk about the main ideas you learned.
  Lunchroom Example: After learning why recycling is important, you could discuss why recycling lunch trays would be helpful to the environment.

---

(8) Multiple Genres: Understanding Story Elements

These skills help us understand the different parts of stories and how they work.

- **(A) Find the Theme or Lesson**
  What it means: Figure out the main lesson or message.

Lunchroom Example: If you hear a story about kids working together to clean the lunchroom, you might say the lesson is "teamwork makes things easier."

- **(B) Describe How Characters Act and Change**
  What it means: Notice how characters behave and what they learn.
  Lunchroom Example: If someone starts out not wanting to eat their vegetables but changes their mind after learning they're healthy, you can discuss that change.
- **(C) Identify Story Parts Like Climax**
  What it means: Recognize parts like the most exciting events and how the story ends.
  Lunchroom Example: In a story about a food fight, the climax might be when the teacher comes in and everyone freezes.
- **(D) Explain the Setting's Impact**
  What it means: Think about how the place or time affects the story.
  Lunchroom Example: If a story takes place in a loud lunchroom, it might make it harder for the characters to hear each other, changing the story's events.

---

(9) Multiple Genres: Understanding Different Types of Texts

These skills help us understand what makes different types of writing special.

- **(A) Recognize Types of Stories**
  What it means: Know what makes different stories unique.
  Lunchroom Example: A fable about manners in the lunchroom might have animals as characters and teach a lesson about being polite.
- **(B) Understand Figurative Language**
  What it means: Notice when words create pictures, like "as hungry as a bear."
  Lunchroom Example: If someone says, "I'm so hungry I could eat a horse," they're not serious; they just mean they're very hungry.
- **(C) Know How Plays Are Structured**
  What it means: Recognize parts of a play, like who's speaking and the scenes.
  Lunchroom Example: If you put on a skit in the lunchroom, each person has lines to say, and the scenes might change from "entering the lunchroom" to "sitting down to eat."
- **(D) Identify Informational Text Features**
  What it means: Recognize things like diagrams or bold words that help explain.
  Lunchroom Example: If you see a chart showing food groups in the lunchroom, it helps you learn what foods are healthy.
- **(E) Identify Parts of an Argument**
  What it means: Spot main points in an argument, like a claim and supporting facts.
  Lunchroom Example: If two kids are debating which lunch item is healthier, one might say "carrots are better than chips because they have vitamins."
- **(F) Recognize Digital Text Features**
  What it means: Notice unique features in online or digital texts, like videos or buttons.
  Lunchroom Example: If you see a video about healthy eating on a screen in the lunchroom, the video can make learning fun and easy to understand.

(10) Author's Purpose and Craft

These skills help us think about why and how an author writes.

- **(A) Explain the Author's Purpose**
  What it means: Understand why the author wrote something.
  Lunchroom Example: A poster about recycling in the lunchroom might be written to encourage kids to recycle more.
- **(B) Explain How Text Structure Helps Purpose**
  What it means: Notice how the way the text is organized helps you understand it better.
  Lunchroom Example: If a poster lists "Do's and Don'ts" for the lunchroom, it's organized to make the rules clear.
- **(C) Notice Pictures or Bold Text**
  What it means: Look at pictures or bold words that make ideas stand out.
  Lunchroom Example: If the lunch menu shows "Today's Special" in bold letters, it helps you see it's the main meal of the day.
- **(D) Describe Imagery or Sound in Language**
  What it means: Notice words that create a picture in your mind or sound interesting.
  Lunchroom Example: If a friend describes their spaghetti as "squishy like worms," you can picture how it feels to eat it.
- **(E) Understand Point of View**
  What it means: Know who is telling the story, like "I" or "they."
  Lunchroom Example: If a kid says, "I felt so hungry," it's their point of view and helps you understand their feelings.
- **(F) Notice Author's Voice**
  What it means: Pay attention to the author's style or mood.
  Lunchroom Example: If a lunchroom story sounds funny, the writer probably wants you to enjoy it and laugh.
- **(G) Recognize Stories Within Stories (Anecdotes)**
  What it means: Spot little stories used to explain a point or give examples.
  Lunchroom Example: If a lunchroom rule poster has a story about a kid cleaning up a spill, it shows why cleaning up is helpful.

These simplified TEKS help kids understand how each skill can be applied in everyday scenarios in the lunchroom, making it more relevant and accessible.

Here's a student-friendly breakdown of the TEKS standards with examples of how each skill can help when <u>dealing with a disagreement with a friend</u>:

(6) Comprehension Skills: Listening, Speaking, Reading, Writing, and Thinking

These skills help us understand and think carefully about what we read, hear, and talk about.

- **(A) Set a Purpose for Reading**
  What it means: Think about why you're reading or listening to something.
  Disagreement Example: If you're listening to a friend explain their side in a disagreement, your purpose might be to understand their feelings.
- **(B) Ask Questions**
  What it means: Asking questions before, during, and after listening helps you learn more.
  Disagreement Example: If your friend says you hurt their feelings, you could ask, "What did I do that made you feel that way?" to understand better.
- **(C) Make Predictions**
  What it means: Guess what might happen based on what you already know.
  Disagreement Example: If your friend is very upset, you might predict that staying calm will help both of you work things out.
- **(D) Create Mental Images**
  What it means: Picture what you're hearing or reading in your mind.
  Disagreement Example: If your friend says, "It felt like you ignored me at lunch," imagine how you would feel in their place.
- **(E) Make Connections**
  What it means: Think about how what you're learning connects to things you know or your experiences.
  Disagreement Example: If your friend says they felt left out, think of a time you felt the same way, which helps you understand them.
- **(F) Use Clues to Figure Out Meaning**
  What it means: Use details to understand things not directly said.
  Disagreement Example: If your friend is quiet and looking away, you might guess they're upset, even if they don't say it.
- **(G) Find Key Ideas**
  What it means: Look for the main points to understand what's most important.
  Disagreement Example: If your friend explains why they're mad, the main idea might be that they felt ignored, which helps you know what to fix.
- **(H) Put Ideas Together to Understand**
  What it means: Combine different ideas to understand the bigger picture.
  Disagreement Example: If you know your friend was upset at lunch and also saw them sitting alone, you can understand that they might have felt left out.
- **(I) Check for Understanding**
  What it means: Make sure you understand, and ask questions if you're confused.

Disagreement Example: If you're not sure why your friend is upset, ask them to explain so you don't misunderstand.

---

(7) Response Skills: Listening, Speaking, Reading, Writing, and Thinking

These skills help us show that we understand what we've read or heard.

- **(A) Make Personal Connections**
  What it means: Relate what you read or learn to your own experiences.
  Disagreement Example: If your friend says they felt embarrassed, think of a time you felt the same way so you can respond with understanding.
- **(B) Write or Share What You Learned**
  What it means: Show you understand by talking about it.
  Disagreement Example: After hearing your friend's side, you could say, "I understand now that I hurt your feelings by not including you."
- **(C) Use Proof from the Conversation**
  What it means: Use specific details to back up what you're saying.
  Disagreement Example: If your friend says you ignored them, you can say, "I'm sorry I didn't see you at lunch; I was busy talking and didn't notice."
- **(D) Retell or Summarize**
  What it means: Share the main parts in your own words.
  Disagreement Example: After your friend explains why they're upset, you might say, "So you're feeling hurt because you felt left out."
- **(E) Take Notes or Draw to Remember**
  What it means: Write down or draw ideas to remember what you learned.
  Disagreement Example: If you're talking to a friend about fixing a misunderstanding, you could write down a plan to include them more often.
- **(F) Use New Words**
  What it means: Use new words you've learned.
  Disagreement Example: If you learn the word "apologize," you could say, "I want to apologize for making you feel bad."
- **(G) Discuss Important Ideas**
  What it means: Talk about the main ideas of what you learned.
  Disagreement Example: After a disagreement, discuss the importance of including everyone to avoid similar problems in the future.

---

(8) Multiple Genres: Understanding Story Elements

These skills help us understand the different parts of stories and how they work.

- **(A) Find the Theme or Lesson**
  What it means: Figure out the main lesson or message.

Disagreement Example: After resolving a disagreement, you might say the lesson is to listen and be kind to friends' feelings.

- **(B) Describe How Characters Act and Change**
  What it means: Notice how characters behave and what they learn.
  Disagreement Example: If a friend was mad but becomes happy after you apologize, talk about how understanding each other's feelings changed the situation.
- **(C) Identify Story Parts Like Climax**
  What it means: Recognize parts like the main events and how the story ends.
  Disagreement Example: In a disagreement, the climax might be when you both say what you need, and the resolution is when you apologize and make up.
- **(D) Explain the Setting's Impact**
  What it means: Think about how the place or time affects the story.
  Disagreement Example: If you argue during recess, the setting means you have a short time to work it out before you have to go back to class.

---

(9) Multiple Genres: Understanding Different Types of Texts

These skills help us understand what makes different types of writing special.

- **(A) Recognize Types of Stories**
  What it means: Know what makes different stories unique.
  Disagreement Example: A story about friendship might teach lessons on kindness, just like real-life arguments with friends can teach us to be better.
- **(B) Understand Figurative Language**
  What it means: Notice when words create pictures, like "fuming with anger."
  Disagreement Example: If your friend says, "I was boiling inside," they don't mean they're hot; it means they felt very upset.
- **(C) Know How Plays Are Structured**
  What it means: Recognize parts of a play, like who's speaking and the scenes.
  Disagreement Example: If you act out a disagreement in a skit, each person has lines to say, and the scenes might go from arguing to apologizing.
- **(D) Identify Informational Text Features**
  What it means: Recognize things like diagrams or bold words that help explain.
  Disagreement Example: If you read a chart about how to apologize, it might include steps like "Listen," "Say Sorry," and "Offer to Make It Right."
- **(E) Identify Parts of an Argument**
  What it means: Spot main points in an argument, like a claim and supporting facts.
  Disagreement Example: If you and your friend are arguing, you might say, "I think you ignored me," and they could respond, "I was focused on something else."
- **(F) Recognize Digital Text Features**
  What it means: Notice unique features in online or digital texts, like videos or buttons.
  Disagreement Example: If you watch a video on "How to Work Things Out with Friends," the video might have examples that show you how to talk calmly.

(10) Author's Purpose and Craft

These skills help us think about why and how an author writes.

- **(A) Explain the Author's Purpose**
  What it means: Understand why the author wrote something.
  Disagreement Example: A story about apologizing might be written to show why saying sorry is important.
- **(B) Explain How Text Structure Helps Purpose**
  What it means: Notice how the way the text is organized helps you understand it better.
  Disagreement Example: If a guide on apologizing has steps listed out, it's structured to make following the steps easier.
- **(C) Notice Pictures or Bold Text**
  What it means: Look at pictures or bold words that make ideas stand out.
  Disagreement Example: If a friendship guide highlights "Respect Each Other" in bold, it's a main idea.
- **(D) Describe Imagery or Sound in Language**
  What it means: Notice words that create a picture in your mind or sound interesting.
  Disagreement Example: If a friend says the argument "felt like a storm," it helps you imagine how intense it was.
- **(E) Understand Point of View**
  What it means: Know who is telling the story, like "I" or "they."
  Disagreement Example: If your friend says, "I felt left out," their point of view helps you understand why they're upset.
- **(F) Notice Author's Voice**
  What it means: Pay attention to the author's style or mood.
  Disagreement Example: If a story about friendship sounds caring, the writer wants to show kindness matters.
- **(G) Recognize Stories Within Stories (Anecdotes)**
  What it means: Spot little stories used to explain a point or give examples.
  Disagreement Example: If a friend tells you a story about a time they felt hurt, it helps you see how similar situations can affect others.

These kid-friendly TEKS explanations use examples from everyday disagreements with friends, helping kids understand how these skills apply in real life and make resolving conflicts easier and more meaningful.

Here's a student-friendly breakdown of these TEKS standards, with examples of <u>how each skill can help in classroom situations:</u>

---

(6) Comprehension Skills: Listening, Speaking, Reading, Writing, and Thinking

These skills help us understand and think about what we read, listen to, and talk about in class.

- **(A) Set a Purpose for Reading**
  What it means: Think about why you're reading or listening to something.
  Classroom Example: If you're reading a story for a reading assignment, your purpose might be to find the main idea or learn something about the topic.
- **(B) Ask Questions**
  What it means: Asking questions before, during, and after helps you learn more.
  Classroom Example: When you're reading a science book, ask questions like "How does this work?" to understand the topic better.
- **(C) Make Predictions**
  What it means: Guess what might happen next based on what you already know.
  Classroom Example: When reading a story, you might predict what a character will do next based on what you've read so far.
- **(D) Create Mental Images**
  What it means: Imagine what you're reading as a picture in your mind.
  Classroom Example: If you read about a forest, picture the trees, animals, and sunlight to make the reading come alive.
- **(E) Make Connections**
  What it means: Think about how what you're learning connects to things you know or your experiences.
  Classroom Example: When reading about a historical event, think of other stories or times in your life that feel similar.
- **(F) Use Clues to Figure Out Meaning**
  What it means: Use details to understand things not directly said.
  Classroom Example: If a character in a story frowns and sighs, you might guess they're upset, even if they don't say so.
- **(G) Find Key Ideas**
  What it means: Look for the main points to understand the most important parts.
  Classroom Example: When reading a textbook, look for bold words or headings to find the main ideas.
- **(H) Put Ideas Together to Understand**
  What it means: Combine what you know to understand things in a new way.
  Classroom Example: If you learn about different animal habitats, combine what you know to understand how animals survive in different environments.
- **(I) Check for Understanding**
  What it means: Make sure you understand, and ask questions if you're confused.

Classroom Example: If you don't understand a math problem, reread the instructions or ask your teacher for help.

---

(7) Response Skills: Listening, Speaking, Reading, Writing, and Thinking

These skills help us show that we understand what we've read or learned.

- **(A) Make Personal Connections**
  What it means: Relate what you read to your own experiences.
  Classroom Example: If you read a story about teamwork, think about a time when you worked with friends on a project.
- **(B) Write or Share What You Learned**
  What it means: Show you understand by talking or writing about it.
  Classroom Example: After learning about recycling, you could write a paragraph about why it's important or share your thoughts with the class.
- **(C) Use Proof from the Text**
  What it means: Use specific details to back up what you're saying.
  Classroom Example: If you say a character is brave, find a part in the story that shows them doing something courageous.
- **(D) Retell or Summarize**
  What it means: Share the main parts in your own words.
  Classroom Example: After reading a chapter in a book, tell your teacher the main points of the story in your own words.
- **(E) Take Notes or Draw to Remember**
  What it means: Write down or draw ideas to remember what you learned.
  Classroom Example: Take notes during a science lesson, or draw a picture to remember the steps of a plant's life cycle.
- **(F) Use New Words**
  What it means: Use new vocabulary you've learned.
  Classroom Example: If you learn the word "ecosystem," use it when discussing how plants and animals interact.
- **(G) Discuss Important Ideas**
  What it means: Talk about the main ideas you learned.
  Classroom Example: After a lesson on kindness, discuss with your class why kindness is important and how it makes school a better place.

---

(8) Multiple Genres: Understanding Story Elements

These skills help us understand the different parts of stories and how they work.

- **(A) Find the Theme or Lesson**
  What it means: Figure out the main lesson or message.

Classroom Example: After reading a story about friendship, you might say the theme is "helping others is important."

- **(B) Describe How Characters Act and Change**
  What it means: Notice how characters behave and what they learn.
  Classroom Example: If a character learns to be brave, talk about how they act at the beginning versus the end of the story.
- **(C) Identify Story Parts Like Climax**
  What it means: Recognize parts like the main events and how the story ends.
  Classroom Example: In a story, the climax might be the exciting part where a character faces their biggest challenge.
- **(D) Explain the Setting's Impact**
  What it means: Think about how the place or time affects the story.
  Classroom Example: If a story takes place in the desert, the setting might make the characters thirsty and tired, which adds to the story's challenges.

---

(9) Multiple Genres: Understanding Different Types of Texts

These skills help us understand what makes different types of writing special.

- **(A) Recognize Types of Stories**
  What it means: Learn what makes different kinds of stories unique.
  Classroom Example: A fable about honesty might have animals as characters and end with a moral or lesson.
- **(B) Understand Figurative Language**
  What it means: Notice when language helps you imagine things, like "as quick as lightning."
  Classroom Example: If a teacher says, "The classroom was a zoo," imagine it being very loud and active, like an animal-filled zoo.
- **(C) Know How Plays Are Structured**
  What it means: Recognize special parts of a play, like characters speaking and stage directions.
  Classroom Example: In a classroom play, you might say lines for your character and know when it's another person's turn to speak.
- **(D) Identify Informational Text Features**
  What it means: Recognize things like bold words or diagrams that explain more.
  Classroom Example: In a textbook, a bolded word like "photosynthesis" is important and may have a diagram to help explain it.
- **(E) Identify Parts of an Argument**
  What it means: Spot main points in an argument, like a claim and supporting facts.
  Classroom Example: If someone argues that "recess is good for kids because it helps them exercise," the claim is that recess is beneficial, and the fact is it helps with exercise.
- **(F) Recognize Digital Text Features**
  What it means: Notice unique features in online or digital texts, like videos or clickable buttons.

Classroom Example: If you're using an educational website, look for videos or diagrams that help explain the lesson.

---

(10) Author's Purpose and Craft

These skills help us think about why and how an author writes.

- **(A) Explain the Author's Purpose**
  What it means: Understand why the author wrote something.
  Classroom Example: If you read a story about teamwork, the purpose might be to show that working together makes tasks easier.
- **(B) Explain How Text Structure Helps Purpose**
  What it means: Notice how the way the text is organized helps you understand it better.
  Classroom Example: If rules for group projects are listed step-by-step, it's structured to make the directions easy to follow.
- **(C) Notice Pictures or Bold Text**
  What it means: Look at pictures or bold words that make ideas stand out.
  Classroom Example: If a poster in class has "Be Kind" in bold letters, it shows it's an important part of classroom rules.
- **(D) Describe Imagery or Sound in Language**
  What it means: Notice words that create a picture in your mind or sound interesting.
  Classroom Example: If a story says "the leaves crunched underfoot," it helps you imagine walking on dry leaves.
- **(E) Understand Point of View**
  What it means: Know who is telling the story, like "I" or "they."
  Classroom Example: If a story is told from a student's point of view, it helps you understand what the student is feeling and experiencing.
- **(F) Notice Author's Voice**
  What it means: Pay attention to the author's style or mood.
  Classroom Example: If a story about science sounds curious and excited, it shows the author wants you to feel excited about learning.
- **(G) Recognize Stories Within Stories (Anecdotes)**
  What it means: Spot little stories used to explain a point or give examples.
  Classroom Example: If a teacher tells a quick story about a time they worked with classmates, it helps you see why teamwork is important.

These kid-friendly TEKS explanations help students understand how each skill applies to classroom activities and make their learning experiences more relevant and engaging.

Here's a student-friendly version of these TEKS standards with examples of <u>how each skill can help with science class</u>:

---

(6) Comprehension Skills: Listening, Speaking, Reading, Writing, and Thinking

These skills help us understand and think about what we read, hear, and talk about, especially when learning new science concepts.

- **(A) Set a Purpose for Reading**
  What it means: Think about why you're reading or listening to something.
  Science Example: When reading a science article about volcanoes, your purpose could be to learn how and why they erupt.
- **(B) Ask Questions**
  What it means: Asking questions before, during, and after reading helps you learn more.
  Science Example: When you read about animals' habitats, you might ask, "How do these animals survive here?" to help understand better.
- **(C) Make Predictions**
  What it means: Guess what might happen based on what you already know.
  Science Example: When learning about weather, you might predict if a storm is coming based on changes in the sky.
- **(D) Create Mental Images**
  What it means: Imagine what you're reading as a picture in your mind.
  Science Example: If you're reading about the rainforest, imagine the dense trees, animals, and rain to understand it better.
- **(E) Make Connections**
  What it means: Think about how what you're learning connects to things you know or your experiences.
  Science Example: When reading about water cycles, think about how the rain helps plants grow in your garden.
- **(F) Use Clues to Figure Out Meaning**
  What it means: Use details to understand things that aren't directly said.
  Science Example: If a science article says that plants need sunlight, soil, and water, you can guess that plants won't grow well in the dark.
- **(G) Find Key Ideas**
  What it means: Look for the main points to understand what's most important.
  Science Example: When studying the solar system, find the key idea about why Earth's orbit around the Sun affects the seasons.
- **(H) Put Ideas Together to Understand**
  What it means: Combine different ideas to understand something new.
  Science Example: If you learn about the parts of a plant, you can combine those ideas to understand how each part helps the plant grow.
- **(I) Check for Understanding**
  What it means: Make sure you understand and ask questions if you're confused.

Science Example: If you don't understand a science experiment's steps, reread the instructions or ask the teacher for help.

---

(7) Response Skills: Listening, Speaking, Reading, Writing, and Thinking

These skills help us show that we understand what we've read or learned.

- **(A) Make Personal Connections**
  What it means: Relate what you read or learn to your own experiences.
  Science Example: If you read about plant life cycles, you might think of a time you planted a seed and watched it grow.
- **(B) Write or Share What You Learned**
  What it means: Show you understand by talking or writing about it.
  Science Example: After learning about recycling, you could write a paragraph on how recycling helps the environment.
- **(C) Use Proof from the Text**
  What it means: Use specific details to back up what you're saying.
  Science Example: If you say that trees help clean the air, find a part in the science text that explains how they do that.
- **(D) Retell or Summarize**
  What it means: Share the main points in your own words.
  Science Example: After learning about weather patterns, tell your teacher the main ideas of how clouds and rain are formed.
- **(E) Take Notes or Draw to Remember**
  What it means: Write down or draw ideas to remember what you learned.
  Science Example: During a lesson about the food chain, you might draw a picture of a predator and prey to understand who eats whom.
- **(F) Use New Words**
  What it means: Use new vocabulary you've learned.
  Science Example: If you learn the word "photosynthesis," use it when talking about how plants make their own food.
- **(G) Discuss Important Ideas**
  What it means: Talk about the main ideas you learned.
  Science Example: After a lesson on the water cycle, discuss with your class why water conservation is important.

---

(8) Multiple Genres: Understanding Story Elements

These skills help us understand the different parts of stories and how they work.

- **(A) Find the Theme or Lesson**
  What it means: Figure out the main lesson or message.
  Science Example: If a story is about animals adapting to survive, the theme might be "adaptation helps survival."
- **(B) Describe How Characters Act and Change**
  What it means: Notice how characters behave and what they learn.
  Science Example: In a science story about a scientist, you could describe how they learned from their experiments.
- **(C) Identify Story Parts Like Climax**
  What it means: Recognize parts like the main events and how the story ends.
  Science Example: In a story about discovering a new planet, the climax might be when the scientists see the planet for the first time.
- **(D) Explain the Setting's Impact**
  What it means: Think about how the place or time affects the story.
  Science Example: In a story about life in the ocean, the underwater setting might make it difficult for characters to breathe, adding challenges.

---

(9) Multiple Genres: Understanding Different Types of Texts

These skills help us understand what makes different types of writing special.

- **(A) Recognize Types of Stories**
  What it means: Learn what makes different kinds of stories unique.
  Science Example: A fable about teamwork might have animals helping each other and end with a lesson about working together.
- **(B) Understand Figurative Language**
  What it means: Notice when words create images, like "as hungry as a wolf."
  Science Example: If a scientist says, "the bacteria spread like wildfire," imagine the bacteria spreading quickly, like flames.
- **(C) Know How Plays Are Structured**
  What it means: Recognize special parts of a play, like characters speaking and stage directions.
  Science Example: If your class performs a skit about the water cycle, each person has lines, and the scene might change from "cloud formation" to "rain."
- **(D) Identify Informational Text Features**
  What it means: Recognize things like bold words or diagrams that explain more.
  Science Example: In a science book, a bold word like "evaporation" is important and might have a diagram to help explain it.
- **(E) Identify Parts of an Argument**
  What it means: Spot main points in an argument, like a claim and supporting facts.

Science Example: If you're reading about climate change, the author might claim that "global warming affects animals' habitats," then use facts to explain.

- **(F) Recognize Digital Text Features**
  What it means: Notice unique features in online or digital texts, like videos or clickable buttons.
  Science Example: When reading an online science article, you might watch a video about volcanoes to better understand eruptions.

---

(10) Author's Purpose and Craft

These skills help us think about why and how an author writes.

- **(A) Explain the Author's Purpose**
  What it means: Understand why the author wrote something.
  Science Example: If you read an article on recycling, the author's purpose might be to show how recycling helps protect nature.
- **(B) Explain How Text Structure Helps Purpose**
  What it means: Notice how the way the text is organized helps you understand it better.
  Science Example: If a science article has steps for an experiment, the structure helps you follow each step correctly.
- **(C) Notice Pictures or Bold Text**
  What it means: Look at pictures or bold words that make ideas stand out.
  Science Example: If a page about planets has "The Solar System" in bold, it tells you this is an important topic.
- **(D) Describe Imagery or Sound in Language**
  What it means: Notice words that create a picture in your mind or sound interesting.
  Science Example: If a story says, "the waves crashed loudly," imagine the powerful noise of waves.
- **(E) Understand Point of View**
  What it means: Know who is telling the story, like "I" or "they."
  Science Example: In a story about an astronaut's journey, understanding it's from the astronaut's point of view helps you see their feelings about space.
- **(F) Notice Author's Voice**
  What it means: Pay attention to the author's style or mood.
  Science Example: If a science text about plants sounds caring and hopeful, the writer likely wants readers to feel that plants are valuable.
- **(G) Recognize Stories Within Stories (Anecdotes)**
  What it means: Spot little stories used to explain a point or give examples.
  Science Example: If a scientist tells a quick story about saving a bird species, it shows why protecting nature is important.

These TEKS in simple language help kids understand how each skill applies to science class, making the learning process clearer and more relevant to their experiences.

Here's a student-friendly breakdown of the TEKS standards with examples of <u>how each skill can help in social studies class</u>:

(6) Comprehension Skills: Listening, Speaking, Reading, Writing, and Thinking

These skills help us understand and think about what we read, listen to, and talk about, especially when learning about history, geography, and cultures.

- **(A) Set a Purpose for Reading**
  What it means: Think about why you're reading or listening to something.
  Social Studies Example: If you're reading about the American Revolution, your purpose might be to learn why it happened and what changed afterward.
- **(B) Ask Questions**
  What it means: Asking questions before, during, and after helps you learn more.
  Social Studies Example: When studying ancient Egypt, you could ask, "How did the pyramids get built?" to understand more about Egyptian culture.
- **(C) Make Predictions**
  What it means: Guess what might happen based on what you already know.
  Social Studies Example: When learning about the Civil Rights Movement, you might predict how new laws helped people gain equal rights.
- **(D) Create Mental Images**
  What it means: Imagine what you're reading as a picture in your mind.
  Social Studies Example: If you're reading about life on the Oregon Trail, imagine the wagons, the landscape, and the long journey.
- **(E) Make Connections**
  What it means: Think about how what you're learning connects to things you know or your experiences.
  Social Studies Example: When reading about the Declaration of Independence, think about how it connects to our rights today.
- **(F) Use Clues to Figure Out Meaning**
  What it means: Use details to understand things that aren't directly said.
  Social Studies Example: If a text mentions "colonists being taxed without a voice," you can infer they were frustrated about unfair laws.
- **(G) Find Key Ideas**
  What it means: Look for the main points to understand what's most important.
  Social Studies Example: When learning about different government systems, find the main idea of each system and how it impacts people's lives.
- **(H) Put Ideas Together to Understand**
  What it means: Combine different ideas to understand something new.
  Social Studies Example: If you learn about different explorers, put the facts together to understand how exploration changed the world.
- **(I) Check for Understanding**
  What it means: Make sure you understand and ask questions if you're confused.

Social Studies Example: If you don't understand a part of a map, ask your teacher to explain it to better understand the geography.

---

(7) Response Skills: Listening, Speaking, Reading, Writing, and Thinking

These skills help us show that we understand what we've read or learned.

- **(A) Make Personal Connections**
  What it means: Relate what you read or learn to your own experiences.
  Social Studies Example: If you learn about people moving to new places for better opportunities, think of a time when you or someone you know moved for a new experience.
- **(B) Write or Share What You Learned**
  What it means: Show you understand by talking or writing about it.
  Social Studies Example: After studying a country's culture, write a paragraph about its customs or share interesting facts with the class.
- **(C) Use Proof from the Text**
  What it means: Use specific details to back up what you're saying.
  Social Studies Example: If you say a leader was brave, find a part in the text that describes the challenges they faced.
- **(D) Retell or Summarize**
  What it means: Share the main points in your own words.
  Social Studies Example: After learning about the Great Depression, tell your teacher the main reasons it happened and its effects.
- **(E) Take Notes or Draw to Remember**
  What it means: Write down or draw ideas to remember what you learned.
  Social Studies Example: During a lesson about Native American tribes, take notes or draw symbols that represent each tribe.
- **(F) Use New Words**
  What it means: Use new vocabulary you've learned.
  Social Studies Example: If you learn the word "democracy," use it when talking about how some countries allow people to vote.
- **(G) Discuss Important Ideas**
  What it means: Talk about the main ideas you learned.
  Social Studies Example: After a lesson on the Constitution, discuss why freedom and rights are important.

---

(8) Multiple Genres: Understanding Story Elements

These skills help us understand different parts of stories and history.

- **(A) Find the Theme or Lesson**
  What it means: Figure out the main lesson or message.
  Social Studies Example: If you read about Martin Luther King Jr., the theme might be "standing up for what is right."
- **(B) Describe How Characters Act and Change**
  What it means: Notice how people behave and what they learn.
  Social Studies Example: When learning about Abraham Lincoln, talk about how he faced challenges to help end slavery.
- **(C) Identify Story Parts Like Climax**
  What it means: Recognize main events and how the story ends.
  Social Studies Example: In a story about a major battle, the climax might be the turning point when one side starts to win.
- **(D) Explain the Setting's Impact**
  What it means: Think about how the place or time affects the story.
  Social Studies Example: If a story takes place during a drought, the dry setting might make it difficult for people to grow food.

---

(9) Multiple Genres: Understanding Different Types of Texts

These skills help us understand what makes different types of writing special.

- **(A) Recognize Types of Stories**
  What it means: Learn what makes different stories unique.
  Social Studies Example: A legend about George Washington might include stories of his bravery and could end with a lesson about leadership.
- **(B) Understand Figurative Language**
  What it means: Notice when words create images, like "as tall as a mountain."
  Social Studies Example: If a story says, "freedom was a bright light," imagine it as something positive and hopeful.
- **(C) Know How Plays Are Structured**
  What it means: Recognize parts of a play, like characters speaking and stage directions.
  Social Studies Example: If you perform a play about a historical event, each person has lines to say, and the scenes may change as time passes.
- **(D) Identify Informational Text Features**
  What it means: Recognize things like bold words or diagrams that explain more.
  Social Studies Example: In a history book, a bold word like "independence" is important and might have a picture or timeline to help explain it.
- **(E) Identify Parts of an Argument**
  What it means: Spot main points in an argument, like a claim and supporting facts.

Social Studies Example: If you read a text about climate change, the claim might be that "humans can help reduce it," and it will give reasons to support this.

- **(F) Recognize Digital Text Features**
  What it means: Notice special features in online or digital texts, like videos or buttons.
  Social Studies Example: If you watch an online video about a historical figure, look for extra information like captions or links for more facts.

(10) Author's Purpose and Craft

These skills help us think about why and how an author writes.

- **(A) Explain the Author's Purpose**
  What it means: Understand why the author wrote something.
  Social Studies Example: If you read an article about environmental protection, the author's purpose might be to show why protecting the planet is important.
- **(B) Explain How Text Structure Helps Purpose**
  What it means: Notice how the way the text is organized helps you understand it better.
  Social Studies Example: If a text on ancient Rome is structured by time periods, it helps you see how Rome changed over time.
- **(C) Notice Pictures or Bold Text**
  What it means: Look at pictures or bold words that make ideas stand out.
  Social Studies Example: In a lesson on voting rights, if "equal rights" is bold, it's a main idea that's important to the lesson.
- **(D) Describe Imagery or Sound in Language**
  What it means: Notice words that create a picture in your mind or sound interesting.
  Social Studies Example: If a story says "the drums of war grew louder," it helps you imagine the tension of the approaching battle.
- **(E) Understand Point of View**
  What it means: Know who is telling the story, like "I" or "they."
  Social Studies Example: In a story from a soldier's point of view, it helps you understand what they might feel during a battle.
- **(F) Notice Author's Voice**
  What it means: Pay attention to the author's style or mood.
  Social Studies Example: If a text about historical heroes sounds admiring and proud, it shows the author respects these people.
- **(G) Recognize Stories Within Stories (Anecdotes)**
  What it means: Spot little stories used to explain a point or give examples.
  Social Studies Example: If a book about bravery includes a quick story about Harriet Tubman, it shows how she displayed courage.

These kid-friendly TEKS explanations help students understand how each skill applies to social studies, making history and cultural lessons more interesting and engaging.

Here's a student-friendly explanation of these TEKS standards with examples of <u>how each skill can help in math class</u>:

(6) Comprehension Skills: Listening, Speaking, Reading, Writing, and Thinking

These skills help us understand and think about what we're learning, especially when we're solving problems or learning new math ideas.

- **(A) Set a Purpose for Learning**
  What it means: Think about why you're learning something.
  Math Example: When starting a lesson on fractions, your purpose might be to understand how to split things equally, like pizza slices or groups of objects.
- **(B) Ask Questions to Understand More**
  What it means: Asking questions helps you understand better.
  Math Example: When learning about shapes, you might ask, "How many sides does a hexagon have?" to make sure you know the differences.
- **(C) Make Predictions Based on What You Know**
  What it means: Guess what might happen based on what you already know.
  Math Example: If you know that multiplication makes numbers bigger, you can predict that multiplying by fractions makes numbers smaller.
- **(D) Picture Ideas in Your Mind**
  What it means: Imagine what you're learning as a picture in your mind.
  Math Example: When learning about geometry, imagine a triangle in your head and picture its three sides and three points.
- **(E) Make Connections to What You Know**
  What it means: Think about how what you're learning connects to things you already know.
  Math Example: If you're learning about measurement, think about when you measure ingredients while cooking or baking.
- **(F) Use Clues to Figure Out Meaning**
  What it means: Use details to understand things that aren't directly said.
  Math Example: When solving word problems, clues in the problem like "in total" or "altogether" help you know to add.
- **(G) Find Key Ideas**
  What it means: Look for the main points to understand what's most important.
  Math Example: When learning how to add fractions, focus on the idea that fractions need the same denominator to be added together.
- **(H) Put Ideas Together to Understand**
  What it means: Combine different ideas to understand something new.
  Math Example: When solving multi-step problems, put together addition, subtraction, and multiplication to find the answer.
- **(I) Check for Understanding**
  What it means: Make sure you understand and ask questions if you're confused.

Math Example: If you're not sure about a math step, re-read the problem or ask the teacher to explain it in another way.

---

(7) Response Skills: Listening, Speaking, Reading, Writing, and Thinking

These skills help us show that we understand what we've read, learned, or worked through.

- **(A) Make Connections to Personal Experiences**
  What it means: Relate what you're learning to your life.
  Math Example: When learning about percentages, think about how sales at a store use percentages to show discounts.
- **(B) Write or Share What You've Learned**
  What it means: Show you understand by talking or writing about it.
  Math Example: After learning about place value, explain to a friend how the value of each number changes based on its position.
- **(C) Use Proof from the Text or Problem**
  What it means: Use specific details to back up what you're saying.
  Math Example: When explaining a solution, point to the steps you followed, like "I added these numbers to get the answer."
- **(D) Retell or Summarize in Your Own Words**
  What it means: Share the main points in your own words.
  Math Example: After solving a multi-step word problem, summarize by saying, "First, I added, then multiplied to find the answer."
- **(E) Take Notes or Draw**
  What it means: Write down or draw ideas to remember what you learned.
  Math Example: If you're solving a complex problem, jot down each step to help you keep track.
- **(F) Use New Words You've Learned**
  What it means: Use new math vocabulary.
  Math Example: After learning about "perimeter," use the word when talking about finding the distance around shapes.
- **(G) Discuss Important Ideas**
  What it means: Talk about the main ideas you learned.
  Math Example: After a lesson on area, discuss why knowing the area of a room can be important, like when buying carpet.

---

(8) Multiple Genres: Understanding Story Elements

These skills help us understand the different parts of math problems, like stories or examples used to explain ideas.

- **(A) Find the Theme or Lesson**
  What it means: Figure out the main idea or lesson in a story problem.
  Math Example: If a story problem shows two friends sharing, the theme might be fairness and equal parts.
- **(B) Describe Changes in Characters or Events**
  What it means: Notice how things or people change in the problem.
  Math Example: In a math problem about saving money, talk about how a character's savings grow over time.
- **(C) Identify Important Parts of the Story**
  What it means: Recognize the main steps in a story or problem.
  Math Example: In a word problem about time, the climax might be the exact time something happens, like when a bus arrives.
- **(D) Explain the Setting's Impact**
  What it means: Think about how the place or time affects the math problem.
  Math Example: In a problem about cooking, the setting (kitchen) means you might use measurements like cups or ounces.

---

(9) Multiple Genres: Understanding Different Types of Texts

These skills help us understand the features and purpose of different types of math problems and explanations.

- **(A) Recognize Different Types of Stories**
  What it means: Learn what makes different kinds of word problems unique.
  Math Example: A fable-like math problem might end with a lesson, like why it's important to double-check answers.
- **(B) Understand Figurative Language**
  What it means: Notice when words create images, like "as easy as pie."
  Math Example: If a problem says, "I could eat a mountain of cookies," imagine a large amount to solve the math.
- **(C) Know How Math Steps Are Organized**
  What it means: Recognize the order and parts of math solutions.
  Math Example: If instructions say to "subtract, then divide," following that order helps solve correctly.
- **(D) Identify Key Parts of Information**
  What it means: Notice important parts like the main question or numbers given.
  Math Example: In a division problem, find the main numbers and the exact question to focus on.
- **(E) Spot Arguments or Claims**
  What it means: See when an explanation includes a claim and facts to back it up.
  Math Example: If a problem explains that "multiplying gives faster results," notice facts that show this is true.
- **(F) Recognize Digital Math Tools**
  What it means: Notice special tools in online math lessons, like calculators or videos.

Math Example: If you're learning online, a video might show you how to multiply fractions, giving more help than text alone.

---

(10) Author's Purpose and Craft

These skills help us think about why and how a math problem is written.

- **(A) Explain the Author's Purpose**
  What it means: Understand why the author wrote something.
  Math Example: If you read a problem about budgeting, the author's purpose might be to show why saving money is important.
- **(B) Explain How Text Structure Helps Purpose**
  What it means: Notice how the way the problem is set up helps you understand it better.
  Math Example: If a problem explains a recipe step-by-step, the structure helps you solve it in the right order.
- **(C) Notice Graphics and Bold Text**
  What it means: Look at pictures or bold words that make ideas stand out.
  Math Example: If a diagram shows parts of a fraction, the picture helps you see what the parts look like.
- **(D) Describe Imagery or Interesting Language**
  What it means: Notice words that make you imagine something or sound fun.
  Math Example: If a problem says, "The hungry ants divided the crumbs," it helps you picture dividing equally.
- **(E) Understand Point of View**
  What it means: Know who is telling the problem, like "I" or "we."
  Math Example: In a story problem about a team, understanding "we" helps you see the group working together.
- **(F) Notice Author's Style**
  What it means: Pay attention to the author's style or tone.
  Math Example: If a math explanation sounds friendly, the writer probably wants you to feel confident about the steps.
- **(G) Recognize Stories Within Stories (Anecdotes)**
  What it means: Spot little stories used to explain a point or give examples.
  Math Example: If a problem includes a short story about a famous mathematician, it shows you how math can be used in real life.

These explanations help students connect each TEKS to situations in math class, making the skills they're learning useful for solving problems, understanding directions, and applying concepts.

Here's a student-friendly breakdown of these TEKS standards with examples of <u>how each skill can be used in music class</u>:

---

(6) Comprehension Skills: Listening, Speaking, Reading, Writing, and Thinking

These skills help us understand and think about what we're learning, especially when practicing music or learning about songs and instruments.

- **(A) Set a Purpose for Learning**
  What it means: Think about why you're learning a song or piece of music.
  Music Example: If you're learning a new song, your purpose might be to get better at reading notes or to prepare for a concert.
- **(B) Ask Questions to Understand More**
  What it means: Asking questions helps you understand better.
  Music Example: When learning about a composer, ask questions like, "What inspired this music?" or "What was happening when this song was written?"
- **(C) Make Predictions Based on What You Know**
  What it means: Guess what might come next based on the rhythm or pattern.
  Music Example: If you know a song has a repeating pattern, predict when it will play again.
- **(D) Picture Ideas in Your Mind**
  What it means: Imagine the music in your mind.
  Music Example: While listening to a song, imagine a story or picture that matches the feeling of the music.
- **(E) Make Connections to What You Know**
  What it means: Think about how the music relates to things you know or feel.
  Music Example: If a song is about nature, think about times you've been outside and how the music captures that feeling.
- **(F) Use Clues to Figure Out Meaning**
  What it means: Use details in the music or lyrics to understand the meaning.
  Music Example: If a song has fast, upbeat sounds, you might understand it's meant to feel exciting.
- **(G) Find Key Ideas**
  What it means: Look for the main idea or feeling in the music.
  Music Example: When learning a new piece, find out if it's happy, sad, or dramatic, so you know how to play it with the right emotion.
- **(H) Put Ideas Together to Understand**
  What it means: Combine different music parts to understand the full piece.
  Music Example: In a band, put together each section's part to understand how they work together to make one song.
- **(I) Check for Understanding**
  What it means: Make sure you understand and ask questions if you're confused.

Music Example: If you don't understand a part of a rhythm, ask your teacher to explain it again so you play it correctly.

---

(7) Response Skills: Listening, Speaking, Reading, Writing, and Thinking

These skills help us show that we understand what we've heard or practiced in music class.

- **(A) Make Personal Connections**
  What it means: Relate what you hear in the music to your own experiences.
  Music Example: If you hear a song about friendship, think of a friend and how the song makes you feel about them.
- **(B) Share What You Learned**
  What it means: Show you understand by talking or writing about it.
  Music Example: After learning about jazz, explain to a friend what makes jazz different from other types of music.
- **(C) Use Proof from the Song**
  What it means: Use specific parts of the music to support what you're saying.
  Music Example: If you say a song sounds sad, mention the slow tempo or minor notes as proof.
- **(D) Retell or Summarize in Your Own Words**
  What it means: Share the main points of what you've learned in music class.
  Music Example: After listening to a symphony, summarize what you heard, like the changes in tempo or the instruments used.
- **(E) Take Notes or Draw to Remember**
  What it means: Write down or draw ideas to remember the music.
  Music Example: If you're learning about musical notes, draw the notes to help remember where they are on the staff.
- **(F) Use New Music Words**
  What it means: Use new music vocabulary you've learned.
  Music Example: After learning about "tempo," use the word when talking about how fast or slow a song is.
- **(G) Discuss Important Ideas**
  What it means: Talk about the main ideas in the music.
  Music Example: After learning about rhythm, discuss how rhythm helps keep a song steady.

---

(8) Multiple Genres: Understanding Music Elements

These skills help us understand the different parts of music, like tempo, melody, and rhythm.

- **(A) Find the Theme or Main Idea**
  What it means: Figure out the main idea or mood of a song.
  Music Example: In a lullaby, the theme might be calmness, so it's played softly to help someone relax.
- **(B) Describe How Sounds Change in Music**
  What it means: Notice how music changes, like going from loud to soft.
  Music Example: In a song with verses and a chorus, describe how the chorus might be louder and more energetic than the verses.
- **(C) Identify Important Parts of the Music**
  What it means: Recognize the main parts, like the introduction or ending.
  Music Example: In a song with a solo, the solo part is usually special and stands out from the rest of the music.
- **(D) Explain the Setting's Impact**
  What it means: Think about how the place or style of music affects how it sounds.
  Music Example: A song meant for a marching band might be loud and rhythmic, fitting for outdoor performances.

---

(9) Multiple Genres: Understanding Different Types of Music

These skills help us understand the features and purpose of different types of music.

- **(A) Recognize Different Types of Songs**
  What it means: Learn what makes different types of music unique.
  Music Example: A folk song might tell a story about nature, while a pop song might focus on feelings.
- **(B) Understand Figurative Language in Lyrics**
  What it means: Notice words that create images, like "as bright as the sun."
  Music Example: In a song lyric that says "fly like an eagle," imagine feeling free and powerful.
- **(C) Know How Musical Performances Are Structured**
  What it means: Recognize the order and parts in a performance.
  Music Example: In a choir, know who sings first, who sings harmony, and how the song flows from beginning to end.
- **(D) Identify Key Parts of Music Information**
  What it means: Notice important parts like the main notes or key signature.
  Music Example: In sheet music, look at the time signature to know how many beats are in each measure.
- **(E) Identify Arguments or Claims in Lyrics**
  What it means: See if the lyrics are making a point or expressing an idea.

Music Example: In a protest song, the lyrics might claim "we can make a change," expressing a strong opinion or hope.

- **(F) Recognize Digital Music Features**
  What it means: Notice special tools in digital music, like sound effects or beats.
  Music Example: In a recorded song, pay attention to the use of sound effects that make it sound more exciting or dramatic.

---

(10) Author's Purpose and Craft in Music

These skills help us think about why and how a song or piece of music is made.

- **(A) Explain the Songwriter's Purpose**
  What it means: Understand why the songwriter wrote the lyrics or music.
  Music Example: If a song is about peace, the songwriter's purpose might be to encourage kindness.
- **(B) Explain How Structure Helps Purpose**
  What it means: Notice how the way the song is organized helps you understand it better.
  Music Example: If a song has verses and a repeating chorus, the structure helps you remember the main message.
- **(C) Notice Important Visuals or Sounds**
  What it means: Look at or listen to things that stand out.
  Music Example: In a music video, watch for colors and scenes that match the mood of the song.
- **(D) Describe Imagery in Lyrics**
  What it means: Notice words in the lyrics that create a picture in your mind.
  Music Example: If a song says "the ocean waves dance," picture waves moving up and down as you listen.
- **(E) Understand Point of View in Lyrics**
  What it means: Know who is singing or talking in the song.
  Music Example: If a song is sung from the first-person point of view ("I feel..."), it helps you connect personally to the singer's emotions.
- **(F) Notice the Songwriter's Style**
  What it means: Pay attention to the songwriter's unique style or voice.
  Music Example: Some songwriters have a playful style, while others might sound more serious or dramatic.
- **(G) Recognize Stories in Songs (Anecdotes)**
  What it means: Spot little stories used in lyrics to explain a point or give examples.
  Music Example: In a country song, a story about a small town might show pride in simple, everyday life.

These kid-friendly explanations help students connect each TEKS standard to experiences in music class, making music lessons more meaningful and enjoyable.

Here's a student-friendly breakdown of these TEKS standards, along with examples that show <u>how each skill can be used in technology class</u>:

---

(6) Comprehension Skills: Listening, Speaking, Reading, Writing, and Thinking

These skills help you understand what you're learning in tech class, whether you're reading instructions or exploring a new program.

- **(A) Set a Purpose for Learning**
  What it means: Decide why you're learning something new in technology class.
  Example: If you're learning coding, your purpose might be to create a game. Knowing this helps you focus on what you need to learn to reach your goal.

- **(B) Ask Questions to Understand Better**
  What it means: Ask questions before, during, and after you work with tech to understand it better.
  Example: When learning how to use a new app, you might ask, "How can I add a picture here?" or "What does this tool do?"

- **(C) Make Predictions Using Features**
  What it means: Guess what a button or tool will do based on its design.
  Example: If you see a button with a camera icon, you might predict it will let you take a picture.

- **(D) Picture Ideas in Your Mind**
  What it means: Imagine how things will look when you use different tech tools.
  Example: If you're making a slideshow, picture how each slide will look so you can create a good presentation.

- **(E) Connect to Personal Experiences**
  What it means: Relate what you're learning to things you already know.
  Example: If you're designing a poster in tech class, think about what makes posters interesting, like colors or images, and add them to your design.

- **(F) Use Clues to Figure Out Meaning**
  What it means: Use details in the technology to understand how it works.
  Example: If a website has a magnifying glass icon, you might realize it's for searching.

- **(G) Find Key Ideas**
  What it means: Find the most important parts of the information.
  Example: When learning about online safety, remember key ideas like "don't share passwords" or "ask permission before downloading."

- **(H) Combine Ideas for New Understanding**
  What it means: Bring different tech skills together to create something new.
  Example: If you know how to add pictures and text in a document, you can combine those skills to create a report.

- **(I) Check for Understanding**
  What it means: Make sure you understand and ask for help if you don't.

Example: If you're confused about using a software tool, ask your teacher or rewatch a tutorial until it makes sense.

---

(7) Response Skills: Listening, Speaking, Reading, Writing, and Thinking

These skills help you respond and share what you understand about tech topics.

- **(A) Make Personal Connections**
  What it means: Relate what you learn in tech class to your life.
  Example: If you're learning to edit photos, think about how you can use these skills for fun projects, like making a family photo album.
- **(B) Show What You've Learned**
  What it means: Write or talk about what you learned in a project or program.
  Example: After creating a digital story, explain to your classmates how you made it and what tools you used.
- **(C) Use Evidence to Support Your Ideas**
  What it means: Use parts of what you read or learn to support what you say.
  Example: If you read about keeping passwords safe, mention the article's tips when explaining why password safety is important.
- **(D) Retell or Summarize**
  What it means: Share the main points of what you learned in a simple way.
  Example: After learning about video editing, you might say, "Video editing lets you add music, cut scenes, and make videos more exciting."
- **(E) Take Notes or Draw to Remember**
  What it means: Write down or draw ideas to remember information.
  Example: Draw icons or symbols for each step in a process, like saving a document, to help remember.
- **(F) Use New Tech Vocabulary**
  What it means: Use new words you've learned in tech, like "download" or "upload."
  Example: After learning about coding, use words like "algorithm" when explaining your project.
- **(G) Discuss Important Ideas**
  What it means: Talk about the big ideas in tech.
  Example: In a discussion about digital privacy, share why it's important to keep personal information safe online.

---

(8) Multiple Genres: Understanding Technology Elements

These skills help you understand different parts of digital stories or projects, like themes or characters.

- **(A) Find the Main Theme or Idea**
  What it means: Figure out the main point or goal of a digital project.
  Example: In a video about recycling, the theme might be "protect the environment."
- **(B) Describe How Parts Change in a Digital Story**
  What it means: Notice how characters or ideas develop in a digital story.
  Example: In an animated story, talk about how the main character learns to solve a problem by the end.
- **(C) Identify Key Parts of the Story or Project**
  What it means: Recognize the main parts, like the beginning, middle, and end.
  Example: In a digital slideshow, point out the introduction, main information, and conclusion.
- **(D) Explain How Settings Impact Projects**
  What it means: Think about how the setting (like the time or place) affects a project.
  Example: If you're making a historical presentation, the setting might help explain why events happened a certain way.

---

(9) Multiple Genres: Recognizing Different Types of Digital Content

These skills help you understand different types of digital content, like blogs, tutorials, or infographics.

- **(A) Recognize Different Types of Stories or Videos**
  What it means: Understand what makes different types of media special.
  Example: An instructional video teaches how to do something, while a vlog is more about sharing experiences.
- **(B) Understand Creative Language in Digital Content**
  What it means: Notice words or phrases that make digital stories more interesting.
  Example: If a tutorial says "as simple as ABC," it's using a phrase to make it seem easy.
- **(C) Know How Projects Are Structured**
  What it means: Recognize the layout and order in digital presentations.
  Example: In a website, know where to find the "Home" page, links, or navigation tools.
- **(D) Identify Important Parts of Informational Content**
  What it means: Recognize key ideas, like the main topic or supporting facts.
  Example: In an infographic about planets, the main idea might be a comparison of their sizes.
- **(E) Spot Arguments or Claims in Digital Texts**
  What it means: See if a digital article is making a strong point.
  Example: In a persuasive blog about recycling, the claim might be "Recycling helps the planet."

- **(F) Recognize Digital Text Features**
  What it means: Notice special features in digital content, like links or buttons.
  Example: In an online tutorial, use the "pause" button if you need extra time to follow along.

---

(10) Author's Purpose and Craft in Digital Content

These skills help you understand why and how digital creators make content.

- **(A) Explain the Creator's Purpose**
  What it means: Understand why someone created the content, like to inform or entertain.
  Example: If a video is teaching how to code, the purpose is to educate you about coding.
- **(B) Explain How Structure Helps Purpose**
  What it means: Notice how the way a digital piece is organized helps the purpose.
  Example: If a tutorial is step-by-step, it's structured to make learning easier.
- **(C) Notice Visuals or Special Features**
  What it means: Look at or listen to things that stand out, like images or sound effects.
  Example: In a presentation, colorful charts might help you understand data better.
- **(D) Describe Imagery in Digital Content**
  What it means: Notice words or visuals that create a picture in your mind.
  Example: If an app uses words like "bright and cheerful," imagine a colorful screen.
- **(E) Recognize Points of View in Digital Stories**
  What it means: Know who is sharing the information or telling the story.
  Example: In a blog post, notice if it's written in "I" or "we" to see who's talking.
- **(F) Notice the Creator's Style**
  What it means: Pay attention to how the creator's way of communicating makes it unique.
  Example: Some creators are more formal, while others use humor to make content fun.
- **(G) Recognize Stories or Examples (Anecdotes)**
  What it means: Spot little stories in digital content used to explain or give examples.
  Example: In a science video, the narrator might share a quick story about an experiment to help explain it.

These simplified TEKS help students connect language arts skills to technology, making digital learning more meaningful and enjoyable.

Here's a student-friendly explanation of these TEKS standards, with examples showing <u>how each skill can be helpful in everyday family situations at home</u>:

(6) Comprehension Skills: Listening, Speaking, Reading, Writing, and Thinking

These skills help you better understand things you read or hear, especially when learning something new or figuring things out with your family.

- **(A) Set a Purpose for Reading**
  What it means: Think about why you're reading or listening to something. *Example:* If you're reading a recipe with your parent, your purpose is to make sure you understand how to make the dish.
- **(B) Ask Questions**
  What it means: Ask questions before, during, and after reading or listening to get more details.
  Example: If your family is planning a trip, ask questions like, "What activities will we do?" or "What should I pack?"
- **(C) Make Predictions**
  What it means: Guess what might happen next based on clues.
  Example: If your family is watching a movie, guess what the main character might do next. It makes the story more fun!
- **(D) Picture Things in Your Head**
  What it means: Imagine what you're reading or hearing to understand it better.
  Example: If someone is describing your new room, picture it in your mind to help imagine where your bed or toys might go.
- **(E) Connect Ideas to Your Life**
  What it means: Think about how the information relates to things you already know or have experienced.
  Example: If you're learning about weather, remember a time it was really stormy or sunny and how it affected your plans.
- **(F) Use Clues to Understand**
  What it means: Use hints in what you read or hear to understand better.
  Example: If your parent says it's too chilly for the beach, you might figure out that it's a good day for indoor games instead.
- **(G) Find Important Details**
  What it means: Look for the key information that matters most.
  Example: When reading instructions for a board game, focus on the main rules to play correctly.
- **(H) Combine Ideas**
  What it means: Put information together to learn something new.
  Example: If you learn both how to plant seeds and how to water them, you understand how to grow a plant.

- **(I) Double-Check Your Understanding**
  What it means: If you don't understand, ask questions or reread.
  Example: If you're learning to make a craft, go over the steps again to be sure you know what to do.

(7) Response Skills: Listening, Speaking, Reading, Writing, and Thinking

These skills help you respond to things you read, see, or hear, showing that you understand and can talk about them.

- **(A) Make Connections to Your Life**
  What it means: Think about how things you read or hear connect to your experiences.
  Example: After watching a show about animals, you might tell your family how it reminds you of your pet or an animal you've seen.
- **(B) Show You Understand**
  What it means: Explain what you learned to show you understand.
  Example: After reading a family recipe, explain to your sibling each step to make the dish.
- **(C) Use Information to Support Ideas**
  What it means: Use parts of what you read or hear to support what you say.
  Example: If you're explaining why it's important to recycle, mention how recycling helps the environment.
- **(D) Retell in Your Own Words**
  What it means: Say what you learned in a simpler way.
  Example: After hearing a story, retell the main parts to your family at the dinner table.
- **(E) Take Notes or Draw Pictures**
  What it means: Write or draw to remember information.
  Example: Draw a picture of a science experiment after learning about it to show the steps.
- **(F) Use New Words You've Learned**
  What it means: Use new words you learn in conversation.
  Example: After learning the word "conservation" in a science lesson, use it when talking about saving water at home.
- **(G) Discuss Key Ideas**
  What it means: Talk about the most important ideas with your family.
  Example: Discuss with your parents why healthy eating is important after learning about it in a book.

(8) Multiple Genres: Literary Elements

These skills help you understand stories, including their themes, characters, and plot.

- **(A) Find the Main Theme or Idea**
  What it means: Figure out the main message of a story or article.
  Example: After reading a story about kindness, share that the theme is about helping others.
- **(B) Explain How Characters Change**
  What it means: Notice how characters act and change in a story.
  Example: In a family story, describe how someone who was nervous in the beginning becomes brave.
- **(C) Identify Story Elements**
  What it means: Recognize parts like the beginning, climax, and end.
  Example: If your family reads a book together, talk about what happened in the middle and how the story ends.
- **(D) Describe How the Setting Affects the Story**
  What it means: Think about how the place or time affects the events in a story.
  Example: If the story is set in winter, explain how the cold affects what the characters can do.

---

(9) Multiple Genres: Recognizing Different Types of Stories and Content

These skills help you understand different types of writing, like stories, poems, or informational articles.

- **(A) Recognize Types of Stories**
  What it means: Understand different kinds of stories, like myths or folktales.
  Example: Recognize that a story about animals with human qualities is a fable.
- **(B) Notice Creative Language**
  What it means: Pay attention to language that makes stories fun or interesting.
  Example: In a family poem, notice phrases like "the moon dances," which make it feel magical.
- **(C) Know How Stories Are Organized**
  What it means: Recognize how stories and scripts are arranged.
  Example: Notice how a family play is organized into acts and scenes.
- **(D) Identify Key Points in Informational Texts**
  What it means: Spot the main ideas in a fact-based article.
  Example: In an article about space, focus on the main facts about planets and stars.
- **(E) Spot Arguments in Texts**
  What it means: Recognize when a writer is trying to convince you of something.
  Example: If an article encourages recycling, identify that the writer is convincing readers to recycle.

- **(F) Recognize Digital Content Features**
  What it means: Notice features in online articles, like videos or links.
  Example: While reading a news article online, click on a link to learn more about the topic.

---

(10) Author's Purpose and Craft

These skills help you understand why authors write the way they do and what they want to communicate.

- **(A) Understand Why the Author Wrote It**
  What it means: Figure out the author's purpose, like to entertain, inform, or persuade.
  Example: If you read a book about animals, know that the purpose is to inform you about different species.
- **(B) Explain How Structure Helps Purpose**
  What it means: Notice how the way something is organized helps its goal.
  Example: A recipe with numbered steps is organized to help you follow each step in order.
- **(C) Recognize Visuals that Help Explain**
  What it means: Look at pictures or charts that help you understand.
  Example: In a science book about weather, a picture of a thunderstorm helps you understand the information.
- **(D) Recognize Words that Create Mental Pictures**
  What it means: Notice words that help you imagine what's happening.
  Example: If a story says, "the fluffy clouds floated," picture the soft clouds in your mind.
- **(E) Recognize Points of View**
  What it means: Notice if the story is told by the character (I) or by someone outside the story (he, she).
  Example: In a story where the character says "I went to the park," recognize it's from the character's point of view.
- **(F) Notice the Author's Style**
  What it means: Pay attention to how the author's style makes their writing unique.
  Example: If a writer uses lots of funny words, you can tell they have a humorous style.
- **(G) Recognize Short Stories (Anecdotes)**
  What it means: Spot little stories the author uses to explain something.
  Example: In a family book about history, the author might tell a quick story to make the facts more interesting.

These simplified TEKS explanations make it easier for students to connect language arts skills to real-life scenarios with their families, making learning more relatable and practical.

Here's a student-friendly breakdown of these TEKS standards, with examples that show <u>how each skill can help in theater class:</u>

(6) Comprehension Skills: Listening, Speaking, Reading, Writing, and Thinking

These skills help you understand and think deeply about scripts, character roles, and scenes.

- **(A) Set a Purpose for Reading**
  What it means: Know why you're reading a script or practicing lines.
  Example: When reading a script for a play, focus on understanding your character's emotions and actions to perform them well.
- **(B) Ask Questions**
  What it means: Ask questions about the script, scene, or character to understand them better.
  Example: If you're confused about why your character is sad, ask, "What happened to my character before this scene?"
- **(C) Make Predictions**
  What it means: Guess what might happen in the story based on the script's details.
  Example: After reading the beginning of a play, you might guess how your character's relationships with others will change.
- **(D) Picture the Scene in Your Head**
  What it means: Imagine the setting, actions, and costumes to get a feel for the scene.
  Example: When reading a scene set in a dark forest, imagine the lighting and mood to understand how to act.
- **(E) Connect to Personal Experiences**
  What it means: Think about how parts of the script relate to your own life.
  Example: If your character is nervous on stage, think of a time you were nervous and use that feeling in your acting.
- **(F) Use Clues to Understand**
  What it means: Use hints in the script to understand your character's actions.
  Example: If the script shows your character's hands shaking, this might mean they're scared or anxious.
- **(G) Find Key Details**
  What it means: Focus on important parts of the script to guide your performance.
  Example: If your character smiles right before delivering a line, this detail might mean they're trying to hide their true feelings.
- **(H) Combine Ideas**
  What it means: Put together different details to create a complete understanding.
  Example: Combine clues about your character's past and current actions to perform the role more naturally.
- **(I) Double-Check Understanding**
  What it means: If you're not sure about something, review the script or ask questions.

Example: If you don't understand a line, ask your teacher or reread the surrounding lines to make sense of it.

---

(7) Response Skills: Listening, Speaking, Reading, Writing, and Thinking

These skills help you react to and understand scripts, characters, and scenes.

- **(A) Make Connections to Yourself**
  What it means: Think about how the story relates to your own life.
  Example: If your character feels brave in a scene, think of a time you were brave to help bring the feeling to life.
- **(B) Show You Understand**
  What it means: Explain what the script or scene means to you.
  Example: Describe how your character's experiences in a play are similar to someone you know.
- **(C) Use Script Details to Support Your Ideas**
  What it means: Use parts of the script to explain your choices in acting.
  Example: If you think your character is happy, use a line where they're smiling to back up your interpretation.
- **(D) Retell the Script in Your Own Words**
  What it means: Summarize the main points to understand the scene better.
  Example: After reading a scene, summarize what happened to get a clear picture of the storyline.
- **(E) Take Notes or Draw**
  What it means: Write down thoughts or sketch ideas to remember details.
  Example: Draw a quick sketch of your character's costume and expressions to help visualize them during rehearsal.
- **(F) Use New Theater Terms**
  What it means: Practice using terms you learn in theater class.
  Example: After learning the term "monologue," practice using it by saying, "I have a monologue to practice today!"
- **(G) Discuss Key Ideas**
  What it means: Talk about the important themes or emotions in the script.
  Example: If a scene is about friendship, talk with classmates about how to show that on stage.

---

(8) Multiple Genres: Literary Elements

These skills help you recognize the parts of a story, like themes, character changes, and the plot.

- **(A) Find the Theme**
  What it means: Figure out the main idea or message in a play.

Example: If a play shows characters forgiving each other, you can say that a theme is forgiveness.

- **(B) Explain How Characters Change**
  What it means: Notice how a character grows or changes in the story.
  Example: If your character starts out shy and then becomes brave, understand why that change happens to show it in your acting.
- **(C) Identify Plot Elements**
  What it means: Recognize parts like the beginning, middle, climax, and end.
  Example: Notice where the most exciting part (climax) happens in a scene, so you can build up to it in your acting.
- **(D) Describe How the Setting Affects the Story**
  What it means: Think about how the place or time changes the story's events.
  Example: If a play is set in a busy city, act with quick movements to match the setting.

(9) Multiple Genres: Recognizing Different Types of Writing

These skills help you understand different types of writing, like stories, poems, or plays.

- **(A) Recognize Types of Stories**
  What it means: Know different kinds of stories like folktales or myths.
  Example: If your play is a fable, understand that it teaches a lesson, and focus on acting that shows the moral.
- **(B) Notice Creative Language**
  What it means: Pay attention to fun language like similes or metaphors.
  Example: If a line says "the stage was a jungle," imagine the scene feeling wild or unpredictable.
- **(C) Understand Script Organization**
  What it means: Recognize how scripts are set up with acts, scenes, and tags.
  Example: Notice which scene or act you're in and look for your character tag so you know when to enter or speak.
- **(D) Find Main Ideas in Informational Texts**
  What it means: Spot important ideas in nonfiction texts.
  Example: If you read an article on theater history, focus on main points like how theater started or how it's changed.
- **(E) Spot Arguments in Texts**
  What it means: Recognize when a text tries to convince you of something.
  Example: If you read about the importance of rehearsals, understand that it's encouraging you to practice.
- **(F) Recognize Digital Content Features**
  What it means: Notice online features like videos or pictures that add information.
  Example: If you watch a video on theater techniques, focus on the visuals to learn new skills.

(10) Author's Purpose and Craft

These skills help you understand why the writer wrote the play or script the way they did.

- **(A) Understand the Author's Purpose**
  What it means: Figure out the reason behind the script—like to entertain or teach.
  Example: If the play is funny, understand the author's purpose was to entertain, so you can act with humor.
- **(B) Explain How the Structure Helps**
  What it means: Notice how the setup of a script or story helps its purpose.
  Example: If a monologue is placed at the climax, understand it's there to show intense emotions.
- **(C) Recognize Visuals and Their Purpose**
  What it means: Look at any pictures or stage directions and why they help explain things.
  Example: If stage directions say to dim the lights, understand it's to create a spooky mood.
- **(D) Notice Words that Paint a Picture**
  What it means: Pay attention to language that helps you imagine the scene.
  Example: If the script describes a "stormy night," use slow, tense actions to match that mood.
- **(E) Recognize Point of View**
  What it means: Notice if the character is speaking from their own view or if they're describing others.
  Example: If your character speaks directly to the audience, think about how that personalizes the story.
- **(F) Notice the Author's Style**
  What it means: Understand the unique style or tone the writer uses.
  Example: If the writer uses old-fashioned language, adjust your acting to match that historical feel.
- **(G) Recognize Little Stories (Anecdotes)**
  What it means: Notice short stories or examples the writer uses to make a point.
  Example: If your character shares a quick story, use it to show their personality or backstory.

These simplified TEKS explanations connect language arts and reading skills to real-life theater situations, helping students understand how to use these skills while performing and interpreting scripts.

Chapter 6

Selections with and without TEKS

Selection, Passage, Article, or Story?

The words "selection," "passage," "article," and "story" are often used interchangeably in education, especially when talking about reading materials—but they do have distinct meanings and implications, particularly in curriculum design and standardized assessments. Here's a clear breakdown:

1. Selection (overarching)

Definition: A selection is a chosen piece of text—either whole or excerpted—that may span multiple genres and often serves as a broader instructional tool.

Usage: The term "selection" is used more broadly in curriculum materials and assessments (like STAAR) to refer to the entire piece students will read and respond to.

Length: Medium to long—may be a short story, a full article, or several pages of an excerpt.

Example: A TEKS-aligned selection from a historical fiction novel used during a reading unit.

Purpose: To assess multiple comprehension skills or serve as the anchor for a full lesson.

Where it's seen: Reading comprehension sections, anchor texts, or unit studies, overarching term used in STAAR assessments.

2. Passage

Definition: A passage is a brief excerpt or snippet taken from a larger text.

Usage: It typically focuses on a specific portion used to highlight a skill or objective (e.g., inferencing, identifying tone).

Length: Usually short.

Example: A paragraph from Charlotte's Web used to teach figurative language.

Purpose: Focused skill practice, close reading, or targeted instruction.

Where it's seen: Common in STAAR test prep, guided reading groups, or warm-ups.

3. Article

Definition: An article is a nonfiction piece of writing found in newspapers, magazines, or digital platforms, intended to inform, explain, or persuade.

Usage: "Article" refers to the genre more than the length. It must have a clear purpose, structure, and usually a central idea.

Length: Varies—can be short or long.

Example: A science article about ecosystems or a persuasive editorial on recycling.

Purpose: Often used to teach text structure, author's purpose, central idea, or argument.

Where it's seen: Nonfiction reading instruction, paired texts, or cross-curricular literacy.

▇ 4. Story

Definition: A story is a narrative text that follows a plot structure—typically including characters, setting, conflict, and resolution.

Usage: Stories are complete narratives—either short stories or full-length books—used to build comprehension and understanding of literary elements.

Length: Can range from short (one page) to long (novels).

Example: "Thank You, Ma'am" by Langston Hughes or a novel like Holes by Louis Sachar.

Purpose: Teach literary elements (plot, theme, character, setting, conflict), author's craft, and narrative writing.

Where it's seen: Fiction units, mentor texts, reading instruction (STAAR), writing modeling.

Poems and plays are referred to poems and plays.

Quick Comparison Table

Term	Genre	Purpose	Common Use	Length
Selection	Fiction or Nonfiction	Assess comprehension & build theme	Anchor texts, test sections	Varies
Passage	Fiction or Nonfiction	Targeted skill practice	Mini-lessons, warm-ups, tests	Short
Article	Nonfiction only	Inform, explain, persuade	Informational text study	Varies
Story	Fiction only	Explore narrative elements	Fiction units, read alouds, mentor texts	Varies

💡 Teach BIG Tip:

When planning instruction using the Full Circle of Language Arts framework:

- Use passages to target habits (phonics, grammar, vocabulary, fluency).
- Use selections to assess application (reading comprehension or writing prompts).
- Use articles to support cross-curricular learning, genre exposure, and argument analysis.
- Use stories to dive deep into character, theme, and emotional growth (BRAKES strategy).

Fictional Story: Never Giving Up (Without TEKS Labels)

The sky was overcast as Mia stood at the starting line for the annual school marathon. She had trained for weeks, but now, facing the long path ahead, doubt started creeping in. Could she really finish this race?

As the whistle blew, Mia took off, feeling the rush of the wind against her face. For the first mile, everything went smoothly. She kept pace with the other runners and felt confident in her stride. But as the second mile began, she felt her legs getting heavy. Her breaths came quicker, and her heart pounded in her chest.

Mia started to fall behind. The other runners seemed to glide effortlessly while she struggled with each step. "I can't do this," she thought, slowing to a walk. The other kids raced ahead, leaving her behind.

Suddenly, Mia heard a voice from the sidelines. It was her coach, shouting, "Keep going, Mia! You can do it! Don't give up!" She paused for a moment, looking at the remaining distance. It seemed impossible. But then she remembered all those afternoons spent practicing, pushing herself, and how proud she felt when she improved just a little more each day.

"I didn't come this far to quit now," Mia said to herself. She took a deep breath and started running again. Her legs ached, but she focused on her goal—the finish line. Slowly, Mia picked up speed, passing a few of the kids who had zoomed by her earlier.

With the finish line in sight, Mia felt a surge of energy. The crowd was cheering, and she sprinted the last few yards, crossing the line with her arms raised high. She didn't finish first, but she finished, and that was the victory she had wanted.

After the race, her coach walked over and said, "Mia, I knew you could do it. It's not about how fast you were—it's about never giving up."

Mia smiled. She had learned something much more important than winning: she had learned the power of perseverance.

Fictional Story: Never Giving Up (With TEKS Labels)

The sky was overcast as Mia stood at the starting line for the annual school marathon. She had trained for weeks, but now, facing the long path ahead, doubt started creeping in. Could she really finish this race? **(6A)**

As the whistle blew, Mia took off, feeling the rush of the wind against her face. For the first mile, everything went smoothly. She kept pace with the other runners and felt confident in her stride. But as the second mile began, she felt her legs getting heavy. Her breaths came quicker, and her heart pounded in her chest. **(6D)**

Mia started to fall behind. The other runners seemed to glide effortlessly while she struggled with each step. "I can't do this," she thought, slowing to a walk. The other kids raced ahead, leaving her behind. **(6F)**

Suddenly, Mia heard a voice from the sidelines. It was her coach, shouting, "Keep going, Mia! You can do it! Don't give up!" She paused for a moment, looking at the remaining distance. It seemed impossible. But then she remembered all those afternoons spent practicing, pushing herself, and how proud she felt when she improved just a little more each day. **(7A)**

"I didn't come this far to quit now," Mia said to herself. She took a deep breath and started running again. Her legs ached, but she focused on her goal—the finish line. Slowly, Mia picked up speed, passing a few of the kids who had zoomed by her earlier. **(6H)**

With the finish line in sight, Mia felt a surge of energy. The crowd was cheering, and she sprinted the last few yards, crossing the line with her arms raised high. She didn't finish first, but she finished, and that was the victory she had wanted. **(7C)**

After the race, her coach walked over and said, "Mia, I knew you could do it. It's not about how fast you were—it's about never giving up." **(6I)**

Mia smiled. She had learned something much more important than winning: she had learned the power of perseverance. **(6G)**

TEKS Breakdown:

1. **6A - Establish Purpose for Reading**: Mia's internal reflection at the starting line sets up the theme of perseverance and introduces the purpose of the story.
2. **6D - Create Mental Images**: The description of Mia's physical struggle as her legs grow heavy helps create a vivid mental image.
3. **6F - Make Inferences**: Mia's self-talk about not being able to continue allows readers to infer her frustration and doubt.
4. **7A - Describe Personal Connections**: Mia recalls her practice sessions and draws personal motivation to keep going.
5. **6H - Synthesize Information**: Mia's decision to start running again after recalling her hard work demonstrates how she synthesizes her past efforts into new determination.
6. **7C - Use Text Evidence**: The coach's encouragement and Mia's internal resolve support the theme of never giving up.
7. **6I - Monitor Comprehension and Adjust**: Mia mentally reassesses her situation, decides not to quit, and makes adjustments by picking up her pace.
8. **6G - Evaluate Key Ideas**: The story wraps up with Mia realizing that finishing the race, not winning, was her true victory.

This labeled and unlabeled version provides students with the opportunity to engage with a fictional story while identifying specific TEKS standards through practical reading comprehension and analysis activities.

Fictional Story: Fairness (Without TEKS Labels)

The air was filled with excitement as students gathered around the blacktop. It was the day of the annual relay race, and each class had carefully chosen their fastest runners. Jason stood at the starting line, feeling a mixture of nervousness and excitement. He glanced at the other runners, wondering if he stood a chance.

As the whistle blew, Jason surged forward, his legs pumping hard against the ground. He quickly gained the lead, and for a moment, he felt invincible. But halfway through the race, disaster struck. His shoelace came undone, causing him to trip and fall. The crowd gasped as Jason tumbled to the ground, clutching his scraped knee.

The other runners rushed past him, but one person stopped. It was Derek, the runner from the other team. Instead of continuing, Derek knelt beside Jason and offered him a hand. "Are you okay?" Derek asked.

Jason nodded, trying to hold back his frustration. "Go ahead and finish the race. You'll win."

Derek shook his head. "That wouldn't be fair. Let's both finish it together."

Jason stared at Derek in disbelief. "But you could win this for your team!"

"It's not about winning," Derek said with a smile. "It's about doing the right thing."

With Derek's help, Jason got to his feet, and the two boys crossed the finish line together, earning cheers from the crowd. Even though they didn't win first place, they won something far more valuable—the respect of their classmates.

Later that day, the principal gathered everyone and said, "What we saw today was true sportsmanship. Winning isn't just about crossing the finish line first; it's about fairness, kindness, and doing what's right."

Jason looked at Derek and realized that fairness wasn't about who won the race, but how you treated others along the way.

Fictional Story: Fairness (With TEKS Labels)

The air was filled with excitement as students gathered around the blacktop. It was the day of the annual relay race, and each class had carefully chosen their fastest runners. Jason stood at the starting line, feeling a mixture of nervousness and excitement. He glanced at the other runners, wondering if he stood a chance. **(6A)**

As the whistle blew, Jason surged forward, his legs pumping hard against the ground. He quickly gained the lead, and for a moment, he felt invincible. But halfway through the race, disaster struck. His shoelace came undone, causing him to trip and fall. The crowd gasped as Jason tumbled to the ground, clutching his scraped knee. **(6D)**

The other runners rushed past him, but one person stopped. It was Derek, the runner from the other team. Instead of continuing, Derek knelt beside Jason and offered him a hand. "Are you okay?" Derek asked. **(6E)**

Jason nodded, trying to hold back his frustration. "Go ahead and finish the race. You'll win." **(6F)**

Derek shook his head. "That wouldn't be fair. Let's both finish it together." **(6G)**

Jason stared at Derek in disbelief. "But you could win this for your team!" **(7A)**

"It's not about winning," Derek said with a smile. "It's about doing the right thing." **(7C)**

With Derek's help, Jason got to his feet, and the two boys crossed the finish line together, earning cheers from the crowd. Even though they didn't win first place, they won something far more valuable—the respect of their classmates. **(7B)**

Later that day, the principal gathered everyone and said, "What we saw today was true sportsmanship. Winning isn't just about crossing the finish line first; it's about fairness, kindness, and doing what's right." **(10A)**

Jason looked at Derek and realized that fairness wasn't about who won the race, but how you treated others along the way. **(6H)**

TEKS Breakdown:

1. **6A - Establish Purpose for Reading**: Jason's internal reflection sets up the theme of fairness and introduces the purpose of the story.
2. **6D - Create Mental Images**: The imagery of Jason tripping and falling creates a vivid picture in the reader's mind.
3. **6E - Make Connections to Personal Experiences**: The moment Derek helps Jason relates to everyday moments when students have the chance to help someone in need.
4. **6F - Make Inferences**: Jason's words about Derek continuing the race allow readers to infer his disappointment and frustration.
5. **6G - Evaluate Key Ideas**: Derek's decision to stay behind shows fairness and sportsmanship, which becomes a key theme in the passage.
6. **6H - Synthesize Information**: Jason's realization at the end of the story shows new understanding that fairness is not just about winning.
7. **7A - Describe Personal Connections**: Jason and Derek's conversation highlights how they connect through sportsmanship.
8. **7B - Write Responses that Demonstrate Understanding**: The boys finishing the race together shows how they understand the value of fairness.
9. **7C - Use Text Evidence**: Derek's dialogue about "doing the right thing" supports the theme of fairness in action.
10. **10A - Explain Author's Purpose**: The principal's speech summarizes the message of fairness and serves as a clear example of the author's intended theme.

With the two versions—one labeled and one not—students will be able to locate and identify TEKS skills while engaging with a meaningful story about fairness and sportsmanship.

Fictional Story: Friendship (Without TEKS Labels)

It was a scorching summer day, and the sun beat down mercilessly on the small park. Jasmine sat on the edge of the sandbox, feeling defeated. Her best friend, Mia, had stopped talking to her ever since their argument last week. Jasmine couldn't even remember what the fight was about, but it left a gaping hole in her heart.

She sighed and picked up a stick, tracing patterns in the sand, her mind swirling with questions. Why had things gone so wrong? Was the friendship beyond repair?

Just then, she saw Mia walking toward the park, kicking a soccer ball. Jasmine's heart raced. Should she wave? Should she apologize? But what if Mia didn't want to be friends anymore?

Mia looked up and caught Jasmine's gaze. For a moment, they just stared at each other. Then Mia slowly approached, the soccer ball still under her arm.

"Hey," Mia said quietly, her voice unsure.

"Hey," Jasmine replied, her voice equally tentative.

Mia shuffled her feet. "I, um, was thinking about last week… and I'm really sorry for what happened."

Jasmine felt a weight lift off her chest. "Me too," she said, smiling. "I don't even remember why we argued. It seems silly now."

Mia grinned. "Do you want to play soccer? We can forget about it and just have fun like we used to."

Jasmine jumped up, her heart lighter than it had been in days. "Yeah, let's go!" she said.

As they kicked the ball back and forth, the tension between them melted away. The warmth of their friendship returned, stronger than ever. Sometimes, Jasmine realized, it wasn't about winning an argument. It was about remembering what really mattered.

That day, in the sweltering summer heat, they rebuilt their friendship, one kick at a time.

Fictional Story: Friendship (With TEKS Labels)

It was a scorching summer day, and the sun beat down mercilessly on the small park. **(6A)** Jasmine sat on the edge of the sandbox, feeling defeated. Her best friend, Mia, had stopped talking to her ever since their argument last week. Jasmine couldn't even remember what the fight was about, but it left a gaping hole in her heart. **(6F)**

She sighed and picked up a stick, tracing patterns in the sand, her mind swirling with questions. **(6B)** Why had things gone so wrong? Was the friendship beyond repair? **(6G)**

Just then, she saw Mia walking toward the park, kicking a soccer ball. Jasmine's heart raced. Should she wave? Should she apologize? **(6C)** But what if Mia didn't want to be friends anymore?

Mia looked up and caught Jasmine's gaze. For a moment, they just stared at each other. Then Mia slowly approached, the soccer ball still under her arm. **(6D)**

"Hey," Mia said quietly, her voice unsure. **(7A)**

"Hey," Jasmine replied, her voice equally tentative.

Mia shuffled her feet. "I, um, was thinking about last week… and I'm really sorry for what happened."

Jasmine felt a weight lift off her chest. "Me too," she said, smiling. "I don't even remember why we argued. It seems silly now." **(7B)**

Mia grinned. "Do you want to play soccer? We can forget about it and just have fun like we used to." **(7E)**

Jasmine jumped up, her heart lighter than it had been in days. "Yeah, let's go!" she said.

As they kicked the ball back and forth, the tension between them melted away. The warmth of their friendship returned, stronger than ever. Sometimes, Jasmine realized, it wasn't about winning an argument. It was about remembering what really mattered. **(6H)**

That day, in the sweltering summer heat, they rebuilt their friendship, one kick at a time. **(8A)**

TEKS Breakdown:

1. **6A - Establish Purpose for Reading**: The theme of friendship is established early as Jasmine reflects on her fractured relationship with Mia.
2. **6B - Generate Questions**: Jasmine's internal questions deepen the reader's understanding of her emotional state and uncertainty.
3. **6C - Make Predictions**: The reader can predict what might happen next as Jasmine debates whether to wave or apologize.
4. **6D - Create Mental Images**: The visual of Jasmine and Mia staring at each other creates a clear image of their tension.
5. **6F - Make Inferences**: Readers can infer that Jasmine is deeply affected by the argument with Mia, even if she can't remember the details.
6. **6G - Evaluate Key Ideas**: Jasmine's realization that the argument was not important shows the key idea of valuing friendship over conflict.
7. **6H - Synthesize Information**: Jasmine's reflection that sometimes it's not about winning an argument but about friendship shows new understanding.
8. **7A - Describe Personal Connections**: Jasmine and Mia's conversation about their argument reflects how people mend broken relationships.
9. **7B - Write Responses that Demonstrate Understanding**: Mia's apology and Jasmine's response show understanding of forgiveness and reconciliation.
10. **7E - Interact with Sources in Meaningful Ways**: The dialogue between Jasmine and Mia allows for interaction that deepens their relationship.
11. **8A - Infer Basic Themes Supported by Text Evidence**: The theme of friendship is clear through Jasmine and Mia's actions to mend their relationship.

By providing these two versions—one labeled and one not—students can practice identifying TEKS skills in a relatable, engaging passage about friendship.

Fictional Story: Responsibility (Without TEKS Labels)

Evan's eyes darted across the crowded classroom as the clock ticked closer to dismissal. Mrs. Brooks had announced that their final group project was due tomorrow, and Evan had barely started his portion. He glanced at his group members, who were busy making last-minute adjustments. They relied on him to finish his part, but he had procrastinated, spending too much time playing video games. Now, he felt the weight of his responsibility pressing down on him.

After school, Evan hurried home. His mom greeted him with a smile and asked about his day, but he barely responded. His mind was racing, thinking about how to pull off the project in time. He sat at his desk and opened his laptop, staring at the blank screen. What if he couldn't finish? What if his group failed because of him?

Just then, his little sister, Lily, knocked on his door. "Evan, can you help me with my homework?" she asked, holding up her math workbook. Evan hesitated. He really needed to focus on his project, but Lily looked up at him with wide eyes. "Please?"

Evan sighed and decided to help her. "Okay, just for a little while," he said. As they worked together on her math problems, Evan realized something. He had been putting off his own work, but now that he was helping Lily, he felt a sense of responsibility growing inside him. If he could help her, surely he could help his group by finishing his part of the project.

After Lily left, Evan got to work. He planned out his project piece carefully, double-checking the requirements and making sure he stayed focused. Slowly but surely, he made progress. By the time he finished, it was well past his bedtime, but he felt a wave of relief. He had finally stepped up.

The next day at school, Evan handed his completed work to his group members. They smiled, grateful for his effort. "Thanks, Evan," one of them said. "We really needed this."

Evan grinned. It wasn't just about getting the project done—it was about taking responsibility and realizing that others were counting on him. In that moment, he learned a valuable lesson: responsibility wasn't just about doing things for yourself, but about doing things for others, too.

Fictional Story: Responsibility (With TEKS Labels)

Evan's eyes darted across the crowded classroom as the clock ticked closer to dismissal. **(6A)** Mrs. Brooks had announced that their final group project was due tomorrow, and Evan had barely started his portion. **(6B)** He glanced at his group members, who were busy making last-minute adjustments. They relied on him to finish his part, but he had procrastinated, spending too much time playing video games. Now, he felt the weight of his responsibility pressing down on him. **(6E)**

After school, Evan hurried home. His mom greeted him with a smile and asked about his day, but he barely responded. His mind was racing, thinking about how to pull off the project in time. He sat at his desk and opened his laptop, staring at the blank screen. **(6C)** What if he couldn't finish? What if his group failed because of him? **(6F)**

Just then, his little sister, Lily, knocked on his door. "Evan, can you help me with my homework?" she asked, holding up her math workbook. Evan hesitated. He really needed to focus on his project, but Lily looked up at him with wide eyes. **(7A)** "Please?"

Evan sighed and decided to help her. "Okay, just for a little while," he said. As they worked together on her math problems, Evan realized something. He had been putting off his own work, but now that he was helping Lily, he felt a sense of responsibility growing inside him. **(7F)** If he could help her, surely he could help his group by finishing his part of the project. **(8A)**

After Lily left, Evan got to work. He planned out his project piece carefully, double-checking the requirements and making sure he stayed focused. **(7E)** Slowly but surely, he made progress. By the time he finished, it was well past his bedtime, but he felt a wave of relief. He had finally stepped up. **(7D)**

The next day at school, Evan handed his completed work to his group members. They smiled, grateful for his effort. "Thanks, Evan," one of them said. "We really needed this." **(6G)**

Evan grinned. It wasn't just about getting the project done—it was about taking responsibility and realizing that others were counting on him. In that moment, he learned a valuable lesson: responsibility wasn't just about doing things for yourself, but about doing things for others, too. **(8B)**

TEKS Breakdown:

1. **6A - Establish Purpose for Reading**: Evan's growing sense of responsibility sets the purpose for the story's message.
2. **6B - Generate Questions**: Evan's internal questions about whether he can finish the project deepen the reader's understanding of his struggle.
3. **6C - Make Predictions**: The blank screen and Evan's panic foreshadow the difficulty he may face in finishing the project.
4. **6E - Make Connections**: Evan's realization of how his actions affect others connects to the reader's own experiences with responsibility.
5. **6F - Make Inferences**: Readers can infer that Evan's procrastination has left him feeling anxious and guilty about the group's project.
6. **6G - Evaluate Key Ideas**: The key idea of responsibility is highlighted when Evan's group thanks him for completing his work.
7. **7A - Describe Personal Connections**: Evan's decision to help his sister, despite his own stress, creates a personal connection to his sense of responsibility.
8. **7D - Retell in Logical Order**: The progression from procrastination to responsibility follows a clear, logical sequence.
9. **7E - Interact with Sources**: Evan interacts with the project's requirements, ensuring that his work meets the necessary standards.
10. **7F - Respond Using Newly Acquired Vocabulary**: Evan's internal realization about responsibility helps him understand its deeper significance.
11. **8A - Infer Basic Themes**: The theme of responsibility is inferred through Evan's growth from procrastination to completing his work.
12. **8B - Explain Character Interactions**: The interaction between Evan and his group members shows how responsibility can build trust and cooperation.

This labeled version allows students to identify and practice specific TEKS standards within a relatable, fictional passage.

Fictional Story: Adaptation (Without TEKS Labels)

The wind howled as Sophia stood on the deck of her new home—a small house nestled by the seaside. It had been just a week since her family moved from the bustling city to this quiet, coastal town. The salty breeze and the cries of seagulls were so different from the sounds of honking cars and busy sidewalks she had grown used to. She wrapped her arms around herself, feeling the chill of the sea air. She wasn't sure she liked it here.

At school, things were even harder. Everyone seemed to have their own close-knit group of friends, and Sophia felt like an outsider. She missed her old friends, the ones she could talk to about anything. Now, she had to start over. The idea of making new friends seemed almost impossible.

One afternoon after school, as she sat at the beach staring at the waves, a girl her age approached her. "Hi, I'm Mia. You're new here, right?" the girl asked with a smile. Sophia nodded, unsure of what to say.

"Want to help me build a sandcastle?" Mia asked, motioning toward a pile of sand near the shore.

Sophia hesitated. She didn't know the first thing about building sandcastles, but Mia seemed friendly. "Sure," she said, getting up.

As they worked together, Mia explained how to pack the sand tightly so it wouldn't collapse. Sophia followed her instructions carefully, and soon they had built a tall, impressive sandcastle. For the first time since moving, Sophia felt a spark of happiness.

Over the next few days, Sophia found herself spending more time with Mia. They explored the beach, collected seashells, and even started meeting up at school. Slowly but surely, Sophia began to feel more at home. She realized that while the town was different, and making new friends was hard, it wasn't impossible. Just like the sandcastle, she had to start with small steps, building piece by piece until things felt solid again.

Sophia smiled as she stood on the deck one evening, the sea breeze no longer cold but refreshing. Maybe change wasn't so bad after all.

Fictional Story: Adaptation (With TEKS Labels)

The wind howled as Sophia stood on the deck of her new home—a small house nestled by the seaside. **(6A)** It had been just a week since her family moved from the bustling city to this quiet, coastal town. **(6E)** The salty breeze and the cries of seagulls were so different from the sounds of honking cars and busy sidewalks she had grown used to. She wrapped her arms around herself, feeling the chill of the sea air. She wasn't sure she liked it here. **(6H)**

At school, things were even harder. Everyone seemed to have their own close-knit group of friends, and Sophia felt like an outsider. **(6F)** She missed her old friends, the ones she could talk to about anything. Now, she had to start over. The idea of making new friends seemed almost impossible. **(6D)**

One afternoon after school, as she sat at the beach staring at the waves, a girl her age approached her. "Hi, I'm Mia. You're new here, right?" the girl asked with a smile. **(7A)** Sophia nodded, unsure of what to say.

"Want to help me build a sandcastle?" Mia asked, motioning toward a pile of sand near the shore.

Sophia hesitated. She didn't know the first thing about building sandcastles, but Mia seemed friendly. **(6C)** "Sure," she said, getting up.

As they worked together, Mia explained how to pack the sand tightly so it wouldn't collapse. Sophia followed her instructions carefully, and soon they had built a tall, impressive sandcastle. **(6G)** For the first time since moving, Sophia felt a spark of happiness. **(7F)**

Over the next few days, Sophia found herself spending more time with Mia. They explored the beach, collected seashells, and even started meeting up at school. Slowly but surely, Sophia began to feel more at home. **(8B)** She realized that while the town was different, and making new friends was hard, it wasn't impossible. **(7D)** Just like the sandcastle, she had to start with small steps, building piece by piece until things felt solid again. **(8A)**

Sophia smiled as she stood on the deck one evening, the sea breeze no longer cold but refreshing. Maybe change wasn't so bad after all. **(7G)**

TEKS Breakdown:

1. **6A - Establish Purpose for Reading**: Sophia's reflection on her move sets up the purpose of the story, centered around adaptation to change.
2. **6E - Make Connections**: Sophia's adjustment to her new home contrasts with her previous life in the city, providing an opportunity for readers to connect to the challenge of moving.
3. **6H - Synthesize Information**: The story builds towards Sophia's growing acceptance of her new environment and friendships, showing how she synthesizes new experiences.
4. **6F - Make Inferences**: Sophia feels like an outsider, leading the reader to infer that she is struggling with the move and her new surroundings.
5. **6D - Create Mental Images**: Descriptions of the seagulls, beach, and sandcastle help the reader create vivid mental images of Sophia's new life.
6. **6C - Make Predictions**: The introduction of Mia suggests a potential shift in Sophia's social situation, leading the reader to predict changes in her feelings.
7. **6G - Evaluate Key Ideas**: Building the sandcastle represents the key idea of adapting to new situations and finding joy in the process.
8. **7A - Describe Personal Connections**: Sophia's interactions with Mia serve as a personal connection, helping her feel more at ease in her new town.
9. **7D - Retell in Logical Order**: The progression of events from Sophia's discomfort to her acceptance follows a logical and clear sequence.
10. **7F - Respond Using Newly Acquired Vocabulary**: Sophia's new experiences help her respond to Mia's kindness, reflecting her shift in perspective.
11. **8B - Explain Character Interactions**: The relationship between Sophia and Mia highlights how character interactions can lead to personal growth and change.
12. **8A - Infer Basic Themes**: The story's theme of adaptation is supported by text evidence, such as Sophia's realization that change isn't always bad.
13. **7G - Discuss Specific Ideas in the Text**: The final reflection on change ties back to the main theme, reinforcing the story's message.

This labeled version allows students to identify how specific TEKS standards are embedded within the story, enhancing comprehension and analytical skills.

Fictional Story: Baseball Game (Without TEKS Labels)

It was a hot summer afternoon, and the sun was beating down on the field. Josh wiped the sweat off his forehead as he stood on the pitcher's mound, gripping the baseball tightly. He took a deep breath, eyes fixed on home plate. His best friend, Tim, was up to bat. Josh knew Tim was good, but he also knew his own strength as a pitcher. He smiled, knowing this would be a great challenge.

The other kids were gathered on the sidelines, watching eagerly. Some were chatting about the upcoming pool party later that day, while others were intensely focused on the game. This wasn't just any game—this was the last game before the championship.

Josh threw his first pitch, a fastball right down the middle. Tim swung hard but missed. The kids cheered as the ball snapped into the catcher's glove. Tim's eyebrows furrowed in concentration, and he adjusted his stance. Josh could feel the pressure building, not just from the heat but from the intensity of the moment.

The second pitch came, this time a curveball. Tim swung again, connecting with a loud crack. The ball soared high into the air. Josh turned, eyes wide, as the ball flew toward the fence in the outfield.

"Go! Go! Go!" everyone shouted. The outfielder raced toward the ball, but it was too late. The ball sailed over the fence for a home run. Tim trotted around the bases with a huge grin on his face as his teammates cheered. Josh couldn't help but smile too, despite being the pitcher who gave up the home run.

"Nice one, Tim!" Josh shouted as Tim crossed home plate. The game was tied now, and it was anyone's to win. Josh shook off the pressure and got ready for the next batter. He knew this was far from over.

Fictional Story: Baseball Game (With TEKS Labels)

It was a hot summer afternoon, and the sun was beating down on the field. Josh wiped the sweat off his forehead as he stood on the pitcher's mound, gripping the baseball tightly. **(6A)** He took a deep breath, eyes fixed on home plate. His best friend, Tim, was up to bat. Josh knew Tim was good, but he also knew his own strength as a pitcher. He smiled, knowing this would be a great challenge. **(6F)**

The other kids were gathered on the sidelines, watching eagerly. Some were chatting about the upcoming pool party later that day, while others were intensely focused on the game. **(6E)** This wasn't just any game—this was the last game before the championship. **(6H)**

Josh threw his first pitch, a fastball right down the middle. **(6C)** Tim swung hard but missed. The kids cheered as the ball snapped into the catcher's glove. Tim's eyebrows furrowed in concentration, and he adjusted his stance. **(6D)** Josh could feel the pressure building, not just from the heat but from the intensity of the moment.

The second pitch came, this time a curveball. Tim swung again, connecting with a loud crack. The ball soared high into the air. **(6G)** Josh turned, eyes wide, as the ball flew toward the fence in the outfield.

"Go! Go! Go!" everyone shouted. The outfielder raced toward the ball, but it was too late. The ball sailed over the fence for a home run. Tim trotted around the bases with a huge grin on his face as his teammates cheered. **(7A)** Josh couldn't help but smile too, despite being the pitcher who gave up the home run.

"Nice one, Tim!" Josh shouted as Tim crossed home plate. **(7D)** The game was tied now, and it was anyone's to win. Josh shook off the pressure and got ready for the next batter. He knew this was far from over. **(7B)**

TEKS Breakdown:

1. **6A - Establish Purpose for Reading**: Josh's focus on the challenge with Tim sets up the purpose of the scene.
2. **6F - Make Inferences**: Josh's internal dialogue about knowing Tim is good but recognizing his own strengths implies their competitive friendship.
3. **6E - Make Connections**: The other kids talking about the pool party adds a layer of connection between the game and real-life events.
4. **6H - Synthesize Information to Create New Understanding**: The reference to the championship game adds meaning to the scene, showing how this game impacts future events.
5. **6C - Make Predictions**: Josh's first pitch suggests something about how the game will unfold, and the reader can predict Tim's next move.
6. **6D - Create Mental Images**: Tim adjusting his stance and the description of the pitch help create vivid images of the game's progression.
7. **6G - Evaluate Details Read to Determine Key Ideas**: The description of the home run allows readers to evaluate Tim's success in the game.
8. **7A - Describe Personal Connections**: Josh's reaction to Tim's success is positive, reflecting the friendship and sportsmanship shared between them.
9. **7D - Retell in Logical Order**: Josh's praise and the game's progression are logically ordered and summarized in a clear sequence.
10. **7B - Write Responses Demonstrating Understanding**: Josh's response to Tim's win shows good sportsmanship and an understanding of the game's emotional ups and downs.

This labeled version helps students identify how specific TEKS standards appear naturally in the passage, offering them insight into reading comprehension and textual analysis.

Fictional Story (Without TEKS Labels)

Ava stood at the edge of the forest, staring into the endless trees. She had always heard stories about this place, tales of strange creatures and lost treasures. Now, it was her turn to explore. She took a deep breath, her heart racing, and stepped onto the narrow dirt path leading into the woods.

As she walked, the trees seemed to close in around her, their branches stretching overhead like twisted fingers. The sound of birds calling and leaves rustling filled the air, but Ava couldn't shake the feeling that something was watching her.

Suddenly, she saw a glint of light ahead. Curiosity pushed her forward, and soon she found herself standing in front of an old stone well. The stones were covered in moss, and a faint glow seemed to emanate from the water deep inside. Ava peered over the edge, her reflection shimmering in the water below.

Without thinking, she reached into her backpack and pulled out a small notebook. She had always written down her thoughts and discoveries, and this moment felt important. "Old stone well in the middle of the forest," she scribbled. "Water glowing, feels mysterious—almost magical."

Just as she finished writing, Ava heard a soft whisper. She spun around but saw nothing. The whisper came again, this time closer. Her pulse quickened. "Who's there?" she called, her voice trembling. There was no answer.

A shadow flickered at the edge of her vision. Ava froze, gripping her notebook tightly. She could hear her own breathing, shallow and quick. Whatever was watching her was close—too close.

Then, out of the shadows, a small figure appeared. It looked like a child, but its eyes were too large, its skin too pale. "Hello," the figure said, its voice soft and echoing.

Ava's fear subsided, replaced by curiosity. "Who are you?" she asked.

"I am the keeper of the well," the figure replied. "Many have come here, but few have seen what you see. You are special."

Ava felt a strange connection to the figure, like it had been waiting for her. "Why am I here?" she asked.

"You seek answers," the figure whispered, "and they are within you." It pointed to her notebook. "Write what you feel, and you will understand."

Ava opened her notebook again, her hand shaking. She began to write, her thoughts spilling onto the page. As she wrote, the forest around her seemed to shift, becoming less threatening, more familiar.

When she looked up, the figure was gone. But Ava no longer felt afraid. She closed her notebook, tucked it back into her bag, and turned to leave the forest, feeling like she had uncovered something important—something just for her.

Fictional Story (With TEKS Labels)

Ava stood at the edge of the forest, staring into the endless trees. **(6A)** She had always heard stories about this place, tales of strange creatures and lost treasures. Now, it was her turn to explore. She took a deep breath, her heart racing, and stepped onto the narrow dirt path leading into the woods. **(6D)**

As she walked, the trees seemed to close in around her, their branches stretching overhead like twisted fingers. The sound of birds calling and leaves rustling filled the air, but Ava couldn't shake the feeling that something was watching her. **(6C)**

Suddenly, she saw a glint of light ahead. **(6G)** Curiosity pushed her forward, and soon she found herself standing in front of an old stone well. The stones were covered in moss, and a faint glow seemed to emanate from the water deep inside. **(6E)** Ava peered over the edge, her reflection shimmering in the water below.

Without thinking, she reached into her backpack and pulled out a small notebook. She had always written down her thoughts and discoveries, and this moment felt important. **(7A)** "Old stone well in the middle of the forest," she scribbled. "Water glowing, feels mysterious—almost magical."

Just as she finished writing, Ava heard a soft whisper. She spun around but saw nothing. The whisper came again, this time closer. Her pulse quickened. "Who's there?" she called, her voice trembling. There was no answer. **(7C)**

A shadow flickered at the edge of her vision. Ava froze, gripping her notebook tightly. She could hear her own breathing, shallow and quick. Whatever was watching her was close—too close.

Then, out of the shadows, a small figure appeared. It looked like a child, but its eyes were too large, its skin too pale. "Hello," the figure said, its voice soft and echoing. **(8B)**

Ava's fear subsided, replaced by curiosity. **(8A)** "Who are you?" she asked.

"I am the keeper of the well," the figure replied. "Many have come here, but few have seen what you see. You are special."

Ava felt a strange connection to the figure, like it had been waiting for her. "Why am I here?" she asked.

"You seek answers," the figure whispered, "and they are within you." **(9E)** It pointed to her notebook. "Write what you feel, and you will understand." **(7E)**

Ava opened her notebook again, her hand shaking. She began to write, her thoughts spilling onto the page. **(6F)** As she wrote, the forest around her seemed to shift, becoming less threatening, more familiar. **(9A)**

When she looked up, the figure was gone. But Ava no longer felt afraid. She closed her notebook, tucked it back into her bag, and turned to leave the forest, feeling like she had uncovered something important—something just for her. **(6H)**

TEKS Breakdown:

1. **6A - Establish Purpose for Reading**: The story begins with Ava's purpose to explore the mysterious forest, setting up her reason for venturing in.
2. **6D - Create Mental Images**: Vivid descriptions of the trees and path help the reader form clear mental images.
3. **6C - Make Predictions**: As Ava walks, she senses something watching her, prompting the reader to make predictions about what might happen next.
4. **6E - Make Connections**: Ava's curiosity about the glowing water connects to her previous knowledge and stories she has heard.
5. **6G - Evaluate Details to Determine Key Ideas**: Ava notices the glint of light, prompting her to explore further, leading to key plot development.
6. **7A - Describe Personal Connections**: Ava writes in her notebook, connecting her personal experience of the mysterious well with her written reflections.
7. **7C - Use Text Evidence to Support Response**: Ava's reaction to the whisper and the shadow show her growing tension, supported by the text's description of her actions.
8. **8A - Infer Themes Supported by Text Evidence**: Ava's journey into the forest and encounter with the figure suggest themes of self-discovery and bravery.
9. **8B - Explain Character Interactions**: The interaction between Ava and the figure hints at a deeper connection and serves to move the plot forward.
10. **7E - Interact with Sources in Meaningful Ways**: Ava's writing helps her process her experience and understand her feelings, showing her connection to the mysterious well.
11. **9E - Explain Characteristics of Argumentative Text**: The figure's statement "the answers are within you" is a claim, encouraging Ava to reflect and find answers.
12. **9A - Recognize Genre-Specific Characteristics**: Ava's magical journey contains elements typical of adventure and fantasy genres, such as the mysterious figure and enchanted forest.
13. **6F - Make Inferences**: Ava uses her intuition and the figure's guidance to uncover the meaning behind her experience.
14. **6H - Synthesize Information to Create New Understanding**: By the end of the story, Ava synthesizes her experience and leaves the forest feeling enlightened.

Fiction Story (Without TEKS Labels)

It was a cloudy afternoon when Emma and her friends decided to visit the old library at the edge of town. The large oak trees that lined the street swayed gently in the wind, casting long shadows over the cracked sidewalk. As they approached the building, Emma couldn't help but feel a sense of excitement mixed with nervousness. The stories she had heard about the library, some filled with mystery and others with adventure, came flooding back to her mind.

Inside, the smell of old books filled the air, and the soft glow from the stained glass windows painted the room in warm hues. Emma's eyes widened as she spotted a book with a gold-trimmed cover on a high shelf. "That's it," she whispered to herself, remembering her grandmother's stories about a magical book hidden in the library. She reached up and took it carefully in her hands, feeling the rough texture of its aged leather.

The group gathered around as Emma opened the book. The pages were covered in beautiful illustrations of far-off lands and creatures unlike any they had ever seen. "It looks like a fairy tale," her friend Jack said, pointing at a picture of a dragon flying over a castle.

"Maybe it is," Emma replied, flipping through the pages. "Or maybe it's a guide to somewhere real."

As they continued to explore the book, something strange happened. The words on the pages began to glow, and the room around them seemed to shift. Suddenly, they were no longer in the library, but standing in a lush green field with mountains in the distance.

"Where are we?" asked Lily, her voice trembling.

"I think," Emma began, "we're inside the story."

The group stood in silence, taking in their new surroundings. In front of them, a narrow path led toward a dense forest. "We have to find a way back," Jack said, trying to remain calm. "But first, we need to figure out what this place is."

Emma nodded, clutching the book to her chest. "Let's stick together and find out what this adventure has in store for us."

Answer Key (With TEKS Labels)

It was a **cloudy afternoon** when Emma and her friends decided to visit the old library at the edge of town. (6A) The large oak trees that lined the street swayed gently in the wind, casting long shadows over the cracked sidewalk. **As they approached the building, Emma couldn't help but feel a sense of excitement mixed with nervousness.** (6C) The stories she had heard about the library, some filled with mystery and others with adventure, came flooding back to her mind. (6E)

Inside, the smell of old books filled the air, and the soft glow from the stained glass windows painted the room in warm hues. (6D) Emma's eyes widened as she spotted a book with a gold-trimmed cover on a high shelf. "That's it," she whispered to herself, remembering her grandmother's stories about a magical book hidden in the library. (6F) She reached up and took it carefully in her hands, feeling the rough texture of its aged leather. (6H)

The group gathered around as Emma opened the book. The pages were covered in beautiful illustrations of far-off lands and creatures unlike any they had ever seen. (7E) "It looks like a fairy tale," her friend Jack said, pointing at a picture of a dragon flying over a castle. (8A)

"Maybe it is," Emma replied, flipping through the pages. "Or maybe it's a guide to somewhere real." (7G)

As they continued to explore the book, something strange happened. The words on the pages began to glow, and the room around them seemed to shift. (6I) Suddenly, they were no longer in the library, but standing in a lush green field with mountains in the distance. (7B)

"Where are we?" asked Lily, her voice trembling. (8B)

"I think," Emma began, "we're inside the story." (8D)

The group stood in silence, taking in their new surroundings. In front of them, a narrow path led toward a dense forest. "We have to find a way back," Jack said, trying to remain calm. "But first, we need to figure out what this place is." (6G)

Emma nodded, clutching the book to her chest. "Let's stick together and find out what this adventure has in store for us." (7C)

TEKS Breakdown:

1. **6A** - Establish Purpose for Reading: The story begins by setting up Emma's purpose for visiting the library and looking for the magical book.
2. **6C** - Predictions: Emma anticipates finding something exciting in the library, and the audience makes predictions about what she might discover.
3. **6E** - Make Connections: Emma's recollections of her grandmother's stories create a connection between her past experiences and the present moment.
4. **6F** - Inferences: Emma infers that the book might be magical based on its appearance and her grandmother's stories.
5. **6D** - Create Mental Images: Descriptions of the old library and glowing words help the reader form vivid mental images.
6. **6I** - Monitoring Comprehension: As the setting changes, both the characters and readers adjust their understanding of the new situation.
7. **7B** - Compare and Contrast: The shift from the library to the magical setting allows for a comparison of these two places.
8. **7C** - Text Evidence: Jack's response to the unfolding events demonstrates a careful observation of the situation, supported by details in the text.
9. **7G** - Important Ideas: Emma's comment about the book possibly being a guide shows her critical thinking about the adventure ahead.
10. **8A** - Themes: The adventure introduces a potential theme of exploration and discovery, supported by the mystery surrounding the magical book.
11. **8B** - Character Interactions: The dialogue between the characters shows how they interact and how their relationships evolve during the adventure.
12. **8D** - Setting's Influence on Plot: The sudden shift in setting drives the plot forward as the characters enter a new, mysterious world.

Nonfiction Article: Never Giving Up (Without TEKS Labels)

Michael Jordan is one of the most famous basketball players of all time, but his journey to success wasn't always smooth. In high school, Jordan tried out for the varsity basketball team as a sophomore but was cut. Many people would have been discouraged, but not Jordan. Instead of giving up, he used this setback as motivation. He worked harder than ever before, practicing day and night, determined to improve his skills and prove himself.

By his junior year, Jordan had not only made the team but was one of the standout players. His incredible dedication paid off, and he went on to play college basketball at the University of North Carolina. From there, he was drafted by the Chicago Bulls, where he became a six-time NBA champion and one of the greatest athletes in history.

Throughout his career, Jordan faced numerous challenges, including injuries and tough losses, but his perseverance remained constant. He famously said, "I've failed over and over and over again in my life. And that is why I succeed." His story teaches us that setbacks are not the end— they are opportunities to push ourselves harder and grow stronger.

Michael Jordan's career exemplifies the importance of never giving up, no matter how difficult the road may seem. His success wasn't just about talent; it was about determination, hard work, and the will to keep going when things got tough.

Nonfiction Article: Never Giving Up (With TEKS Labels)

Michael Jordan is one of the most famous basketball players of all time, but his journey to success wasn't always smooth. **(6A)** In high school, Jordan tried out for the varsity basketball team as a sophomore but was cut. Many people would have been discouraged, but not Jordan. **(6F)** Instead of giving up, he used this setback as motivation. **(6E)** He worked harder than ever before, practicing day and night, determined to improve his skills and prove himself. **(6D)**

By his junior year, Jordan had not only made the team but was one of the standout players. His incredible dedication paid off, and he went on to play college basketball at the University of North Carolina. **(6G)** From there, he was drafted by the Chicago Bulls, where he became a six-time NBA champion and one of the greatest athletes in history. **(6H)**

Throughout his career, Jordan faced numerous challenges, including injuries and tough losses, but his perseverance remained constant. **(6C)** He famously said, "I've failed over and over and over again in my life. And that is why I succeed." **(10A)** His story teaches us that setbacks are not the end—they are opportunities to push ourselves harder and grow stronger. **(10G)**

Michael Jordan's career exemplifies the importance of never giving up, no matter how difficult the road may seem. **(7A)** His success wasn't just about talent; it was about determination, hard work, and the will to keep going when things got tough. **(7B)**

TEKS Breakdown:

1. **6A** - Establish Purpose for Reading: The passage's purpose is to show how Michael Jordan's perseverance led to success.
2. **6D** - Create Mental Images: The reader can visualize Jordan practicing day and night.
3. **6E** - Make Connections to Personal Experiences: Many students can relate to setbacks and using them as motivation.
4. **6F** - Make Inferences: The reader infers that Jordan's cut from the team was a turning point in his motivation.
5. **6G** - Evaluate Key Ideas: Jordan's perseverance was key to his eventual success.
6. **6H** - Synthesize Information: The passage synthesizes information about Jordan's career to create a new understanding of perseverance.
7. **6C** - Make Predictions: Students can predict that hard work leads to success based on Jordan's experiences.
8. **7A** - Describe Personal Connections: Jordan's story reflects real-life experiences of facing challenges.
9. **7B** - Write Responses That Demonstrate Understanding: Jordan's journey shows the theme of perseverance.
10. **10A** - Explain Author's Purpose: The author's purpose is to highlight how never giving up leads to success.
11. **10G** - Identify and Explain the Use of Anecdote: The anecdote about Jordan being cut from the team supports the theme of perseverance.

Nonfiction Article: The Invention of the Light Bulb (Without TEKS Labels)

The invention of the light bulb is one of the most famous stories of perseverance and innovation. Thomas Edison, the American inventor, is often credited with bringing electric light into homes and workplaces, but it wasn't easy. Before Edison, people relied on gas lamps and candles, which were expensive and dangerous. Edison set out to change that. His goal was to create a reliable and affordable source of light.

Edison and his team worked tirelessly on the light bulb, experimenting with thousands of materials to find a filament that would burn brightly and last long. After countless failures, Edison finally found success in 1879. He used carbonized bamboo as the filament, which lasted longer than any other material he had tried. It was this breakthrough that led to the widespread use of electric light.

Edison's light bulb didn't just make life easier—it revolutionized society. Factories could now operate around the clock, cities were safer at night, and people could read and work longer into the evening. The invention of the light bulb was a key step in moving the world into the modern age, and it is a reminder that persistence and hard work can change the world.

Nonfiction Article: The Invention of the Light Bulb (With TEKS Labels)

The invention of the light bulb is one of the most famous stories of perseverance and innovation. **(6A)** Thomas Edison, the American inventor, is often credited with bringing electric light into homes and workplaces, but it wasn't easy. **(6B)** Before Edison, people relied on gas lamps and candles, which were expensive and dangerous. Edison set out to change that. His goal was to create a reliable and affordable source of light. **(6E)**

Edison and his team worked tirelessly on the light bulb, experimenting with thousands of materials to find a filament that would burn brightly and last long. **(6F)** After countless failures, Edison finally found success in 1879. **(6G)** He used carbonized bamboo as the filament, which lasted longer than any other material he had tried. It was this breakthrough that led to the widespread use of electric light. **(6H)**

Edison's light bulb didn't just make life easier—it revolutionized society. **(6I)** Factories could now operate around the clock, cities were safer at night, and people could read and work longer into the evening. **(7A)** The invention of the light bulb was a key step in moving the world into the modern age, and it is a reminder that persistence and hard work can change the world. **(7G)**

TEKS Breakdown:

1. **6A** - Establish Purpose for Reading: The purpose is to understand the invention of the light bulb and how persistence led to its success.
2. **6B** - Generate Questions: What challenges did Edison face in creating the light bulb? How did he overcome them?
3. **6E** - Make Connections: Students can connect this with other examples of inventions or challenges in their own lives.
4. **6F** - Make Inferences: The reader infers that Edison's determination was key to his success.
5. **6G** - Evaluate Details: Key details, like the use of carbonized bamboo, helped Edison create a lasting light bulb.
6. **6H** - Synthesize Information: The passage synthesizes Edison's journey and shows how one invention transformed society.
7. **6I** - Monitor Comprehension: Students can adjust their understanding of how the invention process works by rereading certain sections.
8. **7A** - Describe Personal Connections: Edison's perseverance can be related to personal experiences where hard work led to success.
9. **7G** - Discuss Important Ideas: The passage highlights the theme that perseverance and hard work can lead to revolutionary changes.

Chapter 7

TEKS Standards Categorized by the Four Dimensions

Here's how each of the TEKS standards can be categorized into the four dimensions:

(6) Comprehension skills: listening, speaking, reading, writing, and thinking using multiple texts.

The student uses metacognitive skills to both develop and deepen comprehension of increasingly complex texts.

- **(A)** establish purpose for reading assigned and self-selected texts.
  Dimension 1 - TAUGHT (You are establishing what the purpose is.)
- **(B)** generate questions about text before, during, and after reading to deepen understanding and gain information.
  Dimension 2 - TAP (You must use questions to help guide comprehension, using evidence from the text.)
- **(C)** make and correct or confirm predictions using text features, characteristics of genre, and structures.
  Dimension 3 - THINK (Requires inference skills to predict outcomes and confirm or correct understanding.)
- **(D)** create mental images to deepen understanding.
  Dimension 3 - THINK (Forming mental pictures involves deeper thought and visualization.)
- **(E)** make connections to personal experiences, ideas in other texts, and society.
  Dimension 3 - THINK (Relating text to experiences or societal contexts involves thinking beyond the text.)
- **(F)** make inferences and use evidence to support understanding.
  Dimension 3 - THINK (Inference requires thinking to go beyond the explicit information in the text.)
- **(G)** evaluate details read to determine key ideas.
  Dimension 4 - TOGGLE (You're comparing multiple pieces of information to identify the key ideas.)
- **(H)** synthesize information to create new understanding.
  Dimension 4 - TOGGLE (Combining information from multiple sources requires toggling between ideas.)
- **(I)** monitor comprehension and make adjustments such as re-reading, using background knowledge, asking questions, and annotating when understanding breaks down.
  Dimension 3 - THINK (Requires metacognitive thought and strategy application to adjust understanding.)

(7) Response skills: listening, speaking, reading, writing, and thinking using multiple texts.

The student responds to an increasingly challenging variety of sources that are read, heard, or viewed.

- **(A)** describe personal connections to a variety of sources, including self-selected texts.
  Dimension 3 - THINK (Making personal connections requires thinking beyond the text.)
- **(B)** write responses that demonstrate understanding of texts, including comparing and contrasting ideas across a variety of sources.
  Dimension 4 - TOGGLE (Comparing and contrasting involves toggling between different texts and ideas.)
- **(C)** use text evidence to support an appropriate response.
  Dimension 2 - TAP (You are asked to provide evidence to support your answer.)
- **(D)** retell, paraphrase, or summarize texts in ways that maintain meaning and logical order.
  Dimension 1 - TAUGHT (Retelling or summarizing uses the foundational skill of stating what something is.)
- **(E)** interact with sources in meaningful ways such as notetaking, annotating, freewriting, or illustrating.
  Dimension 3 - THINK (Requires deeper thinking to engage with the text actively.)
- **(F)** respond using newly acquired vocabulary as appropriate.
  Dimension 1 - TAUGHT (Using vocabulary is an application of previously learned definitions and meanings.)
- **(G)** discuss specific ideas in the text that are important to the meaning.
  Dimension 2 - TAP (Using text evidence to discuss key ideas involves tapping into the text.)

(8) Multiple genres: listening, speaking, reading, writing, and thinking using multiple texts--literary elements.

The student recognizes and analyzes literary elements within and across increasingly complex traditional, contemporary, classical, and diverse literary texts.

- **(A)** infer basic themes supported by text evidence.
  Dimension 3 - THINK (Inference requires thinking beyond the text to deduce themes.)
- **(B)** explain the interactions of the characters and the changes they undergo.
  Dimension 2 - TAP (You need to support your understanding of character development with evidence from the text.)
- **(C)** analyze plot elements, including the rising action, climax, falling action, and resolution.
  Dimension 2 - TAP (Analyzing plot involves using evidence to support your understanding.)
- **(D)** explain the influence of the setting, including historical and cultural settings, on the plot.
  Dimension 4 - TOGGLE (You are relating the setting to the plot, requiring you to toggle between these two elements.)

(9) Multiple genres: listening, speaking, reading, writing, and thinking using multiple texts--genres.

The student recognizes and analyzes genre-specific characteristics, structures, and purposes within and across increasingly complex traditional, contemporary, classical, and diverse texts.

- **(A)** demonstrate knowledge of distinguishing characteristics of well-known children's literature such as folktales, fables, legends, myths, and tall tales.
  Dimension 1 - TAUGHT (Demonstrating knowledge of literary characteristics focuses on what something is.)
- **(B)** explain figurative language such as simile, metaphor, and personification that the poet uses to create images.
  Dimension 2 - TAP (You need to support your explanations with textual evidence of figurative language.)
- **(C)** explain structure in drama such as character tags, acts, scenes, and stage directions.
  Dimension 1 - TAUGHT (This focuses on recognizing what the structure of a play is.)
- **(D)** recognize characteristics and structures of informational text, including:
  Dimension 1 - TAUGHT (This requires identifying what certain features in informational texts are.)
  - o **(i)** the central idea with supporting evidence;
    Dimension 2 - TAP (You're asked to find evidence to support the central idea.)
  - o **(ii)** features such as pronunciation guides and diagrams to support understanding;
    Dimension 1 - TAUGHT (Recognizing text features focuses on identifying what they are.)
  - o **(iii)** organizational patterns such as compare and contrast;
    Dimension 4 - TOGGLE (Analyzing organizational patterns like compare and contrast involves understanding how these structures relate to the text.)
- **(E)** recognize characteristics and structures of argumentative text by:
  Dimension 1 - TAUGHT (Recognizing these elements involves understanding what they are.)
  - o **(i)** identifying the claim;
    Dimension 1 - TAUGHT (Identifying the claim involves asking what the claim is.)
  - o **(ii)** explaining how the author has used facts for an argument;
    Dimension 2 - TAP (Using text evidence to explain the argument is a TAP dimension.)
  - o **(iii)** identifying the intended audience or reader;
    Dimension 1 - TAUGHT (Identifying the audience involves asking what the intended audience is.)
- **(F)** recognize characteristics of multimodal and digital texts.
  Dimension 1 - TAUGHT (Recognizing characteristics involves understanding what they are.)

(10) Author's purpose and craft: listening, speaking, reading, writing, and thinking using multiple texts.

The student uses critical inquiry to analyze the authors' choices and how they influence and communicate meaning within a variety of texts.

- **(A)** explain the author's purpose and message within a text.
  Dimension 2 - TAP (You need to support your explanation with evidence from the text.)
- **(B)** explain how the use of text structure contributes to the author's purpose.
  Dimension 4 - TOGGLE (You are relating the structure to the author's purpose, requiring you to toggle between them.)
- **(C)** analyze the author's use of print and graphic features to achieve specific purposes.
  Dimension 2 - TAP (Analyzing how the author uses features requires textual evidence.)
- **(D)** describe how the author's use of imagery, literal and figurative language such as simile and metaphor, and sound devices such as alliteration and assonance achieves specific purposes.
  Dimension 3 - THINK (Understanding why the author uses these devices requires deeper thinking.)
- **(E)** identify and understand the use of literary devices, including first- or third-person point of view.
  Dimension 1 - TAUGHT (Identifying the point of view involves asking what the perspective is.)
- **(F)** discuss how the author's use of language contributes to voice.
  Dimension 3 - THINK (Discussing the author's voice requires thinking and interpreting how language is used.)
- **(G)** identify and explain the use of anecdote.
  Dimension 1 - TAUGHT (This requires identifying what an anecdote is and explaining its purpose.)

4 Dimension Questions for each TEKS

TEKS (6) Comprehension Skills

(A) Establish purpose for reading assigned and self-selected texts:

1. **Definition:** What does it mean to establish a purpose for reading?
2. **Text Evidence:** Find a sentence from the text that helps establish why you are reading the passage.
3. **Why Question:** Why is it important to have a clear purpose before reading?
4. **How Question:** How is having a reading purpose related to staying focused on understanding the text?

(B) Generate questions about text before, during, and after reading to deepen understanding and gain information:

1. **Definition:** What does it mean to generate questions before, during, and after reading?
2. **Text Evidence:** Provide examples of questions you would ask while reading the first paragraph of the text.
3. **Why Question:** Why does asking questions help in understanding the text better?
4. **How Question:** How does generating questions before reading help prepare you for what you will learn?

(C) Make and correct or confirm predictions using text features, characteristics of genre, and structures:

1. **Definition:** What does it mean to make and confirm predictions while reading?
2. **Text Evidence:** Find a section of the text where you can predict what will happen next.
3. **Why Question:** Why is it important to confirm or correct your predictions as you read?
4. **How Question:** How is using text features (like headings or images) related to making accurate predictions?

(D) Create mental images to deepen understanding:

1. **Definition:** What is a mental image, and why is it important while reading?
2. **Text Evidence:** What part of the text helped you create a mental picture of the scene?
3. **Why Question:** Why does creating mental images help with understanding what you read?
4. **How Question:** How does creating mental images help you remember details from the text?

(E) Make connections to personal experiences, ideas in other texts, and society:

1. **Definition:** What does it mean to make connections between the text and your personal experiences?
2. **Text Evidence:** Find an example in the text that reminds you of something in your life or another book you've read.
3. **Why Question:** Why is it important to connect a story or text to your life or the world around you?
4. **How Question:** How does making connections to your experiences help you understand the story better?

(F) Make inferences and use evidence to support understanding:

1. **Definition:** What is an inference, and how do you make one while reading?
2. **Text Evidence:** What can you infer from the character's actions in the text? Use evidence to support your inference.
3. **Why Question:** Why is it important to support your inferences with text evidence?
4. **How Question:** How does making inferences help deepen your understanding of the characters or plot?

(G) Evaluate details read to determine key ideas:

1. **Definition:** What does it mean to evaluate details in a text?
2. **Text Evidence:** Identify the key details in a paragraph that contribute to the main idea.
3. **Why Question:** Why do we need to focus on key ideas when reading?
4. **How Question:** How does focusing on important details help you understand the overall meaning of the text?

(H) Synthesize information to create new understanding:

1. **Definition:** What does it mean to synthesize information?
2. **Text Evidence:** Provide an example where you combined information from two paragraphs to understand the bigger picture.
3. **Why Question:** Why is it important to combine different ideas in a text to form new understanding?
4. **How Question:** How does synthesizing information from different sources or parts of the text help you see the bigger picture?

(I) Monitor comprehension and make adjustments such as re-reading, using background knowledge, asking questions, and annotating when understanding breaks down:

1. **Definition:** What does it mean to monitor comprehension while reading?
2. **Text Evidence:** Find a part of the text where you had to re-read or adjust your understanding.
3. **Why Question:** Why is it necessary to make adjustments to your reading strategy when you don't understand something?
4. **How Question:** How does asking questions and annotating help you when you're struggling with comprehension?

TEKS (7) Response Skills

(A) Describe personal connections to a variety of sources, including self-selected texts:

1. **Definition:** What does it mean to describe personal connections to a text?
2. **Text Evidence:** Find a part of the text that connects to something in your life.
3. **Why Question:** Why is making personal connections important when reading?
4. **How Question:** How do personal connections influence your understanding of the text?

(B) Write responses that demonstrate understanding of texts, including comparing and contrasting ideas across a variety of sources:

1. **Definition:** What does it mean to write responses that compare and contrast different sources?
2. **Text Evidence:** Compare two sources you've read and explain how they are similar or different.
3. **Why Question:** Why is it important to compare and contrast different ideas from multiple texts?
4. **How Question:** How does comparing different sources improve your understanding of a topic?

(C) Use text evidence to support an appropriate response:

1. **Definition:** What is text evidence, and how is it used to support a response?
2. **Text Evidence:** Find a specific quote from the text that supports your response.
3. **Why Question:** Why is it important to use text evidence when making a claim about the text?
4. **How Question:** How does using text evidence make your response stronger?

(D) Retell, paraphrase, or summarize texts in ways that maintain meaning and logical order

1. **Definition**: What is the difference between retelling, paraphrasing, and summarizing a text?
2. **Text Evidence**: What are the most important ideas from the text that should be included in a summary?
3. **Why Question**: Why is it important to maintain the original meaning and logical order when retelling or summarizing a text?
4. **How Question**: How does summarizing a text help you better understand and remember what you read?

(E) Interact with sources in meaningful ways such as notetaking, annotating, freewriting, or illustrating

1. **Definition**: What does it mean to interact with a text, and what are some examples of ways we can do that?
2. **Text Evidence**: Show an example from your notes, annotations, or illustrations that helped you understand a part of the text more clearly.
3. **Why Question**: Why is it helpful to take notes, highlight, or draw when reading a complex text?
4. **How Question**: How does annotating or illustrating a text help you engage with the author's ideas more deeply?

(F) Respond using newly acquired vocabulary as appropriate

1. **Definition**: What does it mean to use newly acquired vocabulary in your speaking or writing?
2. **Text Evidence**: Which new words from the text did you learn, and how can you use one of them in your own sentence?
3. **Why Question**: Why is it important to use new vocabulary words after learning them from a text?
4. **How Question**: How does using new vocabulary help you become a more effective speaker or writer?

(G) Discuss specific ideas in the text that are important to the meaning

1. **Definition**: What does it mean to discuss specific ideas in a text, and how can you tell if an idea is important to the meaning?
2. **Text Evidence**: What is one key idea from the text that you think is important, and what part of the text supports it?
3. **Why Question**: Why is it important to focus on specific ideas when analyzing or talking about a text?
4. **How Question**: How do important ideas in a text help the reader understand the author's message or purpose?

222

TEKS (8) Multiple Genres

(A) Infer basic themes supported by text evidence:

1. **Definition:** What does it mean to infer a theme in a text?
2. **Text Evidence:** Find evidence in the text that supports a theme you've identified.
3. **Why Question:** Why is identifying a theme important for understanding a story?
4. **How Question:** How is the theme of the story related to its characters and their experiences?

(B) Explain the interactions of the characters and the changes they undergo:

1. **Definition:** What does it mean to analyze character interactions and changes?
2. **Text Evidence:** Find a moment in the text where a character undergoes a significant change.
3. **Why Question:** Why is it important to understand how characters change throughout a story?
4. **How Question:** How does a character's change relate to the overall theme of the story?

(C) Analyze plot elements, including the rising action, climax, falling action, and resolution:

1. **Definition:** What are the key elements of a plot, and what do they represent?
2. **Text Evidence:** Identify the climax in the text and explain its significance.
3. **Why Question:** Why is it important to understand the different elements of a plot?
4. **How Question:** How is the resolution of the plot related to the main conflict of the story?

TEKS (9) Multiple Genres - Genres

(A) Demonstrate knowledge of distinguishing characteristics of well-known children's literature such as folktales, fables, legends, myths, and tall tales:

1. **Definition:** What are folktales, fables, legends, myths, and tall tales?
2. **Text Evidence:** Identify a story element that makes the text you're reading a tall tale.
3. **Why Question:** Why are traditional genres like folktales and myths important to understand?
4. **How Question:** How are myths and legends similar, and how are they different in their purpose?

(B) Explain figurative language such as simile, metaphor, and personification that the poet uses to create images

1. **Definition**: What is figurative language, and how do similes, metaphors, and personification help create imagery in poetry?

2. **Text Evidence**: What is one example of figurative language from the poem, and what image does it help you see or feel?
3. **Why Question**: Why do poets use figurative language instead of stating things literally?
4. **How Question**: How does the use of similes, metaphors, or personification affect the mood or meaning of the poem?

(C) Explain structure in drama such as character tags, acts, scenes, and stage directions

1. **Definition**: What are the structural elements of drama, and what do terms like acts, scenes, and stage directions mean?
2. **Text Evidence**: Provide an example from the play that shows how a stage direction or character tag helps the audience understand the action.
3. **Why Question**: Why is it important to include character tags and stage directions in a drama?
4. **How Question**: How do the structure and parts of a drama help the audience understand the story differently than a narrative?

(D) Recognize characteristics and structures of informational text, including:

(i) the central idea with supporting evidence;
(ii) features such as pronunciation guides and diagrams to support understanding; and
(iii) organizational patterns such as compare and contrast)

1. **Definition**: What is informational text, and what are some of its key features and structures?
2. **Text Evidence**: What is the central idea of this informational text, and what evidence does the author provide to support it?
3. **Why Question**: Why do authors of informational texts use diagrams, pronunciation guides, or specific text structures like compare and contrast?
4. **How Question**: How do the features and structure of an informational text help the reader better understand the topic?

(E) Recognize characteristics and structures of argumentative text by:

(i) identifying the claim;
(ii) explaining how the author has used facts for an argument; and
(iii) identifying the intended audience or reader)

1. **Definition**: What is an argumentative text, and what makes it different from other types of writing?
2. **Text Evidence**: What is the author's main claim in this text, and what evidence does the author use to support it?
3. **Why Question**: Why is it important for an author to include facts and evidence in an argumentative text?
4. **How Question**: How can knowing the intended audience help the author make a stronger argument?

(F) Recognize characteristics of multimodal and digital texts

1. **Definition**: What are multimodal and digital texts, and what makes them different from printed texts?
2. **Text Evidence**: What features in this digital or multimodal text (such as audio, images, video, or links) helped you better understand the content?
3. **Why Question**: Why might an author choose to use a digital or multimodal format instead of traditional print?
4. **How Question**: How do the combined features of multimodal or digital texts work together to support the author's message?

TEKS (10) Author's Purpose and Craft

(A) Explain the author's purpose and message within a text:

1. **Definition:** What is an author's purpose?
2. **Text Evidence:** Provide evidence from the text that shows what the author's main message is.
3. **Why Question:** Why is it important to understand the author's purpose?
4. **How Question:** How is the author's purpose related to the structure of the text?

(B) Explain how the use of text structure contributes to the author's purpose

1. **Definition**: What is text structure, and what are some common types used in informational texts?
2. **Text Evidence**: What evidence from the text shows how the structure helps reveal the author's purpose?
3. **Why Question**: Why does the author choose a specific structure (e.g., cause and effect, compare and contrast, chronological order) for this text?
4. **How Question**: How does the text structure make the author's message clearer or more effective?

(C) Analyze the author's use of print and graphic features to achieve specific purposes

1. **Definition**: What are print and graphic features, and how are they used in a text?
2. **Text Evidence**: Which print or graphic feature in the text supports the author's purpose, and what does it show?
3. **Why Question**: Why might an author include bold print, captions, or diagrams in their writing?
4. **How Question**: How do the print and graphic features help readers better understand or visualize the information?

(D) Describe how the author's use of imagery, literal and figurative language such as simile and metaphor, and sound devices such as alliteration and assonance achieves specific purposes

1. **Definition**: What is figurative language, and how is it different from literal language?
2. **Text Evidence**: What is one example of imagery, figurative language, or a sound device in the text, and what effect does it create?
3. **Why Question**: Why does the author use similes, metaphors, or sound devices in this piece of writing?
4. **How Question**: How does the use of figurative language or imagery help the author create a mood, tone, or deeper meaning?

(E) Identify and understand the use of literary devices, including first- or third-person point of view

1. **Definition**: What are literary devices, and what is the difference between first- and third-person point of view?
2. **Text Evidence**: What clues in the text help you identify whether it is written in first or third person?
3. **Why Question**: Why might the author choose a particular point of view to tell the story?
4. **How Question**: How does the point of view influence the way the reader connects with the characters or events?

20 ways to ask the <u>significance/importance</u> of something, with examples:

1. **Why is [X] important?**
   o *Why is the discovery of DNA important in biology?*
2. **What is the significance of...?**
   o *What is the significance of the Treaty of Versailles in world history?*
3. **Why does [X] matter in...?**
   o *Why does biodiversity matter in ecosystem stability?*
4. **What is the value of [X] in...?**
   o *What is the value of teamwork in achieving organizational success?*
5. **What is the purpose of [X] in...?**
   o *What is the purpose of irony in this literary work?*
6. **What is the most likely reason the author uses [X] in….?**
   o *What is the most likely reason the author uses this photograph in this article?*
7. **Why is [X] a key factor in...?**
   o *Why is trust a key factor in building strong relationships?*
8. **What impact did [X] have on...?**
   o *What impact did the internet have on global commerce?*
9. **What difference did [X] make in...?**
   o *What difference did the abolition of slavery make in U.S. society?*
10. **What's the relevance of [X] to...?**
    o *What's the relevance of nutrition to overall health?*
11. **What is the importance of [X] in relation to...?**
    o *What is the importance of free speech in relation to democracy?*
12. **What lasting effects did [X] have on...?**
    o *What lasting effects did the Renaissance have on art and culture?*
13. **Why is [X] significant in shaping...?**
    o *Why is World War II significant in shaping modern geopolitics?*
14. **What is the meaning of [X] in...?**
    o *What is the meaning of symbolism in literature?*
15. **What are the broader implications of [X]?**
    o *What are the broader implications of artificial intelligence on employment?*
16. **Why does [X] play such a pivotal role in...?**
    o *Why does water conservation play such a pivotal role in sustainable development?*
17. **What was the purpose of [X] in...?**
    o *What was the purpose of the Emancipation Proclamation in the U.S.?*
18. **Why is understanding [X] essential to...?**
    o *Why is understanding climate change essential to environmental policy?*
19. **Why is [X] a turning point in...?**
    o *Why is the fall of the Berlin Wall a turning point in modern history?*
20. **What is the overall significance of [X]?**
    o *What is the overall significance of social equality in human rights?*

30 ways to ask <u>how something is related or connected</u>, with examples:

1. **How is [X] related to [Y]?**
   o *How is climate change related to rising sea levels?*
2. **What's the connection between [X] and [Y]?**
   o *What's the connection between diet and heart disease?*
3. **In what way does [X] influence [Y]?**
   o *In what way does technology influence education?*
4. **How does [X] affect [Y]?**
   o *How does inflation affect the cost of living?*
5. **How do [X] and [Y] interact?**
   o *How do supply and demand interact in economics?*
6. **What role does [X] play in [Y]?**
   o *What role does water play in plant growth?*
7. **How are [X] and [Y] connected?**
   o *How are genetics and inherited traits connected?*
8. **How does [X] relate to [Y]?**
   o *How does population growth relate to environmental sustainability?*
9. **What is the relationship between [X] and [Y]?**
   o *What is the relationship between exercise and mental health?*
10. **How are [X] and [Y] interdependent?**
    o *How are education and economic growth interdependent?*
11. **In what way is [X] linked to [Y]?**
    o *In what way is pollution linked to global warming?*
12. **How does [X] tie into [Y]?**
    o *How does technological innovation tie into economic competitiveness?*
13. **What impact does [X] have on [Y]?**
    o *What impact does government policy have on environmental conservation?*
14. **How are [X] and [Y] associated?**
    o *How are poverty and access to education associated?*
15. **How does [X] contribute to [Y]?**
    o *How does deforestation contribute to habitat loss?*
16. **What role does [X] play in shaping [Y]?**
    o *What role does culture play in shaping societal norms?*
17. **How do [X] and [Y] influence each other?**
    o *How do politics and media influence each other?*
18. **How does [X] connect to [Y] in terms of [Z]?**
    o *How does public transportation connect to urban development in terms of sustainability?*
19. **How is [X] intertwined with [Y]?**
    o *How is trade intertwined with international relations?*
20. **What relationship exists between [X] and [Y]?**
    o *What relationship exists between income inequality and crime rates?*

21. **How does [X] correlate with [Y]?**
    o *How does literacy rate correlate with economic development?*
22. **What's the link between [X] and [Y]?**
    o *What's the link between stress and physical health?*
23. **How does [X] reinforce [Y]?**
    o *How does family support reinforce academic success?*
24. **What is the connection between [X] and [Y] in [context]?**
    o *What is the connection between political stability and economic growth in developing nations?*
25. **How is [X] associated with [Y] over time?**
    o *How is technological advancement associated with labor market changes over time?*
26. **How does [X] relate to [Y] in terms of [Z]?**
    o *How does international trade relate to domestic policy in terms of economic growth?*
27. **In what ways do [X] and [Y] overlap?**
    o *In what ways do social movements and political reforms overlap?*
28. **How is [X] integral to [Y]?**
    o *How is electricity integral to modern infrastructure?*
29. **What influence does [X] have on [Y]?**
    o *What influence does advertising have on consumer behavior?*
30. **How do [X] and [Y] work together?**
    o *How do genetics and environment work together to shape behavior?*

These variations provide flexibility in asking about <u>connections and relationships</u> between two or more elements, fostering deeper understanding of how different factors interact or depend on one another.

30 ways to ask <u>how textual evidence is related to a literary element</u>, along with examples:

1. **How does the text support the theme of [X]?**
   - *How does the text support the theme of courage in the story?*
2. **What evidence in the text illustrates the character's [Y]?**
   - *What evidence in the text illustrates the character's loyalty?*
3. **How does the author use [X] to develop the plot?**
   - *How does the author use dialogue to develop the plot?*
4. **What textual evidence reveals the setting of [X]?**
   - *What textual evidence reveals the setting of the novel?*
5. **How does the text demonstrate the use of symbolism?**
   - *How does the text demonstrate the use of the river as a symbol for freedom?*
6. **What details in the text contribute to the mood of [X]?**
   - *What details in the text contribute to the mood of suspense?*
7. **How does the author's language reflect the tone of [X]?**
   - *How does the author's language reflect the tone of melancholy in the poem?*
8. **What evidence in the text shows the conflict between [X] and [Y]?**
   - *What evidence in the text shows the conflict between the protagonist and antagonist?*
9. **How does the text highlight the theme of [X]?**
   - *How does the text highlight the theme of justice?*
10. **What quotes from the text help develop the main character?**
    - *What quotes from the text help develop the main character's personality?*
11. **How does the text illustrate the use of irony in [X]?**
    - *How does the text illustrate the use of irony in the protagonist's actions?*
12. **What part of the text supports the development of the setting?**
    - *What part of the text supports the development of the dystopian setting?*
13. **How does the text evidence the use of foreshadowing in [X]?**
    - *How does the text evidence the use of foreshadowing in the first chapter?*
14. **How does the dialogue in the text reflect the tone of [X]?**
    - *How does the dialogue in the text reflect the tone of sarcasm?*
15. **What textual evidence supports the development of [X] as a theme?**
    - *What textual evidence supports the development of betrayal as a theme?*
16. **How does the author's word choice contribute to the characterization of [X]?**
    - *How does the author's word choice contribute to the characterization of the villain?*
17. **What evidence in the text shows the use of imagery to describe [X]?**
    - *What evidence in the text shows the use of imagery to describe the landscape?*
18. **How does the text depict the resolution of the central conflict?**
    - *How does the text depict the resolution of the conflict between the two families?*
19. **What details in the text develop the theme of [X]?**
    - *What details in the text develop the theme of survival?*
20. **How does the text help establish the mood in [X]?**
    - *How does the text help establish the eerie mood in the haunted house?*

21. **What examples from the text demonstrate the character's internal conflict?**
    o *What examples from the text demonstrate the character's internal conflict over their decision?*
22. **How does the text reveal the climax of the story?**
    o *How does the text reveal the climax of the story between the hero and villain?*
23. **What evidence in the text shows the use of metaphor in [X]?**
    o *What evidence in the text shows the use of metaphor in describing the journey?*
24. **How does the text support the development of the protagonist's motivations?**
    o *How does the text support the development of the protagonist's motivations for revenge?*
25. **What textual evidence shows the shift in tone during [X]?**
    o *What textual evidence shows the shift in tone during the final confrontation?*
26. **How does the text emphasize the theme of [X] through character actions?**
    o *How does the text emphasize the theme of sacrifice through the character's actions?*
27. **What evidence in the text reflects the cultural context of [X]?**
    o *What evidence in the text reflects the cultural context of the 19th century?*
28. **How does the author use figurative language in the text to support [X]?**
    o *How does the author use figurative language in the text to support the theme of transformation?*
29. **What details in the text illustrate the rising action of the plot?**
    o *What details in the text illustrate the rising action of the plot leading to the climax?*
30. **How does the text show the relationship between the protagonist and the setting?**
    o *How does the text show the relationship between the protagonist and the harsh environment?*

Chapter 8

Poster Content for each of the TEKS

Reading with Purpose

TEKS (6): Comprehension Skills

(A) Establish purpose for reading assigned and self-selected texts.

- Ask yourself: *Why am I reading this?*
- Reflect on how your purpose will help you better engage with the text and improve comprehension

I Understand

- I understand that reading is more meaningful when I have a purpose.
- I understand that the purpose for reading changes based on the text I choose or that is assigned.

I Will

- I will set a clear purpose before I begin reading any text.
- I will decide if I am reading to learn, enjoy, or complete a task.
- I will connect my purpose for reading to what I need to understand from the text.

Approach every reading task with intention and focus!

<u>Ask Questions, Find Answers: The Key to Understanding</u>

TEKS (6): Comprehension Skills (B)

Generate questions about text before, during, and after reading.

I Understand

- I understand that asking questions helps me explore the meaning of a text.
- I understand that questioning before, during, and after reading keeps me engaged and improves my comprehension.
- I understand that generating questions helps me connect ideas, clarify confusion, and think critically about the text.

I Will

- **Before Reading:** Ask questions about the title, text features, and what I want to learn.
  Example: What is this text about? What do I already know about this topic?
- **During Reading:** Generate questions to clarify meaning and explore deeper ideas.
  Example: Why did the author include this detail? What might happen next?
- **After Reading:** Reflect on the text by asking questions to analyze and evaluate it.
  Example: What is the main idea? How does this relate to my life or the world?

Great readers ask great questions.
Be curious, stay engaged, and discover meaning!

<u>Predicting with Purpose: A Reader's Superpower</u>

TEKS (6): Comprehension Skills (C)

Make and correct or confirm predictions using text features, characteristics of genre, and structures.

I Understand

- I understand that making predictions helps me engage with the text and think ahead.
- I understand that text features, genre, and structure give clues about what might happen.
- I understand that confirming or correcting my predictions improves my comprehension.

I Will

- **Before Reading:** Use the title, headings, and visuals to predict what the text is about.
  Example: Based on the title and pictures, I think this story is about a journey.
- **During Reading:** Pay attention to clues in the genre and structure to adjust my predictions.
  Example: Since this is a mystery, I predict the main character will solve a problem.
- **After Reading:** Confirm or correct my predictions by comparing them to what actually happens in the text.
  Example: I thought the character would fail, but the ending showed they succeeded.

Activate your imagination and sharpen your comprehension by making informed predictions!

Picture It: Creating Mental Images for Better Understanding

TEKS (6): Comprehension Skills (D)

Create mental images to deepen understanding.

I Understand

- I understand that creating mental images helps me visualize what I read.
- I understand that mental images make the text come alive and improve my understanding.
- I understand that using all my senses when imagining deepens my connection to the text.

I Will

- Use the author's descriptions to picture characters, settings, and events in my mind.
  Example: I imagine the forest as dark and full of towering trees swaying in the wind.
- Use sensory details to hear, see, smell, taste, or feel what is happening in the text.
  Example: I can almost hear the crackling fire and smell the sweet marshmallows roasting.
- Adjust my mental images as I read and gather more details.
  Example: At first, I pictured the character as shy, but now I see them as brave.

Turn words into vivid pictures in your mind—experience the story like you're living it!

Connecting the Dots: Relating Texts to Life

TEKS (6): Comprehension Skills (E)

Make connections to personal experiences, ideas in other texts, and society.

I Understand

- I understand that making connections helps me relate the text to my world.
- I understand that connecting to personal experiences, other texts, and society deepens my understanding.
- I understand that connections make reading more meaningful and engaging.

I Will

- **Connect to Personal Experiences:** Relate the text to my own life and memories.
  Example: This character's journey reminds me of the time I faced a big challenge.
- **Connect to Other Texts:** Find similarities between the text and books, movies, or stories I've read before.
  Example: This story is like another book I read about teamwork and friendship.
- **Connect to Society:** Relate the text to events, issues, or ideas in the world around me.
  Example: This article connects to current events about climate change and its impact.

Every text is a bridge—use your connections to explore and understand it fully!

Read Between the Lines: Making Inferences

TEKS (6): Comprehension Skills (F)

Make inferences and use evidence to support understanding.

I Understand

- I understand that making inferences means figuring out what the author doesn't directly say.
- I understand that inferences are based on clues from the text and my background knowledge.
- I understand that using evidence supports my understanding and helps explain my thinking.

I Will

- Look for clues in the text, such as words, actions, or details, to make inferences.
  Example: The character's trembling hands and quick breathing infer they are nervous.
- Use what I already know to connect the clues to a bigger idea.
  Example: Based on my knowledge of storms, the dark clouds and howling wind suggest danger.
- Support my inferences with evidence from the text.
  Example: I infer the character is kind because the text says they helped a stranger in need.

Think like a detective—combine clues and knowledge to uncover hidden meanings!

Spotlight on Key Ideas: Evaluating Details

TEKS (6): Comprehension Skills (G)

Evaluate details read to determine key ideas.

I Understand

- I understand that not all details in a text are equally important.
- I understand that evaluating details helps me find the key ideas the author wants me to understand.
- I understand that identifying key ideas helps me summarize and focus on the main message.

I Will

- Pay attention to repeated ideas, headings, and important details to determine key ideas.
  Example: The heading "Causes of Pollution" highlights the main ideas in this section.
- Separate supporting details from the key ideas they explain.
  Example: The fact that factories emit smoke is a detail supporting the key idea about pollution.
- Ask myself, "What is the most important takeaway from this text or section?"
  Example: The key idea is that teamwork leads to success, supported by the characters' actions.

Focus on the big picture—find the key ideas that unlock the meaning of the text!

Synthesize to Understand: Building New Ideas

TEKS (6): Comprehension Skills (H)

Synthesize information to create new understanding.

I Understand

- I understand that synthesizing means combining ideas from the text with my own thoughts.
- I understand that synthesis helps me create new understanding and see the bigger picture.
- I understand that by pulling information together, I can gain deeper insights from what I read.

I Will

- Combine details from different parts of the text to form a complete idea.
  Example: By linking the character's actions in the beginning and the ending, I understand their growth.
- Use what I know and what I've read to create new conclusions.
  Example: Based on the evidence about recycling and my experiences, I see how small changes can protect the planet.
- Reflect on how the text connects to larger ideas or themes.
  Example: This story about resilience reminds me how important it is to keep trying in my own life.

Reading is just the beginning—synthesize to discover new ideas and deeper meaning!

Stay on Track: Monitor and Adjust Comprehension

TEKS (6): Comprehension Skills (I)

Monitor comprehension and make adjustments such as re-reading, using background knowledge, asking questions, and annotating when understanding breaks down.

I Understand

- I understand that monitoring my comprehension means checking if I understand the text as I read.
- I understand that when I don't understand something, I need to take action to fix it.
- I understand that making adjustments helps me stay focused and improves my understanding.

I Will

- **Re-read** parts of the text that are confusing to clarify meaning.
  Example: I will go back and re-read the paragraph if I don't understand what happened.
- **Use Background Knowledge** to make connections that help me understand new ideas.
  Example: I know about tornadoes, so I can better understand the text about storm preparation.
- **Ask Questions** when I get stuck to figure out what I need to know.
  Example: Why did the character make this choice? What is the author trying to say here?
- **Annotate** by highlighting important points, writing notes, or summarizing sections.
  Example: I'll underline the key idea and jot down a quick explanation in the margin.

Be an active reader—if you lose your way, adjust and get back on track!

Express Your Understanding: Write to Respond

TEKS (7): Response Skills (A)

Describe personal connections to a variety of sources, including self-selected texts.

I Understand

- I understand that writing responses helps me show what I've learned from texts.
- I understand that comparing and contrasting ideas from different sources deepens my understanding.
- I understand that my responses should clearly explain and connect my thoughts to the text.

I Will

- Write clear responses that explain what I understood from the text.
  Example: The main idea of the story is that teamwork leads to success.
- Compare ideas from different texts to find similarities.
  Example: Both articles emphasize the importance of protecting the environment.
- Contrast ideas from various sources to identify differences.
  Example: While one author believes technology is harmful, the other sees it as beneficial.
- Use evidence from the text to support my responses.
  Example: I know the character is courageous because they stood up for what was right

Your connections bring stories to life—find yourself in every text you read!

Prove Your Point: Use Text Evidence

TEKS (7): Response Skills (B)

Write responses that demonstrate understanding of texts, including comparing and contrasting ideas across a variety of sources.

I Understand

- I understand that using text evidence makes my responses stronger and more convincing.
- I understand that supporting my ideas with evidence shows I understood the text.
- I understand that selecting the right evidence helps me clearly explain my thinking.

I Will

- Find specific quotes or details from the text to support my answers.
  Example: The author states, "Hard work leads to success," which supports my idea about the story's theme.
- Use evidence to explain my thoughts and make connections to the text.
  Example: The detail about the character helping their friend shows they are kind and dependable.
- Ensure my response is clear, logical, and based on the evidence provided in the text.
  Example: I chose this evidence because it directly supports my inference about the character's bravery.

Write your way to deeper understanding—compare, contrast, and connect your ideas!

Tell It Again: Retell, Paraphrase, Summarize

TEKS (7): Response Skills (C)

Use text evidence to support an appropriate response.

I Understand

- I understand that retelling, paraphrasing, and summarizing show my understanding of a text.
- I understand that my responses should keep the text's meaning and follow a logical order.
- I understand that these skills help me focus on the most important ideas in the text.

I Will

- **Retell:** Share the story or text in my own words, keeping all the key details and events.
  Example: First, the character faced a challenge, then they found a solution and succeeded.
- **Paraphrase:** Reword a section of the text to make it simpler while keeping the meaning.
  Example: Instead of "The protagonist exhibited valor," I can say, "The main character was brave."
- **Summarize:** Focus on the main ideas and leave out unimportant details.
  Example: The text is about the importance of teamwork to solve problems.
- Organize my response to ensure it follows the text's original structure.
  Example: I'll explain events in the same order they happened in the story

Strengthen your response by backing it up with evidence—let the text speak for itself!

Engage with Texts: Make Reading Meaningful

TEKS (7): Response Skills (D)

Retell, paraphrase, or summarize texts in ways that maintain meaning and logical order.

I Understand

- I understand that interacting with texts helps me connect with and understand them better.
- I understand that notetaking, annotating, freewriting, and illustrating are tools to express my thoughts.
- I understand that meaningful interaction makes the text more engaging and memorable.

I Will

- **Note-take** by writing down important ideas, questions, and details as I read.
  Example: I'll jot down key events and quotes that stand out to me.
- **Annotate** by highlighting or underlining important parts of the text and adding notes in the margins.
  Example: I'll circle new words and write their meanings or questions next to them.
- **Free write** to reflect on the text and explore my thoughts and ideas.
  Example: I'll write about how the story made me feel and what I learned from it.
- **Illustrate** to visualize ideas, characters, or events from the text.
  Example: I'll draw a timeline of events or a scene from the story to better understand it.

Make it clear, concise, and connected—show your understanding through your own words!

Speak and Write with Confidence: Use New Vocabulary

TEKS (7): Response Skills (E)

Interact with sources in meaningful ways such as notetaking, annotating, freewriting, or illustrating.

I Understand

- I understand that using new vocabulary shows my learning and understanding of the text.
- I understand that applying new words helps me express my thoughts more clearly.
- I understand that expanding my vocabulary makes my responses richer and more precise.

I Will

- Use newly learned words from the text in my responses to show my understanding.
  Example: Instead of saying the character was brave, I'll use the word "courageous" as mentioned in the story.
- Practice new vocabulary by incorporating it into my speaking and writing.
  Example: I'll describe the setting as "serene" instead of just saying "calm."
- Ensure I use the words appropriately and in the correct context.
  Example: If the text describes a "perilous journey," I'll use "perilous" to explain the dangers faced by the characters.

Make your reading active—engage with the text and let your creativity shine!

<u>Dive Deep: Discuss Key Ideas</u>

TEKS (7): Response Skills (F)

Respond using newly acquired vocabulary as appropriate.

I Understand

- I understand that identifying and discussing specific ideas helps uncover the meaning of the text.
- I understand that focusing on important ideas shows my ability to think critically about the text.
- I understand that discussing these ideas helps me connect with the author's message.

I Will

- Identify the most important ideas or themes in the text.
  Example: The story focuses on the importance of perseverance in tough times.
- Explain how these specific ideas contribute to the meaning of the text.
  Example: The character's journey shows that failure can lead to success when you keep trying.
- Support my discussion with details or examples from the text.
  Example: The author shows perseverance when the character overcomes challenges despite setbacks.
- Reflect on why these ideas matter and how they connect to the bigger picture.
  Example: The theme of perseverance reminds us that determination can lead to growth.

Grow your vocabulary—use new words to make your responses powerful and precise!

Uncover the Message: Infer Themes

TEKS (7): Response Skills (G)

Discuss specific ideas in the text that are important to the meaning.

I Understand

- I understand that a theme is the central message or idea the author wants to share.
- I understand that inferring themes means looking beyond the surface of the text.
- I understand that themes are supported by evidence found in the story.

I Will

- Look for clues in the text, such as the characters' actions, dialogue, and the outcomes of events.
  Example: The character's kindness throughout the story suggests the theme of compassion.
- Use text evidence to support the theme I infer.
  Example: I infer the theme is friendship because the story shows the friends helping each other during tough times.
- Reflect on how the theme connects to a bigger idea or lesson.
  Example: The theme of perseverance teaches that challenges can be overcome with determination.

Focus on what matters—discover the big ideas that give the text its power!

Character Connections: Understanding Interactions and Changes

TEKS (8): Multiple Genres - Literary Elements (A)

Infer basic themes supported by text evidence.

I Understand

- I understand that characters' interactions reveal their personalities and relationships.
- I understand that changes in characters show growth, challenges, or lessons learned.
- I understand that explaining these interactions and changes helps uncover the deeper meaning of the story.

I Will

- Identify how characters interact with each other and what these interactions reveal.
  Example: The way the siblings argue but later support each other shows their bond.
- Explain the changes characters go through and what causes these changes.
  Example: The main character becomes more confident after overcoming a major obstacle.
- Use evidence from the text to support my explanation.
  Example: At the beginning, the character is shy, but by the end, they lead a group, showing growth.
- Reflect on how these interactions and changes contribute to the story's themes or message.
  Example: The character's growth highlights the theme of perseverance and self-belief.

Find the heart of the story—discover the themes and back them up with evidence

Breaking Down the Story: Analyzing Plot Elements

TEKS (8): Multiple Genres - Literary Elements (B)

Explain the interactions of the characters and the changes they undergo.

I Understand

- I understand that the plot is the sequence of events that make up a story.
- I understand that analyzing the plot helps me understand how the story develops and resolves.
- I understand that each part of the plot—rising action, climax, falling action, and resolution—plays a key role in the story.

I Will

- **Rising Action:** Identify the events that build tension and lead to the climax.
  Example: The challenges the hero faces create excitement and set up the main conflict.
- **Climax:** Pinpoint the turning point or most intense moment of the story.
  Example: The hero finally confronts their greatest fear during the climax.
- **Falling Action:** Explain how the events after the climax start to resolve the conflict.
  Example: The hero's actions bring peace and understanding to their world.
- **Resolution:** Analyze how the story wraps up and what lessons or outcomes emerge.
  Example: The resolution shows the hero has grown and learned from their journey.

Explore how characters grow and connect—discover their journey within the story!

Setting the Scene: Understanding Its Impact on the Plot

TEKS (8): Multiple Genres - Literary Elements (C)

Analyze plot elements, including the rising action, climax, falling action, and resolution.

I Understand

- I understand that the setting is more than just where and when the story takes place.
- I understand that historical and cultural settings influence the characters, events, and conflicts.
- I understand that analyzing the setting helps me see how it shapes the plot and the story's meaning.

I Will

- Identify the setting, including the time, place, and cultural or historical context.
  Example: The story takes place in the 1800s during the Industrial Revolution.
- Explain how the setting influences the characters' actions and decisions.
  Example: The harsh winter setting forces the characters to work together to survive.
- Analyze how the historical or cultural setting impacts the conflicts or events in the plot.
  Example: The cultural expectations of the time create obstacles for the main character's goals.
- Reflect on how the setting enhances the story's themes or message.
  Example: The historical setting highlights the struggle for equality and justice.

Follow the story's path—understand how each element builds to create an unforgettable journey!

Explore the Classics: Understanding Children's Literature

TEKS (8): Multiple Genres - Literary Elements (D)

Explain the influence of the setting, including historical and cultural settings, on the plot.

I Understand

- I understand that children's literature includes unique genres with their own characteristics.
- I understand that folktales, fables, legends, myths, and tall tales each teach lessons, share cultural values, or entertain in different ways.
- I understand that recognizing these characteristics helps me appreciate and analyze these stories.

I Will

- **Folktales:** Identify stories passed down through generations that reflect cultural traditions.
  Example: Folktales often include simple plots, moral lessons, and magical elements.
- **Fables:** Recognize short stories that use animals or objects to teach a moral.
  Example: "The Tortoise and the Hare" teaches patience and perseverance.
- **Legends:** Explore stories based on historical events or figures, often with exaggerated details.
  Example: Legends like "Robin Hood" combine fact and fiction to inspire bravery.
- **Myths:** Analyze stories that explain natural events, gods, and cultural beliefs.
  Example: Myths such as "Pandora's Box" reveal human traits and consequences.
- **Tall Tales:** Appreciate exaggerated, humorous stories about larger-than-life characters.
  Example: "Paul Bunyan" showcases strength and ingenuity with over-the-top adventures.

See how time and place shape the story—discover the power of the setting in driving the plot!

Painted with Words: Understanding Figurative Language

TEKS (9): Multiple Genres - Genres (A)

Demonstrate knowledge of distinguishing characteristics of well-known children's literature such as folktales, fables, legends, myths, and tall tales.

I Understand

- I understand that figurative language helps create vivid images and deeper meaning in poetry.
- I understand that poets use similes, metaphors, and personification to make their ideas come alive.
- I understand that identifying and explaining figurative language enhances my appreciation of poetry.

I Will

- **Simile:** Recognize comparisons using "like" or "as" that create strong visual images.
  Example: "Her smile was as bright as the sun" compares her smile to sunlight.
- **Metaphor:** Identify direct comparisons that reveal deeper meanings without using "like" or "as."
  Example: "The world is a stage" suggests life is a performance.
- **Personification:** Explain how poets give human traits to objects or ideas to create emotion.
  Example: "The wind whispered through the trees" makes the wind seem alive.
- Use text evidence to explain how figurative language creates images or sets a tone.
  Example: The metaphor "a blanket of stars" makes the night sky feel comforting and magical.

Step into the world of timeless tales—recognize their unique features and lasting impact!

Uncover the Author's Craft: Purpose and Structure

TEKS (9): Multiple Genres - Genres (B)

Explain figurative language such as simile, metaphor, and personification that the poet uses to create images.

I Understand

- I understand that every author writes with a purpose and a message to communicate.
- I understand that the way a text is organized (its structure) supports the author's purpose.
- I understand that identifying these elements helps me better comprehend and analyze the text.

I Will

- **(A) Explain the Author's Purpose and Message:**
  - Determine if the author's purpose is to inform, entertain, persuade, or explain.
    Example: The author wrote this article to inform readers about the effects of climate change.
  - Identify the message or main idea the author wants to convey.
    Example: The message of the story is that teamwork leads to success.
- **(B) Explain the Use of Text Structure:**
  - Recognize text structures like cause and effect, problem and solution, or chronological order.
    Example: The author uses cause and effect to explain how pollution impacts marine life.
  - Explain how the structure supports the author's purpose.
    Example: The problem and solution structure helps the author persuade readers to take action on recycling.

Discover the beauty of poetic language—see how words can paint powerful pictures in your mind!

Author's Purpose and Craft

TEKS 10(A): Author's Purpose and Message

(A) explain the author's purpose and message within a text;

I Understand

- I understand that every author writes with a purpose and a message to communicate.
- I understand that the way a text is organized (its structure) supports the author's purpose.
- I understand that identifying these elements helps me better comprehend and analyze the text.

I Will

- **Determine** if the author's purpose is to inform, entertain, persuade, or explain.
  Example: The author wrote this article to inform readers about the effects of climate change.
- **Identify** the message or main idea the author wants to convey.
  Example: The message of the story is that teamwork leads to success.

Discover how every author writes with intention—unlock the message behind the words and connect with the heart of the text!

Author's Purpose and Craft

TEKS 10(B): Explain the Use of Text Structure to Support the Author's Purpose

(B) explain how the use of text structure contributes to the author's purpose;

I Understand

- I understand that authors organize texts in specific ways to guide readers through their ideas.
- I understand that structure (like compare and contrast or cause and effect) supports the author's message and purpose.
- I understand that analyzing text structure helps me see how ideas build and connect.

I Will

- **Identify** the type of structure used in the text (e.g., sequence, problem and solution, cause and effect, compare and contrast). *Example*: The author uses chronological order to describe the events of the Civil Rights Movement.
- **Explain** how that structure supports what the author is trying to do. *Example*: The cause and effect structure helps show how actions led to real consequences in history.

Discover how structure shapes meaning—see how authors organize their ideas to guide and impact your understanding!

Author's Purpose and Craft

TEKS 10(C): Analyze the Author's Use of Print and Graphic Features to Achieve Specific Purposes

(C) analyze the author's use of print and graphic features to achieve specific purposes;

I Understand

- I understand that authors use features like bold print, headings, graphs, charts, or illustrations to make their writing clearer and more engaging.
- I understand that these features can help highlight key points, organize ideas, or create emphasis.
- I understand that analyzing these features can help me better understand and interpret informational text.

I Will

- **Identify** which print or graphic features are used and describe their function. *Example*: The timeline helps the reader understand when key events happened.
- **Explain** how these features help the author achieve their purpose. *Example*: The diagram makes it easier for the reader to visualize how the heart pumps blood.

Discover how visuals and features add power to words—watch how images, charts, and headings help bring information to life!

Author's Purpose and Craft

TEKS 10(D): Describe How the Author's Use of Imagery, Literal and Figurative Language, and Sound Devices Achieves Specific Purposes

(D) describe how the author's use of imagery, literal and figurative language such as simile and metaphor, and sound devices such as alliteration and assonance achieves specific purposes;

I Understand

- I understand that authors use descriptive language to create mental pictures and emotions in the reader.
- I understand that figurative language (like similes, metaphors, and personification) can help express ideas in powerful ways.
- I understand that sound devices (like alliteration and assonance) make the language more musical and memorable.

I Will

- **Identify** examples of imagery, figurative language, or sound devices in the text.
  Example: The author uses the simile "as fierce as a wildfire" to show how fast the argument escalated.
- **Explain** how that language helps the author achieve a purpose (like creating emotion, building mood, or making the writing more vivid).
  Example: The repetition of the "s" sound adds a soothing rhythm that matches the peaceful mood of the poem.

Discover the beauty of poetic language—see how words can paint powerful pictures in your mind!

Author's Purpose and Craft

(E) Identify and Understand the Use of Literary Devices, Including First- or Third-Person Point of View

(E) identify and understand the use of literary devices, including first- or third-person point of view;

I Understand

- I understand that literary devices are special techniques authors use to make stories more interesting and meaningful.
- I understand that point of view affects how the story is told and what we know about the characters.
- I understand that identifying literary devices helps me better understand the author's choices and the story's message.

I Will

- **Identify** the point of view used in a story (first-person or third-person) and other literary devices like flashback, foreshadowing, or irony.
  Example: The narrator uses first-person point of view, saying "I was terrified when I heard the news."
- **Explain** how that point of view or device affects the way the story is experienced.
  Example: The first-person point of view lets the reader feel closer to the character's emotions and thoughts.

Discover how authors shape stories through point of view—step inside the story and experience it from the inside out!

Chapter 9

Parental Involvement for each of the TEKS

Involving parents in the teaching of the **Language Arts TEKS** can significantly enhance student learning. Here are some of the best ways to engage parents effectively:

---

1. Communicate Clearly and Regularly

- **What to Do:**
    - Share the TEKS goals and expectations in simple, understandable language.
    - Provide regular updates about what students are learning (e.g., newsletters, emails, or parent-teacher conferences).
    - Explain how specific activities at home can support TEKS skills, like reading comprehension or writing practice.
- **Example:** Send a weekly email summarizing focus TEKS (e.g., "This week, we are working on summarizing texts and identifying themes. Encourage your child to practice by summarizing a book or movie they enjoy.").

---

2. Provide Home Activities Aligned with TEKS

- **What to Do:**
    - Share simple, engaging activities that align with TEKS and can be done at home.
    - Include instructions for activities that involve reading, writing, and vocabulary development.
- **Examples:**
    - Reading TEKS: Create a family reading night where parents and children discuss books.
    - Writing TEKS: Encourage children to keep a daily journal or write letters to family members.
    - Vocabulary TEKS: Play word games like Scrabble or Boggle to reinforce new vocabulary.

---

3. Host Parent Workshops

- **What to Do:**
    - Organize workshops to teach parents how to support TEKS learning at home.
    - Provide tips for encouraging reading, guiding writing activities, or discussing texts.
- **Example:** Host a "Helping Your Child with Writing" night where parents learn how to help with brainstorming, drafting, and editing.

4. Leverage Technology and Apps

- **What to Do:**
    - Recommend educational apps, websites, or digital tools that align with TEKS skills.
    - Show parents how to use these resources during parent-teacher meetings or through tutorial videos.
- **Examples:**
    - Suggest apps like Epic! or Raz-Kids for reading practice.
    - Use tools like Quizlet for vocabulary and grammar review.

---

5. Encourage a Literacy-Rich Home Environment

- **What to Do:**
    - Provide tips for creating a home environment that encourages reading and writing.
    - Share book lists, writing prompts, and creative activities parents can use at home.
- **Examples:**
    - Suggest a cozy reading nook and encourage 20 minutes of family reading time each evening.
    - Provide a list of recommended books for different grade levels and TEKS objectives.

---

6. Engage Parents in Classroom Activities

- **What to Do:**
    - Invite parents to participate in classroom literacy activities like reading aloud or helping during writing workshops.
    - Encourage parents to share their own experiences with writing or storytelling.
- **Examples:**
    - Parent volunteers can read books related to current TEKS themes.
    - Parents can join "Author Days" to discuss how writing is used in their professions.

7. Promote Collaboration Through Projects

- **What to Do:**
  - o Assign family-friendly projects that align with TEKS and encourage parental involvement.
  - o Incorporate creative activities that parents and children can complete together.
- **Examples:**
  - o Create a family storybook where each member contributes a page or idea.
  - o Work on a research project together, using online and library resources.

8. Highlight TEKS in Everyday Activities

- **What to Do:**
  - o Show parents how TEKS skills can be reinforced in everyday life.
  - o Connect language arts skills to real-world applications like grocery lists, recipes, or schedules.
- **Examples:**
  - o Have children write a shopping list or plan a family schedule.
  - o Encourage parents to discuss the themes or characters in movies they watch together.

9. Celebrate Progress and Involvement

- **What to Do:**
  - o Share student achievements with parents to show how their support is making a difference.
  - o Recognize families that actively participate in home-based TEKS activities.
- **Examples:**
  - o Send home certificates of recognition for student progress.
  - o Highlight parent involvement in newsletters or at school events.

10. Provide Bilingual and Accessible Resources

- **What to Do:**
  - Offer resources in multiple languages to ensure all families can participate.
  - Make materials accessible for families with limited time or resources.
- **Examples:**
  - Translate activity instructions into families' home languages.
  - Provide take-home materials like reading logs, graphic organizers, or vocabulary flashcards.

---

11. Foster a Partnership Mindset

- **What to Do:**
  - Encourage parents to see themselves as partners in their child's education.
  - Listen to their concerns and ideas, and involve them in goal-setting for their child's language arts progress.
- **Examples:**
  - Invite parents to share what has worked for their child at home.
  - Collaboratively set reading or writing goals during parent-teacher conferences.

By providing resources, creating meaningful opportunities for involvement, and maintaining open communication, teachers can help parents actively support their children in mastering the **Language Arts TEKS**.

For letters in English and Spanish giving parents ideas of conversations they can have and simple projects they can do at home that emphasize particular TEKS go to teachbig.com and read about the online assessment platform.

Chapter 10

Book Recommendations with TEKS Correlated Questions

Book Recommendation: TEKS 6

"The Snowy Day" by Ezra Jack Keats

(A) Establish Purpose for Reading Assigned and Self-Selected Texts

- **How the Book Helps Teach the TEKS:**
  Before reading, ask students why they think they are reading this book. They might say, "To enjoy a story," "To learn about winter," or "To see what the boy does in the snow." Discuss how setting a purpose helps them focus on the story.

(B) Generate Questions About Text Before, During, and After Reading

- **How the Book Helps Teach the TEKS:**
  - **Before Reading:** Ask, "What do you think this story is about based on the title and cover?"
  - **During Reading:** Pause and ask, "What do you think Peter will do next in the snow?"
  - **After Reading:** Ask, "Why do you think Peter saved a snowball? What happened to it?"

(C) Make and Correct or Confirm Predictions Using Text Features, Characteristics of Genre, and Structures

- **How the Book Helps Teach the TEKS:**
  Look at the cover illustration and title together. Ask students to predict what might happen in the story. As they read, they can confirm or adjust their predictions based on what they learn.

(D) Create Mental Images to Deepen Understanding

- **How the Book Helps Teach the TEKS:**
  Encourage students to close their eyes as you describe Peter crunching through the snow or dragging his stick through the snowbanks. Ask them to share what they imagine to deepen engagement with the text.

(E) Make Connections to Personal Experiences, Ideas in Other Texts, and Society

- **How the Book Helps Teach the TEKS:**
  After reading, ask students:
    - "Have you ever played in the snow like Peter? What did you do?"
    - "Does this remind you of any other books about winter or snow?"

(F) Make Inferences and Use Evidence to Support Understanding

- **How the Book Helps Teach the TEKS:**
  Ask students:
    - "Why do you think Peter saved the snowball in his pocket?"
    - "What happened to it, and how do you know?"

(G) Evaluate Details Read to Determine Key Ideas

- **How the Book Helps Teach the TEKS:**
  Guide students to identify the key idea of the book, such as exploring and enjoying simple moments like playing in the snow. Discuss how the illustrations and Peter's actions support this idea.

(H) Synthesize Information to Create New Understanding

- **How the Book Helps Teach the TEKS:**
  After reading, discuss how Peter's experiences in the snow teach us about curiosity and joy. Students can connect this new understanding to how they explore and learn in their own environments.

(I) Monitor Comprehension and Make Adjustments

- **How the Book Helps Teach the TEKS:**
  Encourage students to pause and ask themselves questions as you read aloud:
    - "Does this part make sense to me?"
    - "Why did Peter make the choices he did?"
      Guide them to reread or ask for clarification if they're confused.

Book Recommendation: TEKS 7

"Charlotte's Web" by E.B. White

Why this book?
Charlotte's Web is a timeless story that offers opportunities for students to make personal connections, write responses, use text evidence, summarize key ideas, and engage with the text in creative and meaningful ways. It's accessible for 4th graders and contains rich themes of friendship, kindness, and perseverance.

(A) Describe Personal Connections to a Variety of Sources, Including Self-Selected Texts

- **How the Book Helps Teach the TEKS:**
    - Ask students: "Have you ever had a close friend like Wilbur and Charlotte? How did that friendship make you feel?"
    - Students might connect Wilbur's loneliness on the farm to a time they felt left out and how someone made them feel included.

(B) Write Responses That Demonstrate Understanding of Texts, Including Comparing and Contrasting Ideas Across a Variety of Sources

- **How the Book Helps Teach the TEKS:**
    - Have students compare *Charlotte's Web* to another story about unlikely friendships, such as *The One and Only Ivan* by Katherine Applegate.
    - Prompt: "How are Wilbur and Charlotte's friendship similar to or different from Ivan's friendship with Ruby and Stella?"
    - Students can write responses highlighting themes, character traits, or settings.

(C) Use Text Evidence to Support an Appropriate Response

- **How the Book Helps Teach the TEKS:**
    - Ask: "Why is Charlotte willing to help Wilbur? Use evidence from the text to support your answer."
    - Students might cite Charlotte's line, "You have been my friend. That in itself is a tremendous thing," to support their response.

(D) Retell, Paraphrase, or Summarize Texts in Ways That Maintain Meaning and Logical Order

- **How the Book Helps Teach the TEKS:**
  - Activity: Have students summarize the story in three sentences, focusing on the beginning (Wilbur's life on the farm), middle (Charlotte's plan to save him), and end (Wilbur's survival and Charlotte's legacy).
  - Students can also paraphrase the meaning of Charlotte's famous message, "Some Pig."

(E) Interact with Sources in Meaningful Ways Such as Notetaking, Annotating, Freewriting, or Illustrating

- **How the Book Helps Teach the TEKS:**
  - Ask students to illustrate one of Charlotte's webs with their own creative message that represents Wilbur.
  - Alternatively, they can annotate passages where Charlotte explains her loyalty to Wilbur and jot down what they think about her actions.

(F) Respond Using Newly Acquired Vocabulary as Appropriate

- **How the Book Helps Teach the TEKS:**
  - Introduce words like "radiant" and "terrific" as used in the story. Ask students to use these words in sentences about the book, such as:
    - "Charlotte thought Wilbur was radiant because he was a good friend."

(G) Discuss Specific Ideas in the Text That Are Important to the Meaning

- **How the Book Helps Teach the TEKS:**
  - Host a discussion on the theme of selflessness:
    - "Why does Charlotte work so hard to save Wilbur when it doesn't benefit her? What does this teach us about friendship and helping others?"
  - Encourage students to share their opinions and listen to their peers' perspectives.

Book Recommendation: TEKS 8

"Because of Winn-Dixie" by Kate DiCamillo

Why this book?
Because of Winn-Dixie is a rich story that demonstrates themes, character growth, plot structure, and the influence of setting on a story. It is engaging and relatable for 4th graders, offering opportunities for deep discussion and analysis of literary elements.

(A) Infer Basic Themes Supported by Text Evidence

- **How the Book Helps Teach the TEKS:**
  - The book has clear themes of friendship, forgiveness, and acceptance.
  - Activity: Ask students, "What lesson do you think Opal learns by the end of the story? What evidence supports this?"
    - Students might infer that the theme is about finding family in unexpected places and use Opal's friendships with her neighbors and her relationship with her father as evidence.

(B) Explain the Interactions of the Characters and the Changes They Undergo

- **How the Book Helps Teach the TEKS:**
  - Characters like Opal, her father (the preacher), and Gloria Dump undergo changes through their interactions with each other and Winn-Dixie.
  - Activity: Discuss how Opal changes from being lonely to feeling part of a community because of her relationships with others.
    - Prompt: "How does Winn-Dixie help Opal make friends and connect with her father? How does her father change by the end of the story?"

(C) Analyze Plot Elements, Including the Rising Action, Climax, Falling Action, and Resolution

- **How the Book Helps Teach the TEKS:**
  - The book's structure is clear, making it easy to identify plot elements:
    - **Rising Action:** Opal adopts Winn-Dixie and starts meeting new people.
    - **Climax:** The big storm and Winn-Dixie's disappearance create tension.

- **Falling Action:** Opal searches for Winn-Dixie and reflects on her friendships and father.
- **Resolution:** Winn-Dixie is found, and the party brings everyone together.
  - o Activity: Have students create a plot diagram for the story, identifying key events in each part.

(D) Explain the Influence of the Setting, Including Historical and Cultural Settings, on the Plot

- **How the Book Helps Teach the TEKS:**
  - o The small-town Southern setting influences the plot by creating a close-knit community where everyone knows each other. The setting also provides opportunities for Opal to interact with diverse and quirky characters.
  - o Activity: Discuss how the town's culture and setting impact the story.
    - Prompt: "How might the story change if it were set in a big city? Would Opal still meet people like Gloria Dump or Otis?"

Book Recommendation: TEKS 9

"The Stinky Cheese Man and Other Fairly Stupid Tales" by Jon Scieszka

Why this book?
This book is a collection of humorous retellings of classic folktales, fables, and fairy tales, making it perfect for teaching the characteristics of multiple genres. Its playful language, satirical tone, and unique structure also provide opportunities to explore figurative language, drama elements, informational text features, argumentative writing, and multimodal aspects.

(A) Demonstrate Knowledge of Distinguishing Characteristics of Well-Known Children's Literature

- **How the Book Helps Teach the TEKS:**
    - Each story in the collection is a parody of a well-known folktale, fable, or fairy tale, such as *The Gingerbread Man* or *The Ugly Duckling*.
    - Activity: Ask students to identify the original tale being retold and explain how the parody changes the story's tone or message.
        - Example: Compare *The Gingerbread Man* to *The Stinky Cheese Man* and discuss how the exaggerated humor distinguishes tall tales and parody.

(B) Explain Figurative Language Such as Simile, Metaphor, and Personification

- **How the Book Helps Teach the TEKS:**
    - The stories use playful figurative language, like similes ("The cheese smelled worse than a skunk's gym socks") and personification (e.g., the Cheese Man talks and runs).
    - Activity: Have students highlight examples of figurative language and explain how they create humor or vivid images.

(C) Explain Structure in Drama Such as Character Tags, Acts, Scenes, and Stage Directions

- **How the Book Helps Teach the TEKS:**
  - Some stories mimic a play structure, with characters addressing the reader or interacting in exaggerated ways.
  - Activity: Ask students to rewrite a short tale from the book as a script, adding character tags and stage directions.

(D) Recognize Characteristics and Structures of Informational Text

(i) The Central Idea With Supporting Evidence

- The book includes a mock "Table of Contents" and narrator interruptions that exaggerate the structure of a typical book.
- Activity: Discuss the central idea of a specific tale (e.g., "Not all fairy tales have happy endings") and identify how the story supports it.

(ii) Features Such as Pronunciation Guides and Diagrams

- The book includes playful asides and exaggerated formatting that mimic text features.
- Activity: Have students design a page for a "Stinky Cheese Man Dictionary" with made-up pronunciation guides for silly words from the book.

(iii) Organizational Patterns Such as Compare and Contrast

- Students can compare the parody tales to the original versions, identifying similarities and differences in characters, tone, and plot.
- Activity: Create a Venn diagram comparing *The Ugly Duckling* and *The Really Ugly Duckling* from the book.

(E) Recognize Characteristics and Structures of Argumentative Text

(i) Identifying the Claim

- In the narrator's commentary, there are mock "claims" about how these stories should be told or perceived.
- Activity: Identify a claim the narrator makes (e.g., "These stories are better than the originals") and discuss whether it's supported.

(ii) Explaining How the Author Has Used Facts for an Argument

- Discuss how the exaggerated details in each tale support the claim that the stories are meant to be funny rather than serious.

(iii) Identifying the Intended Audience or Reader

- The humor and playful tone are aimed at a younger audience who might already know the original tales.
- Activity: Ask students, "Who do you think would enjoy this book? Why?"

(F) Recognize Characteristics of Multimodal and Digital Texts

- **How the Book Helps Teach the TEKS:**
  - The book itself includes multimodal elements, such as bold typography, comic illustrations, and unconventional page layouts.
  - Activity: Have students identify how the visual elements (e.g., the size and style of the text) enhance the humor or meaning of the stories.

Summary:

"The Stinky Cheese Man and Other Fairly Stupid Tales" is a versatile book for teaching TEKS (9) because it spans multiple genres, encourages analysis of literary elements, and introduces text structures in a fun and engaging way. Its humor and creative approach make it relatable and enjoyable for students.

Book Recommendation: TEKS 10

"The Day the Crayons Quit" by Drew Daywalt

Why this book?
The Day the Crayons Quit is a humorous and engaging book that uses creative writing, distinct character voices, and playful illustrations to convey meaning. It provides an excellent opportunity to analyze the author's purpose, text structure, print and graphic features, figurative language, and literary devices.

(A) Explain the Author's Purpose and Message Within a Text

- **How the Book Helps Teach the TEKS:**
  - Each crayon writes a letter to Duncan explaining its feelings and frustrations, teaching readers about perspective and communication.
  - Activity: Ask students, "Why do you think the author wrote this book? What message is the author sharing about listening to others or appreciating differences?"
    - Students might respond that the author wants to entertain but also teach the importance of considering others' feelings.

(B) Explain How the Use of Text Structure Contributes to the Author's Purpose

- **How the Book Helps Teach the TEKS:**
  - The book's structure is a series of letters written by the crayons, which allows each crayon to share its unique perspective.
  - Activity: Discuss how the letter format helps the author achieve their purpose. Ask, "How does hearing from each crayon in their own words help us understand the story better?"

(C) Analyze the Author's Use of Print and Graphic Features to Achieve Specific Purposes

- **How the Book Helps Teach the TEKS:**
  - The text includes bold fonts, colorful illustrations, and handwritten-style letters to emphasize each crayon's personality.
  - Activity: Have students examine a page and discuss how the choice of font or color helps express the crayon's feelings.
    - Example: "How do the bright colors of the red crayon's letter make its frustration with overuse clear?"

(D) Describe How the Author's Use of Imagery, Literal and Figurative Language, and Sound Devices Achieves Specific Purposes

- **How the Book Helps Teach the TEKS:**
  - The book uses figurative language like exaggeration (e.g., "I'm so short and stubby I can't even see over the box!") to create humor and empathy.
  - Activity: Identify examples of figurative language, such as metaphors or personification, and discuss how they help readers understand the crayons' emotions.
    - Example: "Why does the peach crayon's description of being 'naked' make us laugh and feel bad for it at the same time?"

(E) Identify and Understand the Use of Literary Devices, Including First- or Third-Person Point of View

- **How the Book Helps Teach the TEKS:**
  - Each letter is written in the first person, giving the crayons distinct voices and making their complaints more personal and relatable.
  - Activity: Ask students to rewrite one of the letters in third person. Discuss how the point of view change affects the tone or message of the story.

Chapter 11

Nonfiction, TEKS-Based
(Science and Social Studies)
SelectionPractice with *Stop-Gap*
ELAR TEKS Comprehension Questions

Practice Passage with Stop Gap Comprehension Questions

Nonfiction Passage: The Free Enterprise System (TEKS 6)

Introduction

The free enterprise system is an economic system where people are free to make their own choices about what to buy, sell, and produce. This system encourages creativity, competition, and innovation. Imagine a lemonade stand in your neighborhood. The person running the stand decides how much to charge for each cup, what ingredients to use, and how to attract customers. These choices are part of the free enterprise system.

(A) Establish Purpose for Reading Assigned and Self-Selected Texts

Teacher Prompt:

"Before we keep reading, let's think about why we're learning about the free enterprise system. Why might understanding this system be important for us? How can this knowledge help us in real life?"

How the System Works

In a free enterprise system, businesses compete to provide the best products or services. This competition benefits customers because it encourages businesses to keep prices fair and improve their products. For example, imagine two pizza shops on the same street. Each one wants to attract more customers, so they might offer lower prices, better ingredients, or special deals.

(B) Generate Questions About Text Before, During, and After Reading

Teacher Prompt:

"Can you think of a question about how competition works in the free enterprise system? For example, why would two pizza shops want to compete? What might happen if one shop doesn't compete?"

The Role of Consumers and Producers

In a free enterprise system, consumers (buyers) and producers (sellers) play key roles. Consumers decide what they want to buy based on price, quality, and personal preferences. Producers create goods or services to meet those demands. For instance, if people in your neighborhood love chocolate chip cookies, a bakery might decide to start selling them.

(C) Make and Correct or Confirm Predictions Using Text Features, Characteristics of Genre, and Structures

Teacher Prompt:
"Based on what we just read, what do you think might happen if the bakery's cookies become very popular? What clues in the text helped you make that prediction?"

Opportunities and Challenges

The free enterprise system creates opportunities for people to start businesses and earn money. However, it also comes with challenges. If a business doesn't provide good products or charge fair prices, customers might go elsewhere. For example, if a lemonade stand sells sour lemonade for a high price, people might choose to buy from a different stand.

(D) Create Mental Images to Deepen Understanding

Teacher Prompt:
"Close your eyes for a moment and imagine two lemonade stands on the same street. One has a big sign, smiling workers, and tasty lemonade. The other looks messy and sells sour drinks. Which stand would you choose? Why?"

How It Connects to Our Lives

You interact with the free enterprise system every day. When you choose where to shop or what to buy, you're participating as a consumer. If you've ever sold something, like cookies at a bake sale, you've been a producer.

(E) Make Connections to Personal Experiences, Ideas in Other Texts, and Society

Teacher Prompt:
"Can you think of a time when you made a choice as a consumer, like deciding what snack to buy at the store? Or have you ever been a producer, like selling something at a fundraiser?"

Key Ideas of the Free Enterprise System

The free enterprise system is built on choice, competition, and opportunity. It gives people the freedom to make decisions and encourages businesses to work hard to meet the needs of consumers.

(F) Make Inferences and Use Evidence to Support Understanding

Teacher Prompt:
"Why do you think the free enterprise system encourages people to work hard? What evidence from the text supports your answer?"

Synthesis and New Understanding
Understanding the free enterprise system helps us see how businesses and consumers affect each other. By making smart choices, both groups can benefit. For example, when businesses create great products and consumers buy them, everyone succeeds.

(G) Evaluate Details Read to Determine Key Ideas
Teacher Prompt:
"What do you think is the most important idea we've read about the free enterprise system so far? Why is that idea important?"

(H) Synthesize Information to Create New Understanding
Teacher Prompt:
"How do businesses and consumers work together in the free enterprise system? Can you explain this idea in your own words?"

Conclusion: Monitoring Understanding
Learning about the free enterprise system helps us understand how choices and competition shape our world. If something doesn't make sense, we can reread, ask questions, or think about what we already know to help us understand.

(I) Monitor Comprehension and Make Adjustments

Teacher Prompt:
"Did anything we read confuse you? What strategy could you use to figure it out? For example, you could reread a section, ask for help, or look for clues in the text."

Summary:

This passage and its questions guide students through the TEKS, helping them set a purpose, ask questions, make predictions, connect ideas, and evaluate key concepts about the free enterprise system.

Nonfiction Passage: Patriotic Symbols and Landmarks of Texas (TEKS 7)

Introduction
Texas is a state rich in history, pride, and unique symbols that reflect its heritage. From the mighty Texas flag to historic landmarks like the Alamo, these symbols remind us of the state's independence and resilience. Let's explore some of the most important patriotic symbols and landmarks of Texas.

The Texas Flag
The Texas flag is one of the most recognized state flags in the United States. Known as the "Lone Star Flag," it features a single white star that represents Texas's struggle for independence and its pride as a former republic. The red stripe symbolizes bravery, the white stands for purity, and the blue represents loyalty.

Teacher Prompt for (A): Describe Personal Connections to a Variety of Sources
"Have you ever seen the Texas flag flying outside a building or at an event? How did it make you feel? Does it remind you of any other flags you've seen?"

The Alamo
The Alamo is a historic site in San Antonio that symbolizes the bravery and sacrifice of Texans during their fight for independence from Mexico in 1836. Although the defenders of the Alamo lost the battle, their courage inspired others to continue the fight for freedom, leading to Texas's victory in the Texas Revolution.

Teacher Prompt for (B): Write Responses Demonstrating Understanding of Texts
"If you compare the Texas flag to the Alamo, how are they similar? How are they different in what they represent?"

The Bluebonnet
The bluebonnet is the state flower of Texas and is known for its vibrant blue blossoms that blanket fields and hills in the spring. It represents the natural beauty of Texas and is often seen as a symbol of renewal and hope.

Teacher Prompt for (C): Use Text Evidence to Support an Appropriate Response
"Why do you think the bluebonnet is an important symbol for Texas? Can you use details from the text to explain your answer?"

San Jacinto Monument

The San Jacinto Monument stands near Houston and marks the site of the final battle of the Texas Revolution, where Texas secured its independence. The 567-foot monument is topped with a 220-ton star, symbolizing the Lone Star State.

Teacher Prompt for (D): Retell, Paraphrase, or Summarize Texts

"Can you summarize why the San Jacinto Monument is an important landmark in Texas history? Try to include the key details without retelling the whole passage."

Texas Longhorn

The Texas Longhorn, a breed of cattle known for its long, curved horns, represents the ranching history and rugged spirit of Texas. The Longhorn is often used as a mascot for sports teams and a symbol of strength and determination.

Teacher Prompt for (E): Interact with Sources in Meaningful Ways

"Draw a quick sketch of the Texas Longhorn or write down one word that you think describes its importance to Texas. How does this activity help you connect with what you read?"

The Texas State Capitol

The Texas State Capitol in Austin is not only the largest capitol building in the United States but also a symbol of Texas's government and independence. Its towering dome and pink granite exterior make it a standout landmark.

Teacher Prompt for (F): Respond Using Newly Acquired Vocabulary as Appropriate

"Use one of these words in a sentence about the Texas State Capitol: 'symbol,' 'independence,' or 'landmark.' For example, 'The Capitol is a landmark that symbolizes Texas's independence.'"

Conclusion

Patriotic symbols and landmarks like the Texas flag, the Alamo, and the bluebonnet remind us of Texas's rich history and culture. They serve as a way for Texans to connect with their past and feel proud of their state.

Teacher Prompt for (G): Discuss Specific Ideas in the Text That Are Important to the Meaning

"What do you think is the most important idea in this passage? Why do you think symbols like the flag or landmarks like the Alamo are so meaningful to Texans?"

Nonfiction Passage: The Duty of Civic Participation (TEKS 8)

Introduction
Civic participation means taking part in activities that help your community, state, or nation. This includes voting, volunteering, and staying informed about important issues. Just like characters in a story, individuals have a role to play in shaping the events that happen around them. Without active participation, communities and governments cannot thrive.

The Power of One Vote
In the United States, citizens have the right to vote for their leaders and on important issues. Voting is a way to make your voice heard and contribute to decisions that affect everyone. History shows us that every vote counts. For example, in 1845, Texas joined the United States by just a few votes in Congress. Imagine how different history might have been if some people hadn't participated.

Teacher Prompt for (A): Infer Basic Themes Supported by Text Evidence
"What theme can you infer from the story of Texas joining the United States? How does this example show the importance of every individual's participation?"

Working Together for Change
In addition to voting, citizens can participate in civic affairs by volunteering or attending public meetings. For instance, a group of neighbors might work together to build a new park or clean up their community. When individuals unite for a cause, they can make a big difference.

Teacher Prompt for (B): Explain the Interactions of the Characters and the Changes They Undergo
"How do the neighbors in this example work together, and how might their efforts change the community? Can you think of a time when working with others helped achieve a goal?"

A Story of Civic Engagement
Think about a story where people faced a challenge and came together to solve it. For example, during the Civil Rights Movement of the 1960s, individuals worked tirelessly to achieve equal rights for all citizens. The movement involved peaceful protests, speeches, and new laws. This effort reached its climax with landmark victories like the Civil Rights Act, which changed the lives of millions.

Teacher Prompt for (C): Analyze Plot Elements, Including Rising Action, Climax, Falling Action, and Resolution
"What is the rising action in the story of the Civil Rights Movement? What event might you identify as the climax? How did the falling action and resolution shape the country?"

The Influence of Time and Place

The role of civic participation often depends on the setting. In times of war, citizens may show their support by conserving resources or joining the armed forces. During elections, the focus shifts to campaigns and voting. Cultural settings also play a role—some communities might prioritize environmental causes, while others focus on education or healthcare.

Teacher Prompt for (D): Explain the Influence of the Setting, Including Historical and Cultural Settings, on the Plot

"How does the setting influence the type of civic participation people might engage in? Can you think of a historical or cultural setting that changed how people participated in civic affairs?"

Conclusion

Participating in civic affairs is a duty that connects us all. Whether it's voting, volunteering, or working together for change, our actions shape the future of our communities and our nation. Just like in a story, every character's role matters, and together, we can create a better outcome.

Teacher Wrap-Up Questions:

- For (A): "What is the overall theme of this passage about civic participation? How do the examples support that theme?"
- For (B): "How do people working together create change, and what can we learn from their interactions?"
- For (C): "If this passage were a story, how would you identify the key plot elements?"
- For (D): "How does the setting of this passage—local, state, or national levels—affect the type of civic participation discussed?"

Summary

This passage and its questions help students connect the duty of civic participation to literary elements like theme, character interaction, plot structure, and setting. By analyzing real-life examples through the lens of literary analysis, students can deepen their understanding of both the importance of civic engagement and the TEKS skills being practiced.

Nonfiction Passage: The Scientific Method (TEKS 9)

Introduction
The scientific method is a process that helps scientists answer questions and solve problems. It's like a recipe with steps that guide us to find the truth about the world around us. By observing, questioning, experimenting, and analyzing, scientists can uncover new knowledge and understand how things work.

The Steps of the Scientific Method
The scientific method follows a logical order of steps:

1. **Ask a Question**: Start with a question about something you want to learn.
2. **Do Research**: Gather information about the topic.
3. **Form a Hypothesis**: Make an educated guess about what you think will happen.
4. **Conduct an Experiment**: Test your hypothesis by running experiments.
5. **Analyze Data**: Look at the results and see what they tell you.
6. **Draw a Conclusion**: Decide whether your hypothesis was correct.

Teacher Prompt for (D)(i): The Central Idea With Supporting Evidence
"What is the central idea of this section? Can you find evidence in the text that explains why these steps are important?"

A Practical Example: Growing Plants
Let's imagine you want to know how sunlight affects plant growth.

- Your question is, "Do plants grow taller with more sunlight?"
- You do research and find that plants use sunlight to make food.
- Your hypothesis might be, "If a plant gets more sunlight, it will grow taller."
- To test this, you place one plant in full sunlight and another in shade. You water both equally and measure their growth every day.

Teacher Prompt for (D)(iii): Organizational Patterns Such as Compare and Contrast
"How does this example compare the effects of sunlight on the two plants? What is similar and different about the conditions for each plant?"

Using Diagrams to Understand the Process
Diagrams often help explain complex ideas. Here is a basic diagram of the scientific method:

1. Question → 2. Research → 3. Hypothesis → 4. Experiment → 5. Analyze → 6. Conclusion

Teacher Prompt for (D)(ii): Features Such as Pronunciation Guides and Diagrams
"How does this diagram make it easier to understand the scientific method? What steps would you add or emphasize?"

The Scientific Method in Everyday Life
The scientific method isn't just for scientists. Imagine you want to know which type of paper airplane flies the farthest. You could follow the scientific method:

- Ask: "What paper design flies farthest?"
- Hypothesize: "A plane with long wings will fly farther than a short one."
- Experiment: Test different designs and measure how far they fly.
- Analyze: Compare your results to see which design worked best.

Teacher Prompt for (A): Demonstrate Knowledge of Distinguishing Characteristics of Well-Known Texts
"How is this explanation of the scientific method like a folktale or fable? What lessons can we learn from using these steps?"

The Scientific Method as a Drama
If the scientific method were a play, each step would be a different scene.

- **Act 1**: The scientist asks a question.
- **Act 2**: Research provides background information.
- **Act 3**: The hypothesis is formed.
- **Act 4**: Experiments begin, with trials and errors.
- **Act 5**: Data is analyzed.
- **Act 6**: The story ends with a conclusion.

Teacher Prompt for (C): Explain Structure in Drama Such as Character Tags, Acts, and Scenes
"If this were a play, who would the main character be? How do the different acts help tell the story of the scientific method?"

The Argument for Using the Scientific Method

The scientific method is important because it helps people solve problems logically and accurately. Scientists argue that this method ensures fair testing and reliable results. For example, using the scientific method to test a new medicine means scientists can be sure it works before giving it to patients.

Teacher Prompt for (E)(i): Identifying the Claim

"What claim does the author make about the scientific method? Why do you think this claim is important?"

Teacher Prompt for (E)(ii): Explaining How the Author Has Used Facts for an Argument

"What facts from the passage support the idea that the scientific method is a reliable process?"

Conclusion

The scientific method is a step-by-step guide for solving problems, whether you're a scientist or a student. It teaches us to ask questions, test ideas, and learn from the results. By following these steps, anyone can explore the world and discover new things.

Teacher Prompt for (F): Recognize Characteristics of Multimodal and Digital Texts

"How might a video or animation about the scientific method help us understand it better? What features would you include if you created one?"

Summary

This passage introduces the scientific method while highlighting TEKS (9). It uses informational text, examples, and connections to drama and argumentation to help students analyze structures, evaluate central ideas, and explore how genre-specific characteristics enhance understanding. The prompts encourage active engagement, critical thinking, and creative connections.

Nonfiction Passage: The Food Chain and Its Importance (TEKS 10)

Introduction

Every living thing is connected in nature, and one of the most important ways this happens is through the food chain. A food chain shows how energy is passed from one living thing to another. From the tiniest plants to the largest predators, every level of the food chain plays a role in keeping the ecosystem balanced.

Producers: The Foundation of the Food Chain

The food chain starts with **producers**, like plants, algae, and some bacteria. These organisms make their own food using sunlight through a process called photosynthesis. They are the foundation of the food chain because they provide energy for all other levels.

Teacher Prompt for (A): Explain the Author's Purpose and Message
"What do you think the author's purpose is in explaining the role of producers? How does the author want us to feel about plants and their importance in the food chain?"

Consumers: Energy Movers

The next level of the food chain includes **consumers**, which are animals that eat plants or other animals. Consumers can be divided into three categories:

1. **Herbivores**: Animals like deer and rabbits that eat only plants.
2. **Carnivores**: Animals like lions and hawks that eat other animals.
3. **Omnivores**: Animals like bears and humans that eat both plants and animals.

Each consumer depends on the level before it to survive, forming a chain of energy transfer.

Teacher Prompt for (B): Explain How the Use of Text Structure Contributes to the Author's Purpose
"How does dividing consumers into categories help the author explain this part of the food chain? Why do you think the author organized it this way?"

Decomposers: Nature's Clean-Up Crew

At the end of the food chain are **decomposers**, like fungi and bacteria. These organisms break down dead plants and animals, returning nutrients to the soil. Without decomposers, the food chain would collapse, and the earth would be covered in waste.

Teacher Prompt for (C): Analyze the Author's Use of Print and Graphic Features
"If the author included a diagram of the food chain, how would it help you understand the role of decomposers? What other features could the author use to make this part clearer?"

A Balanced Ecosystem

Each level of the food chain is like a link in a chain. If one link breaks, the entire chain can fall apart. For example, if there are fewer plants, herbivores like deer might not have enough food. Without enough herbivores, carnivores like wolves might also struggle to survive. This delicate balance shows how every part of the food chain helps the others.

Teacher Prompt for (D): Describe the Author's Use of Imagery and Figurative Language
"Why do you think the author described the food chain as a 'delicate balance'? How does this phrase help you picture its importance?"

An Energy Journey

Think of energy in the food chain like a relay race. The sun gives energy to plants, which pass it to herbivores, which pass it to carnivores. This journey of energy keeps life moving. Without this constant transfer, life on Earth couldn't exist.

Teacher Prompt for (D): Analyze Figurative Language
"How does the metaphor of a 'relay race' help you understand how energy moves through the food chain? Can you think of another metaphor that could describe this process?"

Who's Telling the Story?

This passage uses a **third-person point of view** to explain the food chain. This helps the author provide facts and details from an outside perspective, giving readers a clear and objective view of the topic.

Teacher Prompt for (E): Identify and Understand the Use of Literary Devices, Including First- or Third-Person Point of View
"How does the third-person point of view help the author explain the food chain? How might the passage change if it were written in the first person, like from the perspective of a plant or an animal?"

Conclusion

The food chain is a powerful reminder of how everything in nature is connected. Each level has a role, and when all the links work together, life can thrive. From producers to decomposers, every part of the chain is essential for keeping the ecosystem healthy.

Teacher Wrap-Up Questions:

- For (A): "What message is the author trying to share about the food chain? How does the author want you to feel about its importance?"
- For (B): "Why do you think the author chose to divide the passage into sections? How does this help you understand the topic better?"
- For (C): "What graphic or print feature could help explain this topic more clearly, and why?"
- For (D): "What is one example of figurative language in the text, and how does it make the writing more engaging or clear?"
- For (E): "How does the use of third-person point of view help the author's explanation? Would first-person have been as effective?"

Summary

This passage uses clear explanations and structured sections to demonstrate the importance of the food chain while incorporating prompts to explore **author's purpose and craft**. The prompts guide students to analyze the text, its structure, and the author's use of literary tools for better understanding.

<u>Chapter 12</u>

Escape Room Cumulative Project

(to be used with a book of your choice)

BIG Projects to Review Before the TEST

Station Activities to Review the TEKS

This project fosters teamwork, comprehension, and an appreciation for the TEKS standards through a fun and interactive escape room adventure!

Escape Room Project: "Unlocking the TEKS Treasure" Overview

Objective:
Students work collaboratively to solve a series of TEKS-based puzzles, unlocking the "treasure" of the Enchanted Library by identifying and applying specific TEKS from sections 6, 7, 8, 9, and 10.

Setup:

1. **Room Design:**
   - Create a themed classroom with "Enchanted Library" decorations, such as old books, glowing lights, and mysterious symbols.
   - Divide the room into stations, each with a challenge tied to a specific TEKS.
2. **Storyline:**
   Students are tasked with finding the "Key to Knowledge" by solving puzzles that test their comprehension, analysis, and connection skills.
3. **Tools:**
   Provide students with clipboards, answer sheets, and small props (e.g., keys, locks, or envelopes) for physical interaction.

Challenges:

1. **Station 1: Predict and Infer (TEKS 6B, 6C, 6F)**
   Task:
   - Students read an excerpt from the passage and predict what happens next.
   - Infer why the book glows based on details in the text.
   Solution:
   - Write down predictions and infer the purpose of the glowing book to unlock the station.

---

2. **Station 2: Analyze Literary Elements (TEKS 8A, 8B, 8C)**
   Task:
   - Identify the theme of the passage.
   - Analyze how Sarah's character changes throughout the story.
   - Break down the plot structure (rising action, climax, resolution).
   Solution:
   - Write the correct answers on a provided scroll to receive a puzzle piece.

3. **Station 3: Connect and Respond (TEKS 6E, 7A, 7G)**
   Task:
   - o Make connections between the story and students' own experiences or other texts.
   - o Discuss the main ideas in the text and their importance.
   Solution:
   - o Share responses aloud or write them to earn a code that opens the next clue.

4. **Station 4: Figurative Language and Genre (TEKS 9B, 9C, 10D)**
   Task:
   - o Identify examples of figurative language (e.g., simile, metaphor) in the passage.
   - o Explain the genre of the story and its distinguishing characteristics.
   Solution:
   - o Match figurative phrases to their meanings and correctly identify the genre to unlock the next station.

5. **Station 5: Author's Purpose and Craft (TEKS 10A, 10B, 10E)**
   Task:
   - o Explain the author's purpose and message within the story.
   - o Describe how the setting influences the story's meaning.
   - o Identify whether the text is written in first- or third-person point of view.
   Solution:
   - o Write the correct answers in an "author's notebook" to receive the final key.

Final Task: Unlock the Treasure

- Combine all the puzzle pieces and clues from each station to solve a riddle about the power of stories.
- Use the solution to "unlock" a treasure chest containing certificates, bookmarks, or small prizes.

Assessment:

- Each station aligns with specific TEKS and allows students to demonstrate mastery in creative ways.
- Collaboration and critical thinking are emphasized, making the experience engaging and educational.

Detailed Story: "The Enchanted Library and the Key to Knowledge"

In the quietest corner of an ancient city, hidden beneath the cobblestone streets, there was a library unlike any other. The Enchanted Library had no ordinary books. Its shelves were lined with volumes that whispered secrets, glowed with light, or floated just out of reach. Legends said that the library held the *Key to Knowledge*, an artifact said to unlock boundless wisdom for those worthy of wielding it.

Sarah, a curious and determined student, stumbled upon the library while exploring the city with her friends. As she pushed open the creaking iron door, a soft glow illuminated her face. Inside, rows of books shimmered like stars, their covers etched with symbols she couldn't yet understand.

At the center of the library stood a pedestal, and on it rested a large, leather-bound book titled *The Key to Knowledge*. Beneath the title, golden text shimmered:
"Knowledge is earned, not given. Only those who can think, infer, analyze, and connect will find the key."

As Sarah approached the pedestal, the book opened on its own. A whisper filled the room:
*"To unlock the Key to Knowledge, you must answer these questions:

1. What is the message hidden within this story?
2. How do the characters in this tale influence each other?
3. What clues in the setting help you understand the events that unfold?"*

Sarah's heart raced as more glowing words appeared in the air:

- *Predict what will happen next.*
- *Infer why the library chooses who can enter.*
- *Analyze how the rising action leads to the resolution.*

Suddenly, the library seemed to shift. Shelves moved, books flew open, and symbols glowed on the walls. It was as if the library itself was alive, testing her ability to comprehend its secrets.

Her first challenge appeared before her: a glowing path of stepping stones leading deeper into the library. Each stone bore a riddle:
"Describe how this story connects to your world."
"Retell the events that led you here."
"Explain the author's purpose in sharing this tale."

Sarah realized the library wasn't just testing her knowledge—it was teaching her to think critically, connect ideas, and express her thoughts. As she answered each question, the path lit up, guiding her closer to the Key to Knowledge.

Finally, Sarah reached the heart of the library, where a golden chest rested. On its lid, the final question shimmered:
"What will you do with the knowledge you unlock?"

Sarah smiled, understanding that the library's true treasure wasn't just the key—it was the skills she had developed along the way.

Key Elements of the Story for the Escape Room Project

1. **Comprehension Skills (TEKS 6):**
   o Students can predict what happens next, infer the library's purpose, and synthesize information from the story.
2. **Response Skills (TEKS 7):**
   o Students are asked to connect the story to their own experiences, summarize events, and discuss key ideas.
3. **Literary Elements (TEKS 8):**
   o Analyze themes (e.g., the value of knowledge), character interactions, and the influence of the setting.
4. **Genres (TEKS 9):**
   o Identify the story's fantasy genre, explore its figurative language, and evaluate its structure.
5. **Author's Purpose and Craft (TEKS 10):**
   o Explain the author's purpose, analyze how the setting enhances the narrative, and identify the narrative point of view.

This passage is rich with opportunities for analysis and critical thinking, aligning perfectly with the escape room's TEKS-focused challenges.

Additional Creative TEKS projects designed to align with the Texas Essential Knowledge and Skills (TEKS) while engaging students in meaningful and enjoyable learning activities:

1. Living Museum (TEKS 6, 7, 8, 9, 10)

- **Description:** Students select a historical figure, literary character, or influential author to research. They write a monologue in the first person, summarizing key facts, themes, or contributions and how they connect to broader concepts. On presentation day, students "become" their chosen figure, setting up a museum display and reciting their monologue.
- **Why It Works:** Integrates comprehension, response, literary analysis, and genre exploration. Encourages research, writing, and oral presentation skills.

2. TEKS Bingo Review (TEKS 6, 7, 8, 9, 10)

- **Description:** Create a bingo board where each square represents a TEKS skill (e.g., "Make an inference," "Identify a theme," "Explain figurative language"). Students complete reading activities and check off the corresponding squares as they master each skill. Add challenges for a competitive twist.
- **Why It Works:** Reinforces multiple skills in a low-pressure, game-based format.

3. Genre Exploration Scrapbook (TEKS 8, 9)

- **Description:** Students create a digital or physical scrapbook featuring examples of different genres (e.g., folktales, poetry, drama). For each entry, they identify key characteristics, analyze themes or plot elements, and add creative responses such as illustrations, photos, or personal reflections.
- **Why It Works:** Combines creativity with genre analysis and literary comprehension.

4. Collaborative Story Circle (TEKS 6, 7, 8)

- **Description:** In groups, students create a story collaboratively. Each student contributes a paragraph or scene, focusing on a specific TEKS skill (e.g., describing the setting, analyzing character development, or introducing figurative language). The final product is shared with the class.
- **Why It Works:** Promotes teamwork, writing skills, and TEKS-aligned analysis in a creative way.

5. Book Character Trial (TEKS 7, 8, 10)

- **Description:** Students hold a mock trial for a character from a book they've read. Assign roles like prosecution, defense, judge, and jury. Students must use text evidence to argue their points, aligning with TEKS response and comprehension skills.
- **Why It Works:** Engages critical thinking, textual analysis, and persuasive skills while encouraging collaboration.

---

6. Multimedia Book Review (TEKS 7, 9)

- **Description:** Students create a video, podcast, or website to review a book they've read. They analyze themes, characters, and literary devices while explaining the author's purpose and message. Include visuals, music, or interviews for added creativity.
- **Why It Works:** Integrates technology, critical thinking, and communication skills.

---

7. TEKS Poetry Café (TEKS 8, 9, 10)

- **Description:** Students write original poems using figurative language (e.g., similes, metaphors, alliteration) and perform them in a "poetry café" setting. They can also analyze published poems for similar elements, tying their creative work to literary analysis.
- **Why It Works:** Encourages creative expression while reinforcing analysis of figurative language and sound devices.

---

8. Story Map Relay (TEKS 6, 8)

- **Description:** Create a large story map (on paper or digitally) with blank sections for setting, plot, characters, themes, and conflicts. In small groups, students move through stations to fill in the sections using text evidence from a chosen story.
- **Why It Works:** Interactive and collaborative, reinforcing comprehension and literary analysis skills.

9. Argumentative Text Debate (TEKS 9E)

- **Description:** Provide students with an argumentative text. Assign them sides (agree/disagree) and have them debate the claim using text evidence. Include an analysis of the author's intended audience and use of facts to support the argument.
- **Why It Works:** Builds critical thinking, speaking, and comprehension skills in an engaging format.

10. Create a Graphic Novel (TEKS 7, 8, 9)

- **Description:** Students turn a short story, chapter, or historical event into a graphic novel. They must identify key plot elements, summarize events, and use text features to convey meaning creatively.
- **Why It Works:** Combines literary analysis with visual storytelling and genre exploration.

11. Theme Analysis Escape Box (TEKS 8A, 10A)

- **Description:** Students work in teams to solve puzzles inside a "locked box" by identifying themes in various texts and supporting their answers with evidence. Each correct answer unlocks a new clue.
- **Why It Works:** Builds teamwork and critical thinking while reinforcing TEKS standards on themes and text evidence.

12. Author's Craft Art Exhibit (TEKS 10C, 10D)

- **Description:** Students select a story and create visual representations of the author's use of imagery, figurative language, or sound devices. Each piece includes an explanation of how these craft elements achieve specific purposes.
- **Why It Works:** Encourages deeper analysis and creative interpretation of literary devices.

13. Compare and Contrast Texts Carousel (TEKS 7, 9)

- **Description:** Set up stations with excerpts from different texts. Students rotate in groups, comparing and contrasting themes, structures, and genres at each station. They record findings on shared charts or posters.
- **Why It Works:** Encourages movement, collaboration, and focused text analysis.

14. TEKS Travel Log (TEKS 6, 7, 8, 10)

- **Description:** Students create a "travel log" documenting their learning journey through a story or unit. For each "destination," they describe a key skill (e.g., making predictions, identifying themes) and reflect on how it helps them understand the text.
- **Why It Works:** Reinforces metacognition and connects skills to real-world applications.

15. Digital TEKS Scavenger Hunt (TEKS 6, 7, 8, 9, 10)

- **Description:** Students complete a scavenger hunt using online resources or a digital platform like Google Classroom. Clues and tasks align with specific TEKS, such as finding examples of figurative language or identifying the author's purpose in a given text.
- **Why It Works:** Combines technology with TEKS-focused skills for an interactive experience.

These projects align with multiple TEKS strands and encourage creativity, collaboration, and critical thinking. They can be adapted for different grade levels and tailored to fit various classroom settings.

Station Activities Based on a Central Passage

Passage: "The Never-Ending Journey of Water"

Water is one of Earth's most precious resources, moving through a cycle that keeps life thriving. This process, called the water cycle, has no beginning or end—it's a continuous journey.

It all starts with **evaporation**, when the sun heats water in oceans, rivers, and lakes, turning it into vapor that rises into the atmosphere. Plants also play a role in this step through a process called **transpiration**, where they release water vapor into the air.

Once in the atmosphere, the vapor cools and forms tiny droplets, creating clouds in a process called **condensation**. These droplets gather and grow until they become too heavy to stay in the sky. When that happens, they fall to Earth as **precipitation**—rain, snow, sleet, or hail.

But where does the water go once it reaches the ground? Some of it soaks into the soil, replenishing underground reserves in a process called **infiltration**, while some flows over the surface as **runoff**, heading back to rivers, lakes, and oceans. The cycle then begins again, showing how water constantly moves and transforms, supporting all forms of life.

Station Activities Based on TEKS

Station 1: Comprehension Skills (TEKS 6)

- **Activity Name:** "Water Cycle Detective"
- **Task:**
  - Read the passage and answer comprehension questions:
    1. What causes evaporation in the water cycle?
    2. Predict what might happen if the condensation stage didn't occur.
    3. Make a mental image of the water cycle and draw it on paper.
  - **Objective:** Practice making inferences, predictions, and mental images based on text.
  - **Materials:** Passage handout, paper, colored pencils.

Station 2: Response Skills (TEKS 7)

- **Activity Name:** "Connections to Water"
- **Task:**
  - Write a short response to the following prompts:
    1. Describe a time when you noticed one of the stages of the water cycle in real life (e.g., rain, morning dew).
    2. Compare and contrast the roles of evaporation and infiltration.
    3. Summarize the passage in your own words, maintaining logical order.
  - **Objective:** Develop personal connections, summarize, and compare ideas in the text.
  - **Materials:** Journals or response sheets.

Station 3: Literary Elements (TEKS 8)

- **Activity Name:** "The Water Cycle Story"
- **Task:**
  - Analyze the passage as a story:
    1. Infer the theme of the water cycle (e.g., "Nature's Balance").
    2. Explain how water changes throughout the journey, like a "character" in the story.
    3. Identify the stages of the cycle as plot elements: rising action (evaporation), climax (precipitation), and resolution (runoff).
  - **Objective:** Explore literary elements like theme, character interaction, and plot in a nonfiction context.
  - **Materials:** Graphic organizer.

Station 4: Multiple Genres (TEKS 9)

- **Activity Name:** "Water Cycle Genre Lab"
- **Task:**
  - Examine different formats of the water cycle:
    1. Compare the passage to a diagram of the water cycle (informational text features).
    2. Identify the use of personification in the phrase, "The cycle begins again, showing how water constantly moves and transforms."
    3. Write a short poem or a dramatized script about the water cycle.
  - **Objective:** Analyze how the water cycle is presented in different genres and formats.
  - **Materials:** Diagram, poem template, script outline.

Station 5: Author's Purpose and Craft (TEKS 10)

- **Activity Name:** "Author's Toolbox"
- **Task:**
  - Answer these questions:
    1. What is the author's purpose in writing this passage? (Inform, explain, or persuade?)
    2. Identify and explain how figurative language (e.g., "The never-ending journey of water") enhances understanding.
    3. Discuss how the use of headings like "evaporation" and "precipitation" helps structure the passage.
  - **Objective:** Evaluate the author's purpose, use of craft, and structural elements.
  - **Materials:** Annotated passage, discussion questions.

Wrap-Up Activity: Escape the Water Cycle Room

- After completing all stations, students receive a clue tied to each station's activity. For example:
  - Station 1 clue: "What stage transforms vapor into droplets?" (*Condensation*)
  - Station 2 clue: "Summarize the process that replenishes underground reserves." (*Infiltration*)
  - Station 3 clue: "What stage of the plot corresponds to rain?" (*Climax*)
  - Station 4 clue: "What literary device is used in the phrase, 'water constantly moves and transforms'?" (*Personification*)
  - Station 5 clue: "What is the author's primary purpose in this passage?" (*Inform*)

Students use the collected answers to solve a final riddle, unlocking the "Key to the Water Cycle" and escaping the room.

Appendix

A

Use the following TEKS for the activity that follows.

8D (grades 3-5), **7D** (grades 6-8), **6D** (grades 9-12)

3rd - explain the influence of the setting on the plot.

4th - explain the influence of the setting, including historical and cultural settings, on the plot.

5th - analyze the influence of the setting, including historical & cultural settings, on the plot.

6th - analyze how the setting, including historical and cultural settings, influences character and plot development.

7th - analyze how the setting influences character and plot development. *

8th - explain how the setting influences the values and beliefs of characters.

9th - analyze how the setting influences the theme.

10th - analyze how historical and cultural settings influence characterization, plot, and theme across texts.

11th - analyze how the historical, social, and economic context of setting(s) influences the plot, characterization, and theme.

12th - evaluate how the historical, social, and economic context of setting(s) influences the plot, characterization, and theme.

TEKS Analysis Worksheet (Chapters 1-5)

Level 1 TEKS Analysis: The Basics

Step 1: Understanding the TEKS

1. Write the TEKS Standard:

2. What does this TEKS mean in your own words?

Step 2: Key Components of the TEKS

3. List the important nouns (concepts or topics).

4. List the important verbs (skills or actions).

5. Are there any breakout words to note?
   - Circle or underline words such as "and," "including," "or," and "such as," and explain what they mean in this context.

Step 3: Vertical Alignment

6. What is the same about this TEKS for the previous grade level?

7. What is the same about this TEKS for the next grade level?

8. What is different about this TEKS for the previous grade level?

9. What is different about this TEKS for the next grade level?

Step 4: Instructional Planning

10. How will you explain or introduce this TEKS to your students in three sentences or less?

<u>TEKS Question Worksheet</u> (Chapters 6-7)

Level 2: Developing TEKS/STAAR Questions

TEKS 10(D)

Describe how the author's use of imagery, literal and figurative language such as simile and metaphor, and sound devices such as alliteration and assonance achieves specific purposes.

Step 1: Identify Breakout Words

- **Focus**: List the words or phrases that make this TEKS a breakout TEKS. Look for key words like **and**, **including**, **or**, and **such as** that clarify specific components.

Your List:

1.

2.

3.

Step 2: Recall of Content (Dimension 1: Taught)

- **Focus**: Create questions that require students to recall what they've been taught about literary devices like imagery, figurative language, and sound devices.

Your Questions:

1.

2.

3.

Step 3: Textual Evidence (Dimension 2: Tap)

- **Focus**: Develop questions that ask students to identify and provide textual evidence of the author's use of imagery, figurative language, or sound devices.

Your Questions:

1.

2.

3.

Step 4: Why Questions (Dimension 3: Think)

- **Focus**: Create questions that prompt students to think critically about the reasons behind the author's choices.

Your Questions:

1.

2.

3.

Step 5: How Questions (Dimension 4: Toggle)

- **Focus**: Develop questions that explore relationships, such as how two literary devices or techniques work together or how they impact the text.

Your Questions:

1.

2.

3.

TEKS Application/Reflection Worksheet (Chapters 8-12)

Level 3 TEKS Analysis: A Deeper Study

1. **What evidence would demonstrate mastery of this TEKS?**
   - o List 2–3 examples of student work or behaviors that would show students have met this TEKS.

2. **What challenges might students face with this TEKS?**
   - o Identify possible obstacles and strategies to overcome them.

3. **How does this TEKS connect to other TEKS?**
   - o Name other TEKS that relate or build upon this one (e.g., foundational skills or extensions).

4. **What instructional strategies would best support this TEKS?**
   - o List specific methods or tools (e.g., group work, graphic organizers, anchor charts).

5. **What formative assessments could you use to check understanding of this TEKS?**
   - o Suggest quick checks (e.g., exit tickets, think-pair-share).

6. **What real-world connections can you make to help students understand this TEKS?**
   - o Brainstorm examples from daily life, current events, or careers.

7. **How does this TEKS align with state assessment expectations?**
   - o Note any key words or concepts that connect to tested items.

8. **What resources or materials will you need to teach this TEKS effectively?**
   - o List books, technology, visuals, or other supports.

Appendix

B

The following pages contain an instructional planning worksheet that focuses on **aligned instruction implications**.

1. This is a fantastic form to fill out in a PLC or as an individual teacher creating lesson plans to make sure that each of the breakout TEKS are being addressed accordingly.
2. A new worksheet is needed for each breakout.
3. Several worksheets may be needed for each of the individual TEKS if they have multiple breakouts.
4. This form can be used with any content area and cross curricularly.

TEKS Unpacking & Instructional Planning Worksheet

Teacher Name: _____ **Grade Level:** _____

Subject: _____ **TEKS:** _____

◆ 1. Full TEKS Language with highlighting
Paste or write the full wording of the standard here, and denote only one breakout if needed:

_____

◆ 2. Verbs (What students must do)
List the action words in the TEKS. These guide the level of thinking students must use.
Examples: explain, analyze, evaluate

_____

◆ 3. Nouns / Content (What students must know)
What concepts, topics, or skills are students expected to understand?
Examples: plot, character motivation, setting, text evidence

_____

◆ 4. Cognitive Complexity
Choose one system below to determine rigor. You can use either DOK (Depth of Knowledge) or the Teach BIG 4 Dimensions.

✔ DOK Level (science/math):
☐ Recall (DOK 1)
☐ Skill/Concept (DOK 2)
☐ Strategic Thinking (DOK 3)
☐ Extended Thinking (DOK 4)

OR

✔ Teach BIG 4 Dimensions (RLA/social studies):
☐ Taught (knowledge/recall)
☐ Tap (evidence required)
☐ Think (inference required))
☐ Toggle (connection required)
(Briefly explain your selection(s)):

◆ 5. Sample "I can" or "I will" Statement(s)

Write 1–2 student-friendly learning targets that clearly reflect the TEKS.

Examples:

"I can explain how the setting affects the story."

"I can describe how two characters respond to the same event."

◆ 6. Aligned Instructional Implications

What do you need to teach and model in order to meet the TEKS?

What supports or techniques will you use to help all students master it?

Aligned Instructional Implications Chart

Use this chart to connect TEKS-aligned content to instructional strategies and expected student outcomes.

◆ Aligned (TEKS Concept)	🔧 Instructional (Strategy/Tool)	💡 Implications (Student Outcome)
Setting and Plot	Anchor charts and ways to connect them	Students can relate the effects of settings on a plot

◆ 7. Assessment Ideas

How will you know if students have mastered this standard?

List formative (daily) and/or summative (quiz/test) ideas that are TEKS-aligned.

Examples:

– Exit ticket prompt using sentence stem

– Constructed response with text evidence

– Multiple-choice question in STAAR format

Reflections:

How Does Teach BIG Empower Teachers? A Must-Have Resource with Comprehensive: ELAR TEKS Lesson Plans:

Teaching the **English Language Arts and Reading (ELAR) TEKS** is a monumental task, with **242 breakout TEKS** spanning foundational language skills, reading, writing, and research. To help educators meet these demands with confidence and clarity, we've created a series of **dedicated books**, each focused on specific TEKS, offering **complete lesson plans** tailored to the unique requirements of every standard.

Why These Books Are Essential for Teachers

1. **Comprehensive Coverage of the TEKS**:
   Each book is structured around the **knowledge and skills statements** and delves into the **individual breakout TEKS**, ensuring teachers understand the **anatomy of the TEKS** and can deliver targeted instruction.
2. **Lesson Plan Cycle Included in Every Plan**:
   Each lesson follows a thoughtfully designed instructional cycle to help teachers maximize student engagement and learning outcomes:
   - **Knowledge and Skills Statement Focus**: Clear connections to the overarching TEKS goal to guide the lesson's purpose.
   - **TEKS Breakout-Specific Activities**: Breakouts such as "explain the author's purpose" or "use adverbs to convey degree" are addressed explicitly, providing depth that isn't readily available elsewhere.
   - **Direct Instruction**: Detailed teacher scripts for introducing concepts step-by-step with clarity.
   - **Guided Practice**: Collaborative activities where students engage in structured learning alongside their peers.
   - **Independent Practice**: Opportunities for students to apply their skills independently, reinforcing mastery.
   - **Reflection and Closing**: Prompts for students to share their understanding and solidify learning, ensuring that both teachers and students meet the TEKS expectations.
   - **Extension Activities**: Creative and engaging challenges to deepen understanding and promote critical thinking.

3. **Focus on All 13 TEKS Categories**:
   The books are divided into sections based on the TEKS categories, ensuring a well-rounded approach:
   - **Foundational Skills**: Vocabulary, fluency, and phonics.
   - **Comprehension and Response**: Reading comprehension, literary elements, and genre-specific analysis.
   - **Composition**: Writing process and genre-focused writing skills.
   - **Research and Inquiry**: Developing critical thinking through research tasks.
   - **Author's Purpose and Craft**: Unlocking how authors communicate meaning through purposeful choices.
4. **Tailored for Busy Teachers**:
   With ready-to-use lesson plans, editable activities, and clear connections to the TEKS, these books reduce preparation time while boosting instructional effectiveness.

The Power of Breaking Down the TEKS

By understanding the **242 breakout TEKS** in 4th-grade ELAR, teachers gain the ability to:

- Address each skill individually and thoroughly.
- Ensure no part of the TEKS is overlooked, from foundational language skills to advanced comprehension strategies.
- Teach with confidence, knowing every lesson aligns perfectly with state standards.

What Teachers Will Gain

- **Clarity**: A roadmap to navigating the complexity of the TEKS.
- **Engagement**: Activities designed to captivate and inspire students.
- **Results**: Proven strategies to help students meet and exceed expectations.

Whether you're focusing on **fluency**, **composition**, or **research**, these books offer everything you need to **transform your TEKS instruction into an impactful experience**. With every TEKS meticulously addressed, these resources ensure you and your students are always on the path to success.

Each of the TEKS-specific lesson books can be found on amazon.com.

Made in the USA
Monee, IL
01 August 2025

22364715R00175